Poetry from Chaucer to Spenser

Blackwell Essential Literature

Old and Middle English Poetry

Poetry from Chaucer to Spenser

Renaissance Poetry

Restoration Comedy

Poetry from 1660 to 1780

Romantic Poetry

Victorian Poetry

Poetry from Chaucer to Spenser

Edited by Duncan Wu

based on
Chaucer to Spenser:
An Anthology of Writings
in English 1375–1575

edited by Derek Pearsall

Editorial Offices:
108 Cowley Road, Oxford OX4 1JF, UK
Tel: +44 (0)1865 791100
350 Main Street, Malden, MA 02148-5018, USA
Tel: +1 781 388 8250

First published 2002 by Blackwell Publishers Ltd.

Library of Congress Cataloging-in-Publication Data has been applied for.

ISBN 0-631-22986-8 (hbk) ISBN 0-631-22987-6 (pbk)

A catalogue record for this title is available from the British Library

Set in 8/10pt Galliard
by Kolam Information Services Pvt. Ltd, Pondicherry, India
Printed and bound at T.J. International Ltd, Padstow, Cornwall

For further information on
Blackwell Publishers, visit our website:
www.blackwellpublishers.com

Contents

Series Editor's Preface viii

Introduction 1
Duncan Wu

Geoffrey Chaucer (*c.*1343–1400)

From The Canterbury Tales 7
The General Prologue 7
The Wife of Bath's Prologue and Tale 27
The Pardoner's Prologue and Tale 57

William Langland (fl.1375–1380)

From The Vision of Piers Plowman *(C-text)* 72
Prologue 72
Passus III 77
Passus V 79
Passus VI 82

The Gawain Poet (fl.1390)

Sir Gawain and the Green Knight: *Fit 3* 88

Robert Henryson (*c.*1430–*c.*1505)

The Testament of Cresseid 112
The Fables 128
The Fox and the Wolf 128
The Wolf and the Wether 133

William Dunbar (*c.*1456–*c.*1515)

Meditation in Winter 139
Christ in Triumph 140
From The Golden Targe 141

From The Treatise of the Two Married Women and the Widow 144
'Timor Mortis Conturbat Me' 152

Sir Thomas Wyatt (1503–1542)

'The longe love, that in my thought doeth harbar' 155
'Who-so list to hunt, I knowe where is an hynde' 155
'Farewell, Love, and all thy lawes for ever' 156
'My galy charged with forgetfulnes' 156
'Madame, withouten many wordes' 156
'They fle from me that sometyme did me seke' 157
'What no, perdy, ye may be sure!' 157
'Marvaill no more all-tho' 158
'Tho I cannot your crueltie constrain' 159
'To wisshe and want and not obtain' 159
'Some-tyme I fled the fyre that me brent' 160
'The furyous gonne in his rajing yre' 161
'My lute, awake! perfourme the last' 161
'In eternum *I was ons determed'* 162
'Hevyn and erth and all that here me plain' 163
'To cause accord or to agre' 164
'You that in love finde lucke and habundaunce' 164
'What rage is this? what furour of what kynd?' 165
'Is it possible' 165
'Forget not yet the tryde entent' 166
'Blame not my lute for he must sownde' 167
'What shulde I saye' 168
'Spight hath no powre to make me sadde' 169
'I abide and abide and better abide' 170
'Stond who-so list upon the slipper toppe' 170
'Throughout the world, if it wer sought' 170
'In court to serve decked with freshe aray' 171

Henry Howard, Earl of Surrey (1517–1547)

'When ragyng love with extreme payne' 172
'The soote season, that bud and blome furth bringes' 173
'Set me wheras the sonne doth perche the grene' 173
'Love, that doth raine and live within my thought' 173
'Alas, so all thinges nowe do holde their peace' 174
'Geve place, ye lovers, here before' 174
Epitaph for Wyatt 175

Edmund Spenser (1552–1599)

From The Shepherd's Calendar 177
January 177

Index of Titles and First Lines 180

Series Editor's Preface

The Blackwell Essential Literature series offers readers the chance to possess authoritative texts of key poems (and in one case drama) across the standard periods and movements. Based on correspondent volumes in the Blackwell Anthologies series, most of these volumes run to no more than 200 pages. The acknowledged virtues of the Blackwell Anthologies are range and variety; those of the Essential Literature series are authoritative selection, compactness and ease of use. They will be particularly helpful to students hard-pressed for time, who need a digest of the poetry of each historical period.

In selecting the contents of each volume particular attention has been given to major writers whose works are widely taught at most schools and universities. Each volume contains a general introduction designed to introduce the reader to those central works.

Together, these volumes comprise a crucial resource for anyone who reads or studies poetry.

Duncan Wu
St Catherine's College, Oxford

Introduction

Duncan Wu

Chaucer's age was an eventful one. When he was born in *c.*1343 the Hundred Years' War with France was in progress (it had begun in 1337 and would continue until 1453). During his lifetime (Chaucer died in 1400), Richard II was deposed and murdered by Bolingbroke, the future Henry IV; the Peasants' Revolt of 1381 against the unpopular poll tax made the voices of working people heard for the first time in modern history; English (as opposed to Latin or Anglo-Norman French) was established as the language of the legal system; and the plague (also known as the Black Death) ravaged Europe, killing an estimated 25 million people by the end of the century.

Chaucer's father had been a wine merchant and deputy to the king's butler, and Chaucer moved in similar circles. He became first a page to Elizabeth, Countess of Ulster, then joined Edward III's army as a soldier (he was taken prisoner at the siege of Reims, but the king paid a ransom and won his release). After his marriage into John of Gaunt's family in 1366 he enjoyed Gaunt's patronage, making a successful career as a high-ranking civil servant, and going on diplomatic missions for the king.

His career abated towards the end of his life, leaving him with more time in which to work on his great literary achievement, *The Canterbury Tales*, written during the last thirteen years of his life and left unfinished at his death. It tells the story of a group of pilgrims travelling from London to Canterbury to visit the tomb of St Thomas Becket, Archbishop of Canterbury, murdered on the steps of the high altar in Canterbury cathedral at the instigation of Henry II. Chaucer used the East Midland dialect of English spoken in London, but finding it somewhat impoverished was compelled to draw on foreign influences, particularly French. To an extent, therefore, his achievement is linguistic. But the really important thing about his work is that it enshrines a profound and compassionate understanding of human nature. We no longer have summoners or pardoners but what makes Chaucer's characters immediately recognizable is their truth to the human spirit. His poetry speaks of the follies and inconsistencies, as much as of the virtues, of the human heart – and those things are enduring. In the General Prologue the moral slide begins with the Prioress, through no more than hints, including her name (Eglentyne, meaning 'briar rose', which seems unsuitable for a nun) – a lack of proportion is suggested by her grief if anyone struck one of her dogs, and what are we to make of her gold brooch bearing the tag, 'Amor vincit omnia'? She is followed by more obvious examples of moral ambiguity: a monk who 'loved venerye' and was 'a prykasour aright'; friar Huberd who 'maked ful many a mariage/Of yonge wommen at his owene cost'; a Franklin who was 'Epicurus owene sone'; a Miller whose nose had grown 'A werte, and theron stood a tuft of heerys,/Reede as the bristles of a sowes eerys'; the Summoner who was 'hoot . . . and lecherous as a sparwe'; and a Pardoner who is said to be 'a geldyng or a mare'. The language, as much as the sharp observation of humanity, is the triumph of the General Prologue. As Derek Pearsall points out, the succession of individual character sketches would in the hands of a lesser artist be a recipe for monotony and boredom,

> but Chaucer plucks triumph from seemingly certain disaster by observing no apparently predictable order, by varying the angle of approach, by concentrating in different portraits on different kinds of detail, by beginning and ending the portraits in different ways. He speaks of the pilgrims with an immediacy and spontaneity that suggests he has just met them, throwing in apparently arbitrary and meaningless detail, like the Cook's *mormal* (386), and frank confession of ignorance, as of the Merchant's name (284), as guarantees of 'authenticity'.[1]

That sense of human life passing before our eyes in the here-and-now is the essence of Chaucer's achievement in the *Tales* as a whole, and can be seen in the tales of the Wife of Bath and the Pardoner, included here, with their respective prologues, in their entirety. It is what has most impressed readers of his work over the centuries, particularly the Romantics, who rediscovered Chaucer principally through poetry anthologies. In 1824 William Hazlitt remarked that Chaucer was of 'the first class of poetry' because he 'describes the common but individual objects of nature and the strongest and most universal, because spontaneous workings of the heart'.[2] Wordsworth called Chaucer 'the morning star of [England's] literature',[3] and Blake, who was inspired to paint a panoramic view of London featuring all the Canterbury Pilgrims in the order Chaucer introduced them (now at Pollock House in Glasgow), commented:

> Of Chaucer's characters, as described in his Canterbury Tales, some of the names or titles are altered by time, but the characters themselves for ever remain unaltered, and consequently they are physiognomies or lineaments of universal human life, beyond which Nature never steps. Names alter, things never alter. . . . As Newton numbered the stars, and as Linneus numbered the plants, so Chaucer numbered the classes of men.[4]

Blake might have said 'classes of women' too, for they are well represented in the *Tales*, and never more memorably than in the shape of Alisoun, the 'Gat-tothed' Wife of Bath, whose prologue and tale are presented here in full. Hers is a brilliant portrait of resourcefulness in a man's world, as she relates how she has played on the vanity and weakness of her five husbands to gain wealth – 'They hadde me yeven hir land and hir tresoor' (l. 204). The Pardoner's Tale is designed to illustrate the tag he repeats endlessly: 'radix malorum est cupiditas' (love of money is the root of all evil). It is a stock tale in Western and Eastern culture, designed to do no more than promote the Pardoner's cause; it is as if he has no life but in the act of performing his professional duties.

Troilus and Criseyde, written about 1381–6, is Chaucer's finest complete work. Pearsall presents four extracts from it in his excellent anthology, and anyone with a serious interest in Chaucer will find it helpful to begin a study of the poem there. (For

1 Derek Pearsall (ed.) *Chaucer to Spenser: An Anthology* (Oxford: Blackwell, 1999), p. 80.

2 William Hazlitt, *Select British Poets* (1824).

3 *The Prose Works of William Wordsworth* ed. W. J. B. Owen and Jane Worthington Smyser (3 vols, Oxford: Clarendon Press, 1974), ii. 12.

4 *The Complete Poetry and Prose of William Blake* ed. David V. Erdman, commentary by Harold Bloom (Garden City, NY: Doubleday, 1982), pp. 532–3.

reasons of space I am unable to do justice to it here, and have preferred to omit it from this selection.)

William Langland was slightly older than Chaucer, but besides that little is known of his life. He was apparently born in the Malvern Hills in Worcestershire, educated at the Benedictine school in Malvern, was married, and probably took minor orders in London. Langland devoted much of his life to learning and writing but did not live in an ivory tower, for *The Vision of Piers Plowman*, one of the greatest religious poems in the language, is acutely sensitive to social and political conditions of the time. It is written in the unrhymed alliterative mode, made more accessible by a loosening of the metre and a simplified diction. The poem is presented as a series of dream visions focused on the social and spiritual predicaments of later fourteenth-century England. It begins with the poet going out on a May morning in the Malverns; to the east he sees the rising sun and a tower, to the west a deep valley where death dwells. In between he finds a field full of folk, rich and poor. As the poem proceeds it combines scathing criticism of political and ecclesiastical corruption – issues that agitated many of Langland's readers – with allegorical episodes featuring such figures as Conscience, Reason and the Seven Deadly Sins; it mixes scatological satire with theology, religious poetry with political comment. There are three principal versions: a short, early text dating from the 1360s (A); a major revision and elaboration from the late 1370s (B); and a less 'literary' version of B (C) dating from the 1380s, apparently intended to bring its doctrinal issues into clearer focus. Pearsall's first four extracts from the C-text are presented here; he presents six more in his anthology.[5]

Sir Gawain and the Green Knight, the greatest of the Arthurian romances, was written by an unknown author (the *Gawain* poet)[6] in the latter half of the fourteenth century, perhaps *c.*1390. Its hero, Sir Gawain, is a devout but humanly imperfect Christian who wins a test of arms, resists temptation by a lord's wife, but succumbs to an offer of invulnerability. The poem uses its narrative to explore questions of propriety, honour and morality. It is written in Lancashire dialect (including some words of Scandinavian origin), using alliterative verse broken into irregular stanzas by brief rhyming passages. Fit 3 of the poem is presented here in its entirety.

Some of the most impressive poetry of the fifteenth century was produced in Scotland. Robert Henryson, a graduate of Glasgow University, was a schoolmaster in Dunfermline and probably a notary public before he died *c.*1505. This selection includes a complete text of *The Testament of Cresseid*, written before 1492; it was at one time printed with Chaucer's *Troilus and Criseyde*, of which it was regarded as the sequel. Henryson's analysis of Chaucer's poem seems to have been that in refusing to offer a final judgement on Criseyde it was, in effect, harsher on her than it should have been. All but annihilated by her ruin, Cresseid's pitiful state as she walks the streets 'With cop and clapper' leads Henryson to appeal to the pagan gods that govern her world:

> On fair Cresseid quhy hes thow na mercie,
> Quhilk was sa sweit, gentill and amorous? (ll. 325–6)

Cresseid may not deserve such mercy, and the mention of her amorousness rather undercuts his plea. But Henryson cannot refrain from redeeming her, at least in a

5 See Pearsall, *Chaucer to Spenser*, pp. 182ff.

6 The same author is believed to have written three other poems, *Patience*, *Cleanness* and *Pearl*.

symbolic sense: at the end, she is allowed to bequeath to Troilus the ruby ring that he gave her as a love-token in Book III of Chaucer's poem. It raises the possibility that she might be released from the merciless pagan ethos to which she has been condemned, and admitted instead to the Christian morality of forgiveness. If Henryson is in essence a Christian moralist, that is in no way to criticize him; he is one of the most stimulating and compelling of poets, as is evident from his fables, two of which are presented here: *The Fox and the Wolf* and *The Wolf and the Wether.*

William Dunbar, poet at the court of the Scottish James IV (1488–1513) from about 1500 until the king's death at Flodden, was a graduate of St Andrews and a priest. One of the most accomplished writers of his time, his verse reflects an enormous range of expertise. *The Treatise of the Two Married Women and the Widow*, for instance, is one of the best examples of the *chanson de la mal mariée* in Scots Medieval poetry. This genre, transplanted from France, usually has an older woman advising two younger women who bemoan their husbands' inadequacies (often sexual). Dunbar's characters are particularly well characterized, thanks partly to the influence of the Wife of Bath's Prologue. Like Chaucer's character, the first wife haggles with her husband over sex, and likes to be seen on pilgrimages. But it is the widow who is most Chaucerian of all; her views on the tribulations of marriage owe a lot to the Wife of Bath, and she goes one step further in declaring war on the male sex. Indeed, the men get the worst of it; as Pearsall notes, the poem has more words for '(man with) floppy penis' than one could believe existed. And it is funniest as the women draw on the full resources of their tongue to insult their husbands in the most scurrilous terms:

> I have ane wallidrag, ane worme, ane auld wobat carle,
> A waistit wolroun, na worth bot wourdis to clatter;
> Ane bumbart, ane dron-bee, ane bag full of flewme,
> Ane skabbit skarth, ane scorpioun, ane scutarde behind . . .
> He dois as dotit dog that dankys on all bussis
> And liftis his leg apon loft, thoght he nought list pische.
> (ll. 89–92, 186–7)

Meditation in Winter is a more personal work in which, troubled by thoughts of death, Dunbar dramatizes his psychological state through a deft and imaginative use of allegorical personages such as Despair and Patience. It is most disturbing when Age addresses the poet, telling him that 'thow hes compt to mak/Of all thi tyme thow spendit heir' (ll. 34–5). The ability to express a deeply personal anxiety is what makes '*Timor mortis conturbat me*' so moving. And in addition to being an accomplished writer of satirical and personal poetry, one finds in such poems as *Christ in Triumph* religious verse of immense power; here, Dunbar describes the triumph of the risen Christ and the Harrowing of Hell. Works in all these genres – satirical, religious, meditative – were part of Dunbar's duties as a court poet.

Between Chaucer's death in 1400 and the accession of Henry VIII in 1509, many writers came and went, but the most important event in the literary world during that time was a technical innovation: William Caxton, born in 1422, learnt the mechanics of printing in Cologne during 1470–2, and towards the end of 1476 set up his printing-press at Westminster. During his lifetime he would publish much of the literature available to him, including the work of Chaucer, Malory, Lydgate and Gower. It would change the business of writing forever.

Wyatt and Surrey were beneficiaries of the new technology, as their works were printed in Richard Tottel's *Songes and Sonnettes* (1557) (known also as *Tottel's Miscellany*). Poets of the same court, they are often considered as a pair, but are in fact distinct. Wyatt is by far the more versatile and accomplished. He is often regarded as a love poet, and indeed the salient experiences he describes are the emotional disturbance of falling in love, the expectation of rejection, pleading, and protest and lamentation at betrayal. His sonnets, songs and satires speak eloquently of these things, and with a powerful and individual voice that testifies to his knowledge of them (we know that he had an affair with Anne Boleyn, and separated from his wife, whom he charged with adultery). But to insist on his status purely as a love poet would be misleading. He was twice imprisoned in the Tower, though released on each occasion and eventually returned to royal favour. His poetry is thus preoccupied with the political aspects of love – the means by which power is transferred from one person to another, how games signify interest between potential lovers, and how casual interactions can turn sour or even dangerous – a matter of life or death.

One of the things that makes Wyatt such a stimulating writer is his inventiveness. He introduced the Petrarchan sonnet into English literature, and was the first sonneteer in the language. Had he not lived, Shakespeare might not have written his great sonnets. Throughout his work Wyatt is fascinated by the rhythm of words; against the tendency to regularize metre he takes pleasure in thwarting metrical expectation. Moreover, his use of idiomatic registers can be ingenious – 'What no, perdy, ye may be sure!'. When Tottel came to publish his poems a decade after his death he took the liberty of regularizing the metre, much to their detriment. For instance, Wyatt's most famous poem, which in manuscript reads

> They fle from me that sometyme did me seke
>   With naked fote stalking in my chambre.
> I have sene theim gentill, tame and meke
>   That nowe are wyld and do not remember

becomes in Tottel

> They flee from me, that sometime did me seke,
> With naked foote stalking *within* my chamber.
> *Once have I seen* them gentle, tame, and meke,
> That now are wild, and do not *once* remember...

Tottel's 'improvements' are marked in italics; they are an attempt to impose system on Wyatt's unpredictable, musical harmonies. The effect is mechanical and perfunctory where the original is a constant revelation, integral to Wyatt's distinctive voice. Wyatt's ear is not at fault: he meant his poetry to avoid monotonous repetition. Although some editors have followed Tottel's example, including Quiller-Couch in his *Oxford Book of English Verse*, recent scholars, including Pearsall, have returned to the manuscripts to reveal Wyatt's genius in its true colours.

Though a less able poet, Surrey worked in many of the same genres, including the love sonnet. On the other hand, he had a more tumultuous life, being imprisoned on three occasions for riotous conduct in court, wounded in France during the wars, and finally beheaded on a trumped-up charge of treason at the age of thirty. Compared with Wyatt his poetic manner is relaxed and urbane. Good though his best sonnets are, his most important achievement may be his translation of the second and fourth books of the *Aeneid* into blank verse, of which he was the inventor. The metre would be picked up by Marlowe, Shakespeare and Jonson in their plays, and by Milton, Wordsworth, Keats and Tennyson, among others, in poetry.

'Of all the poets, he is the most poetical', Hazlitt wrote of Spenser.[7] He was right, although at first sight *The Shepherd's Calendar* (1579) may seem like an old-fashioned, even clumsy work. In order to appreciate Spenser's achievement fully, it is useful to bear in mind that at the time he was writing, poetry had lost its way. Wyatt died in 1542, Surrey in 1547; Elizabeth I ascended to the throne in 1558. Little of lasting importance had happened in poetry since Henry VIII's time, and the achievements of Langland and, to some extent, Chaucer had become obscured. Spenser was the first to articulate the aspirations of the Elizabethan period. He did this most successfully in *The Faerie Queene*, but was to create its poetic manner in his first published work, *The Shepherd's Calendar* (of which *January* is presented here entire). Spenser writes twelve 'eclogues', one for each month of the year, and in each varies theme and manner, from the satirical manner of *May*, where he attacks religious abuses, to the high style of *October*. The formality of the verse is due partly to the fact that this was a classical imitation conceived in the manner of Theocritus for informal publication within the coterie of Sir Philip Sidney. Spenser was highly conscious of its place within a classical genre, and published it with an essay about the pastoral eclogue. The display of erudition, to which Spenser's glosses also contribute, is part and parcel of his exploitation of the comparatively new medium of print, and an element of his ambition that the poem open the way to court circles. That ambition would fail not because of Spenser's literary ability, but because the fall from favour of the Earl of Leicester (on whom Spenser was dependent) led to effective exile in Ireland where Spenser served, for most of the rest of his life, as secretary to the Lord Deputy. It was a blessing in disguise, for that exile made possible the great enterprise of *The Faerie Queene*, which would remain incomplete at his death.

In *January* we encounter Colin Clout, a solitary shepherd pained by 'his unfortunate love' for Rosalind. It is in many respects an archetypal situation, to which Shakespeare would return in *As You Like It*.

I am much indebted to Derek Pearsall in what follows, and anyone with a serious interest in this poetry should turn to his anthology, listed below, for fuller scholarly treatment. The editor also wishes to thank Dr. Jeremy Dimmick for assistance with the proof-reading of this volume.

Further Reading

Hattaway, Michael (ed.) (2001) *A Companion to English Renaissance Literature and Culture* (Oxford: Blackwell).

Pearsall, Derek (ed.) (1999) *Chaucer to Spenser: A Critical Reader* (Oxford: Blackwell).

Pearsall, Derek (ed.) (1999) *Chaucer to Spenser: An Anthology of Writings in English 1375–1575* (Oxford: Blackwell).

7 Hazlitt, *Select British Poets*, ii. 196.

Geoffrey Chaucer (c.1343–1400)

From *The Canterbury Tales*

The General Prologue

Whan that Averill with his shoures soote
The droghte of March hath perced to the roote
And bathed every veyne in swich lycour
Of which vertu engendred is the flour;
Whan Zephirus eek with his sweete breeth
Inspired hath in every holt and heeth
The tendre croppes, and the yonge sonne
Hath in the Ram his half cours yronne,
And smale foweles maken melodye,
That slepen al the nyght with open iye
(So priketh hem nature in hir corages),
Thanne longen folk to goon on pilgrymages
And palmeres for to seeken straunge strondes,
To ferne halwes, kouthe in sondry londes;
And specially from every shires ende
Of Engelond to Caunterbury they wende,
The holy blisful martir for to seke
That hem hath holpen whan that they weere seeke.
  Bifel that in that sesoun on a day,
In Southwerk at the Tabard as I lay
Redy to weenden on my pilgrymage
To Caunterbury with ful devout corage,
At nyght was come into that hostelrye
Wel nyne and twenty in a compaignye
Of sondry folk, by aventure yfalle
In felaweshipe, and pilgrymes weere they alle,
That toward Caunterbury wolden ryde.
The chambres and the stables weeren wyde
And wel we weeren esed at the beste.

1 April, sweet. **3** such liquid. **4** By whose power. **6** grove and field. **7** new shoots. **9** birds. **10** eye. **11** hearts. **13** professional pilgrims, foreign shores. **14** distant shrines, well known. **18** helped, sick. **19** It befell. **25** fallen by chance. **29** accommodated.

And shortly, whan the sonne was to reste,
So hadde I spoken with hem everichoon
That I was of hir felaweshipe anoon,
And maade forward erly for to ryse,
To take oure wey ther as I yow devyse.
But nathelees, while I have tyme and space,
Er that I ferther in this tale pace,
Me thynketh it acordant to resoun
To telle yow al the condicioun
Of eech of hem, so as it seemed me,
And whiche they weere and of what degree
And eek in what array that they weere inne;
And at a knyght thanne wol I first bigynne.
A KNYGHT ther was, and that a worthy man,
That fro the tyme that he first bigan
To ryden out, he loved chivalrye,
Trouthe and honour, fredom and curteisye.
Ful worthy was he in his lordes werre,
And therto hadde he ryden, no man ferre,
As wel in Cristendom as hethenesse,
And evere honured for his worthynesse.
At Alisaundre he was whan it was wonne;
Ful ofte tyme he hadde the bord bigonne
Aboven alle nacions in Pruce;
In Lettow hadde he reysed and in Ruce,
No Cristen man so ofte of his degree.
In Gernade at the seege eek hadde he be
Of Algizir, and ryden in Belmarye.
At Lyeys was he and at Satalye
Whan they weere wonne, and in the grete see
At many a noble arivee hadde he bee.
At mortal batailles hadde he been fiftene
And foghten for oure feyth at Tramyssene
In lystes thryes and ay slayn his foo.
This ilke worthy knyght hadde been also
Somtyme with the lord of Palatye
Agayn another hethen in Turkye,
And everemoore he hadde a sovereyn prys.
And thogh that he weere worthy, he was wys,
And of his poort as meke as is a mayde,
Ne nevere yet no vileynye he sayde
In al his lyf unto no manere wight.

33 agreement. **34** where, tell. **36** proceed. **40** social rank. **46** generosity of spirit. **47** war. **48** farther. **52** headed the table. **53** national companies of knights. **54** campaigned. **60** military landing. **63** jousting competitions. **66** against. **67** reputation. **69** demeanour. **70** rudeness. **71** creature.

He was a verray parfit gentil knyght.
   But for to tellen yow of his array,
Hise hors weere goode but he ne was nat gay.
Of fustian he wered a gypoun
Al bismotered with his haubergeoun,
For he was laate comen from his viage
And wente for to doon his pilgrymage.
   With hym ther was his sone, a yong SQUYER,
A lovere and a lusty bachiler,
With lokkes crulle as they weere leyd in presse;
Of twenty yeer he was of age, I gesse.
Of his stature he was of evene lengthe
And wonderly delyvere and of greet strengthe.
      And he hadde been somtyme in chivachye
In Flaundres, in Artoys and Picardye,
And born hym wel, as in so litel space,
In hope to stonden in his lady grace.
Embrouded was he, as it weere a meede
Al ful of fresshe floures, white and reede.
Syngynge he was or floytynge al the day:
He was as fressh as is the monthe of May.
Short was his gowne, with sleves longe and wyde.
Wel koude he sitte on hors and faire ryde.
He koude songes make and wel endite,
Juste and eek daunce and wel portreye and write.
So hoote he loved that by nyghtertale
He slepte namoore than dooth a nyghtyngale.
Curteys he was, lowely and servysable,
And carf biforn his fader at the table.
   A YEMAN he hadde and servantz namo
At that tyme, for hym liste ryde so,
And he was clad in coote and hood of greene.
A sheef of pecok arwes, bright and keene,
Under his belt he bar ful thriftily
(Wel koude he dresse his takel yemanly:
His arwes drowped noght with fetheres lowe),
And in his hand he bar a myghty bowe.
A not-heed hadde he, with a broun visage.
Of wodecraft koude he wel al the usage.
Upon his arm he bar a gay bracer
And by his syde a swerd and a bokeler
And on that oother syde a gay daggere

72 true. **74** horses. **77** journeying. **80** gallant knight-to-be. **81** curled. **83** moderate height. **84** agile. **85** on mounted expeditions. **87** himself, time. **88** lady's. **89** Embroidered, meadow. **95** compose. **96** Joust. **97** at night-time. **99** eager to serve. **100** carved. **101** no more. **104** sharp. **105** properly. **106** look after. **107** drooped in flight. **109** close-cropped ('nut'). **111** archer's arm-guard.

Harneysed wel and sharpe as poynt of spere,
A Cristofre on his brest of silver sheene.
An horn he bar, the bawdryk was of greene:
A forster was he, soothly, as I gesse.
Ther was also a Nonne, a PRIORESSE,
That of hir smylyng was ful symple and coy;
Hir gretteste ooth was but by seinte Loy;
And she was clepyd madame Eglentyne.
Ful wel she soong the servyce dyvyne,
Entuned in hir nose ful semely;
And Frenssh she spak ful faire and fetisly –
After the scole of Stratford at the Bowe,
For Frenssh of Parys was to hire unknowe.
At mete wel ytaught was she withalle:
She leet no morsel from hir lyppes falle
Ne wette hir fyngres in hir sauce deepe.
Wel koude she carye a morsel and wel keepe
That no drope ne fille upon hir brest.
In curteisye was set ful muchel hir lest.
Hir over-lyppe wyped she so cleene
That in hir coppe ther was no ferthyng seene
Of grece, whan she dronken hadde hir draghte.
Ful semely after hir mete she raghte.
And sikerly she was of greet desport
And ful plesaunt and amyable of port
And peyned hire to countrefete chiere
Of court, and been estatlich of manere
And to been holden digne of reverence.
But for to speken of hir conscience,
She was so charitable and so pitous
She wolde wepe if that she sawe a mous
Caught in a trappe, if it weere deed or bledde.
Of smale houndes hadde she that she fedde
With rosted flessh, or mylk and wastel-breed;
But soore wepte she if oon of hem weere deed
Or if men smoot it with a yerde smerte;
And al was conscience and tendre herte.
Ful semely hir wympel pynched was,
Hir nose tretez, hir eyen greye as glas,
Hir mouth ful smal and therto softe and reed.

114 Ornamented. **115** bright. **116** shoulder strap. **119** unaffected and demure. **121** called. **122** sang. **124** elegantly. **125** After the fashion of. **127** mealtimes. **130** take care. **132** good manners, delight. **134** speck. **135** grease. **136** for her food, reached. **137** excellent deportment. **138** bearing. **139** the manners. **140** dignified. **142** moral sensibility. **147** fine white bread. **149** stick, painfully. **151** pleated. **152** well-formed.

But sikerly she hadde a fair forheed,
It was almoost a spanne brood, I trowe,
For, hardily, she was nat undergrowe.
Ful fetys was hir cloke, as I was war.
Of smal coral aboute hir arm she bar
A peyre of bedes, gauded al with greene,
And theron heeng a brooch of gold ful sheene
On which ther was first writen a crowned A
And after *Amor vincit omnia.*
  Another NONNE with hire hadde she
That was hire chapeleyne, and preestes thre.
  A MONK ther was, a fair for the maystrye,
An outrydere, that lovede venerye,
A manly man, to been an abbot able.
Ful many a deyntee hors hadde he in stable,
And whanne he rood, men myghte his brydel heere
Gyngle in a whistlynge wynd as cleere
And eek as loude as dooth the chapel belle
There as this lord is kepere of the selle.
The rule of Seint Maure or of Seint Beneyt,
Bycause that it was oold and somdeel streyt,
This ilke Monk leet oolde thynges pace
And heeld after the newe world the space.
He yaf noght of that text a pulled hen
That seith that hunterys been none holy men,
Ne that a monk, whan he is recchelees,
Is likned til a fissh that is waterlees –
This is to seyn, a monk out of his cloystre.
But thilke text heeld he nat worth an oystre.
And I seyde his opynyon was good.
What sholde he studie and make hymselven wood
Upon a book in cloystre alwey to poure
Or swynke with his handes and laboure
As Austyn bit? How shal the world be served?
Lat Austyn have his swynk to hym reserved!
Therfore he was a prykasour aryght:
Grehoundes he hadde as swift as fowel in flyght;
Of prikyng and of huntyng for the haare
Was al his lust, for no cost wolde he spaare.
I saugh his sleves purfiled at the hond
With grys, and that the fyneste of a lond,
And for to festne his hood under his chyn

155 hand-span. **156** certainly. **157** elegant, aware. **159** string (rosary). **165** a fine one surpassing all others. **174** strict. **175** go (hang). **176** the while. **177** plucked. **179** heedless of his rule. **184** mad. **185** pore. **186** work. **187** commands. **189** a really enthusiastic huntsman. **191** coursing. **192** delight. **193** hemmed with fur. **194** grey squirrel fur.

He hadde of gold ywroght a ful curious pyn;
A love-knotte in the gretter ende ther was.
His heed was balled, that shoon as any glas,
And eek his face, as he hadde been enoynt.
He was a lord ful fat and in good poynt,
His eyen steepe, and rollynge in his heed,
That stemed as a fourneys of a leed,
Hise bootes souple, his hors in greet estaat.
Now certeynly he was a fair prelat.
He nas nat paale as is a forpyned goost:
A fat swan loved he best of any roost.
His palfrey was as broun as is a berye.
  A FRERE ther was, a wantowne and a merye,
A lymytour, a ful solempne man.
In alle the ordres foure is noon that kan
So muche of daliaunce and fair langage:
He hadde maked ful many a mariage
Of yonge wommen at his owene cost;
Unto his ordre he was a noble post.
Ful wel biloved and famylier was hee
With frankeleyns overal in his contree
And eek with worthy wommen of the town,
For he hadde power of confessioun,
As seyde hymself, moore than a curaat,
For of his ordre he was licenciaat.
Ful swetely herde he confessioun
And plesant was his absolucioun:
He was an esy man to yeve penaunce
Ther as he wiste to have a good pitaunce.
For unto a povre ordre for to yeve
Is signe that a man is wel yshryve,
For if he yaf, he dorste make avaunt,
He wiste that a man was repentaunt.
For many a man so hard is of his herte
He may nat weepe, thogh that he soore smerte:
Therfore instede of wepynge and preyeres
Men moote yeve silver to the povre freres.
His typet was ay farsed ful of knyves
And pynnes, for to yeven faire wyves.
And certeynly he hadde a murye noote:
Wel koude he synge and pleyen on a roote;
Of yeddynges he bar outrely the prys.

196 intricately made. **198** bald. **200** condition. **201** bulging. **202** That gleamed like a furnace-fire under a lead cauldron. **209** (self-)important. **214** support. **216** landowners. **224** offering. **226** confessed. **227** make bold to say. **230** he suffers painfully. **233** dangling tip of his hood, stuffed. **235** pleasant voice. **236** fiddle. **237** songs, absolutely, prize.

His nekke whit was as the flour-de-lys;
Therto he stroong was as a championn.
He knew the tavernes wel in every town
And every hostiler and tappestere
Bet than a lazer or a beggestere,
For unto swich a worthy man as he
Acorded nat, as by his facultee,
To have with syke lazers aqueyntaunce.
It is nat honeste, it may noght avaunce,
For to deelen with no swich poraille,
But al with riche and sellerys of vitaille.
And overal, ther as profit sholde aryse,
Curteys he was and lowely of servyse;
Ther was no man nowheer so vertuous.
He was the beste beggere of his hous,
And yaf a certeyn ferme for the graunt –
Noon of his bretheren cam ther in his haunt.
For thogh a wydwe hadde noght a sho,
So plesant was his '*In principio*'
Yet wolde he have a ferthyng er he wente:
His purchaas was wel bettre than his rente.
And rage he koude, as it weere right a whelp.
In love-dayes koude he muchel help,
For there he was nat lyk a cloystrer
With a threedbare cope, as is a povre scoler,
But he was lyk a maister or a pope.
Of double worstede was his semycope,
And rounded as a belle out of the presse.
Somwhat he lypsed for his wantownesse
To make his Englyssh sweete upon his tonge,
And in his harpyng, whan that he hadde songe,
Hise eyen twynkled in his heed aryght
As doon the sterres in the frosty nyght.
This worthy lymytour was cleped Huberd.
  A MARCHANT was ther with a forked berd,
In motlee, and hye on hors he sat,
Upon his heed a Flaundryssh bevere hat,
His bootes clasped faire and fetisly.
Hise resons he spak ful solempnely,
Sownyng alwey th' encrees of his wynnyng.
He woolde the see weere kept for anythyng
Bitwixen Myddelburgh and Orewelle.
Wel koude he in eschaunge sheeldes selle.

241 innkeeper, barmaid. **244** official position. **246** be of any advantage. **247** poor people. **248** victuals (provisions). **256** 'take', official income. **257** lark about, puppy. **261** university teacher. **262** short cloak. **264** affectation. **267** exactly. **271** parti-coloured cloth. **272** Flemish. **273** elegantly. **274** opinions. **275** Going on about. **276** protected above all things.

This worthy man ful wel his wit bisette:
Ther wiste no wight that he was in dette,
So estaatly was he of his governaunce
With his bargaynes and with his chevysaunce.
Forsoothe he was a worthy man withalle,
But sooth to seyn I noot how men hym calle.
  A CLERC ther was of Oxenford also,
That unto logyk hadde longe ygo.
As leene was his hors as is a rake,
And he was noght right fat, I undertake,
But looked holwe and therto sobrely.
Ful threedbare was his overeste courtepy,
For he hadde geten hym yet no benefice
Ne was so worldly for to have office.
For hym was levere have at his beddes heed
Twenty bookes clad in blak or reed
Of Aristotle and his philosophye
Than robes riche or fithele or gay sautrye.
But al be that he was a philosophre,
Yet hadde he but litel gold in cofre;
But al that he myghte of his frendes hente,
On bookes and on lernynge he it spente
And bisily gan for the soules preye
Of hem that yaf hym wherwith to scoleye.
Of studye took he moost cure and moost heede.
Noght oo word spak he moore than was neede
And that was spoke in forme and reverence
And short and quyk and ful of heigh sentence.
Sownynge in moral vertu was his speche,
And gladly wolde he lerne and gladly teche.
  A SERGEAUNT OF LAWE, waar and wys,
That often hadde been at the Parvys,
Ther was also, ful ryche of excellence.
Discreet he was and of greet reverence –
He seemed swich, hise wordes weeren so wyse.
Justice he was ful often in assise
By patente and by pleyn commissioun.
For his science and for his heigh renoun
Of fees and robes hadde he many oon.
So greet a purchasour was nowher noon:
Al was fee symple to hym in effect;
His purchasyng myghte nat been infect.

279 put his mind to things. **281** dignified. **282** financial dealing. **286** dedicated himself. **289** gaunt. **290** top coat. **293** he would rather. **296** fiddle, psaltery (kind of harp). **297** although. **299** get. **302** be a scholar. **303** care. **305** with due formality. **306** serious meaning. **307** All to do with. **309** prudent. **315** royal appointment, full. **316** knowledge. **318** land-buyer. **319** free from constraints on possession. **320** invalidated on a technicality.

Nowher so bisy a man as he ther nas
And yet he seemed bisyer than he was.
In termes hadde he caas and doomes alle
That from tyme of kyng William weere falle.
Therto he koude endite and make a thyng,
Ther koude no wight pynchen at his writyng;
And every statut koude he pleyn by roote.
He rood but hoomly in a medlee coote,
Girt with a ceynt of sylk, with barres smale;
Of his array telle I no lenger tale.
  A FRANKELEYN was in his compaignye.
Whit was his berd as is the dayesye;
Of his complexcion he was sangwyn.
Wel loved he by the morwe a sope in wyn:
To lyven in delyt was evere his wone,
For he was Epicurus owene sone,
That heeld opynyoun that pleyn delit
Was verray felicitee parfit.
An housholdere, and that a greet, was hee;
Seint Julyan he was in his contree.
His breed, his ale, was alweys after oon;
A bettre envyned man was nevere noon.
Withouten bake mete was nevere his hous,
Of fressh fissh and flessh, and that so plentevous
It snewed in his hous of mete and drynke,
Of alle deyntees that men koude bithynke.
After the sondry sesons of the yeer
So chaunged he his mete and his soper.
Ful many a fat partrych hadde he in muwe
And many a breem and many a luce in stuwe.
Wo was his cook but if his sauce weere
Poynaunt and sharpe, and redy al his geere!
Hys table dormaunt in his halle alway
Stood redy covered al the longe day.
At sessions ther was he lord and sire;
Ful ofte tyme he was knyght of the shire.
An anlaas and a gipser al of sylk
Heeng at his girdel, whit as morne mylk.
A shirreve hadde he been, and countour.
Was nowheer swich a worthy vavasour.
  An HABERDASSHERE and a CARPENTER,

323 proper legal written form, cases and decisions. **325** compose, draw up a legal document. **326** find a flaw in. **327** fully by heart. **328** parti-coloured. **329** belt, narrow stripes. **334** piece of bread. **335** wont. **337** pure pleasure. **340** (patron saint of hospitality). **341** of the same high standard. **342** stocked with wine. **349** bird-pen. **350** pike, fish-pond. **352** spicy. **353** permanently in place. **357** dagger, purse. **359** sheriff, county tax auditor. **360** county landowner.

A WEBBE, a DYERE, and a TAPYCER –
And they weere clothed alle in oo lyveree
Of a solempne and a greet fraternytee.
Ful fressh and newe hir geere apyked was:
Hir knyves weere chaped noght with bras
But al with silver, wroght ful cleene and wel,
Hir girdles and hir pouches everydel.
Wel seemed eech of hem a fair burgeys
To sitten in a yeldehalle on a deys.
Everych, for the wisdom that he kan,
Was shaply for to been an alderman,
For catel hadde they ynogh and rente,
And eek hir wyves wolde it wel assente;
And ellis certeyn weere they to blame.
It is ful fair to been yclepyd 'madame'
And goon to vigilies al bifore
And have a mantel realliche ybore.
  A COOK they hadde with hem for the nones
To boille the chiknes with the marybones
And poudre-marchaunt tart and galyngale.
Wel koude he knowe a draghte of London ale.
He koude rooste and seethe and broille and frye,
Maken mortreux and wel bake a pye.
But greet harm was it, as it thoughte me,
That on his shyne a mormal hadde he.
For blankmanger, that maade he with the beste.
  A SHIPMAN was ther, wonyng fer by weste;
For aught I woot he was of Dertemouthe.
He rood upon a rouncy, as he kouthe,
In a gowne of faldyng to the knee.
A daggere hangyng on a laas hadde he
Aboute his nekke, under his arm adown.
The hoote somer hadde maad his hewe al brown.
And certeynly he was a good felawe:
Ful many a draghte of wyn hadde he drawe
Fro Burdeux-ward whil that the chapman sleepe.
Of nyce conscience took he no keepe:
If that he faught and hadde the hyer hond
By watre he sente hem hoom to every lond.
But of his craft to rekene wel his tydes,
His stremys and his daungers hym bisydes,

362 weaver, carpet-maker. **365** adorned. **366** mounted. **369** tradesman-citizen. **370** guild-hall, dais. **372** fit. **373** property, income. **379** for the occasion. **380** marrow-bones. **381** (spices). **384** stews. **386** ulcerous sore. **387** As for thick milky chicken stew. **388** dwelling far in the west. **389** Dartmouth (in Devon). **390** nag, as best he could. **391** coarse cloth. **392** strap. **397** Bordeaux, merchant, slept. **402** currents.

His herberwe and his moone, his lodmenage,
Ther was noon swich from Hulle to Cartage.
Hardy he was and wys to undertake;
With many a tempest hadde his beerd been shake.
He knew alle the havenes, as they weere,
Fro Gootlond to the cape of Fynysteere,
And every cryke in Britaigne and in Spayne.
His barge yclepyd was the Mawdelayne.
With us ther was a DOCTOUR OF PHISYK,
In al this world ne was ther noon hym lyk,
To speken of phisyk and of surgerye.
For he was grounded in astronomye.
He kepte his pacient a ful greet deel
In houres by his magyk natureel.
Wel koude he fortunen the ascendent
Of hise ymages for his pacient.
He knew the cause of every maladye,
Weere it of hoot or coold or moyste or drye,
And where it engendred and of what humour;
He was a verray parfit practisour.
The cause yknowe, and of his harm the roote,
Anoon he yaf the sike man his boote.
Ful redy hadde he hise apothecaryes
To senden hym his drogges and his letuaryes,
For eech of hem maade oother for to wynne –
Hir frendshipe was noght newe to bigynne.
Wel knew he the oolde Esculapyus,
And Deyscorides and eek Rufus,
Olde Ypocras, Haly and Galyen,
Serapion, Razis and Avycen,
Averroys, Damascien and Constantyn,
Bernard and Gatesden and Gilbertyn.
Of his diete mesurable was hee,
For it was of no superfluytee
But of greet norissynge and digestible.
His studye was but litel on the Bible.
In sangwyn and in pers he clad was al,
Lyned with taffata and with sendal,
And yet he was but esy of dispence:
He kepte that he wan in pestilence.
For gold in phisyk is a cordial,
Therfore he loved gold in special.
A good WYF was ther of bisyde BATHE,

403 harbour, art of navigation. **404** Cartagena (in Spain). **405** prudent in his undertakings. **409** inlet, Brittany. **410** sailing-ship. **422** practitioner. **424** remedy. **426** medicines. **428** recently begun. **439** rich cloth of red and grey-blue. **440** (kinds of silk). **441** moderate in spending. **443** Since, health-giving drink.

But she was somdel deef, and that was scathe.
Of clooth-makynge she hadde swich an haunt
She passed hem of Ipres and of Gaunt.
In al the parysshe wyf ne was ther noon
That to the offrynge bifore hire sholde goon,
And if ther dide, certeyn so wrooth was shee
That she was out of alle charitee.
Hir coverchiefes ful fyne weere of grownd:
I dorste swere they weyeden ten pownd
That on a Sonday weeren upon hir heed.
Hir hosen weeren of fyn scarlet reed,
Ful streyte yteyd, and shoes ful moyste and newe.
Boold was hir face and fair and reed of hewe.
She was a worthy womman al hir lyve:
Housbondes at chirche dore she hadde fyve,
Withouten oother compaignye in yowthe –
But therof nedeth noght to speke as nowthe.
And thries hadde she been at Jerusalem;
She hadde passed many a straunge strem.
At Rome she hadde been, and at Boloyne,
In Galyce at Seint Jame, and at Coloyne:
She koude muchel of wandrynge by the weye.
Gat-tothed was she, soothly for to seye.
Upon an amblere esily she sat,
Ywympled wel, and on hir heed an hat
As brood as is a bokeler or a targe,
A foot-mantel aboute hir hypes large,
And on hir feet a peyre of spores sharpe.
In felaweshipe wel koude she laughe and carpe.
Of remedies of love she knew, perchaunce,
For she koude of that art the olde daunce.
   A good man was ther of religioun
And was a povre PERSOUN OF A TOUN,
But riche he was of holy thoght and werk.
He was also a lerned man, a clerk,
That Cristes gospel trewely wolde preche;
His parisshens devoutly wolde he teche.
Benygne he was and wonder diligent
And in adversitee ful pacient
And swich he was ypreved ofte sythes.
Ful looth weere hym to cursen for his tythes,
But rather wolde he yeven, out of doute,

446 a pity. **447** skill. **450** offertory (offering made at the altar). **453** linen head-coverings, texture. **457** tightly laced, supple. **462** just now. **464** foreign. **468** with teeth set wide apart. **469** easy-paced horse. **471** shield. **474** chatter. **475** as it happened. **476** the old tricks. **485** times. **486** he was, excommunicate. **487** without doubt.

Unto his povre parisshens aboute
Of his offrynge and eek of his substaunce;
He koude in litel thyng have suffisaunce.
Wyd was his parisshe, and houses fer asonder,
But he ne lafte noght, for reyn ne thonder,
In siknesse nor in meschief to visite
The ferreste in his parisshe, muche and lyte,
Upon his feet, and in his hond a staf.
This noble ensample to his sheep he yaf
That first he wroghte and afterward he taughte.
Out of the gospel he tho wordes caughte
And this figure he added eek therto,
That if gold ruste, what sholde iren do?
For if a preest be foul, on whom we truste,
No wonder is a lewed man to ruste,
And shame it is, if a preest take keepe,
A shiten shepherde and a clene sheepe.
Wel oghte a preest ensample for to yive
By his clennesse how that his sheep sholde lyve.
He sette noght his benefice to hyre
And leet his sheep encombred in the myre
And ran to Londoun unto Seinte Poules
To seeken hym a chauntrye for soules,
Or with a breetherede to been withhoolde,
But dwelte at hoom and kepte wel his foolde,
So that the wolf ne maade it noght myscarye:
He was a sheepherde and noght a mercenarye.
And thogh he hooly weere and vertuous
He was to synful men noght despitous
Ne of his speche daungerous ne digne
But in his techyng discreet and benygne.
To drawen folk to hevene with fairnesse,
By good ensample, this was his bisynesse.
But it weere any persone obstynaat,
What-so he weere, of heigh or lowe estaat,
Hym wolde he snybben sharply for the nonys.
A bettre preest I trowe ther nowher noon ys.
He wayted after no pompe and reverence
Ne maked hym a spyced conscience,
But Cristes loore and hise apostles twelve
He taughte, but first he folwed it hymselve.
With hym ther was a PLOWMAN, was his broother,
That hadde ylad of donge ful many a foother;

492 neglected. **493** distress. **494** farthest, great and small. **499** metaphor. **502** an ignorant layman. **504** dirty. **508** left. **511** retained (as a chaplain). **516** contemptuous. **517** disdainful, haughty. **521** if there were. **523** rebuke. **525** looked for. **526** over-fastidious. **530** hauled, cartload.

A trewe swynkere and a good was he,
Lyvynge in pees and parfit charitee.
God loved he best with al his hoole herte
At alle tymes, thogh hym gamed or smerte,
And thanne his neighebore right as hymselve.
He wolde thresshe and therto dyke and delve,
For Cristes sake, for every povre wight,
Withouten hyre, if it laye in his myght.
His tythes payde he ful faire and wel,
Bothe of his propre swynk and his catel.
In a tabard he rood upon a mere.
  Ther was also a REVE and a MILLERE,
A SOMONOUR and a PARDONER also,
A MAUNCIPLE and myself – ther weere namo.
  The MILLERE was a stout carl for the nones;
Ful byg he was of brawen and eek of bones –
That proeved wel, for overal ther he cam
At wrastlynge he wolde have alwey the ram.
He was short-shuldred, brood, a thikke knarre:
Ther was no dore that he noolde heve of harre
Or breke it at a rennynge with his heed.
His beerd as any sowe or fox was reed
And therto brood, as thogh it weere a spaade.
Upon the cope right of his nose he haade
A werte, and theron stood a tuft of heerys,
Reede as the bristles of a sowes eerys;
Hise nosethirles blake weere and wyde.
A swerd and a bokeler baar he by his syde.
His mouth as greet was as a greet fourneys:
He was a janglere, a golyardeys,
And that was moost of synne and harlotryes.
Wel koude he stelen corn and tollen thryes,
And yet he hadde a thombe of gold, pardee.
A whit coote and a blew hood wered hee.
A baggepipe wel koude he blowe and sowne
And therwithal he broghte us out of towne.
  A gentil MAUNCIPLE was ther of a Temple,
Of which achatours myghte take exemple
For to been wyse in byynge of vitaille;
For wheither that he payde or took by taille,

534 whether it pleased or pained him. **536** ditch and dig. **538** pay. **540** own, possessions. **541** sleeveless tunic, mare. **545** fellow. **546** muscle. **547** was very evident, everywhere. **548** (given as a prize). **549** compactly built, a thick-set fellow. **550** hinge. **551** by running at it. **554** top. **555** hairs. **556** ears. **557** nostrils. **560** loud-mouth, teller of coarse tales. **561** bawdiness. **562** extract three times the usual extra levy. **564** blue. **565** make a noise with. **568** purchasers. **569** buying. **570** on credit (tally).

Algate he wayted so in his achaat
That he was ay biforn and in good staat.
Now is nat that of God a ful greet grace
That swich a lewed mannes wit shal pace
The wysdom of an heepe of lerned men?
Of maistres hadde he mo than thryes ten,
That weeren of lawe expert and curious,
Of whiche ther weere a dozeyne in that hous
Worthy to been stywardes of rente and lond
Of any lord that is in Engelond,
To make hym lyve by his propre good
In honour dettelees (but if he weere wood),
Or lyve as scarsly as hym lyst desire,
And able for to helpen al a shire
In any caas that myghte falle or happe –
And yet this Maunciple sette hir aller cappe.
  The REVE was a sclendre coleryk man.
His beerd was shave as neigh as ever he kan;
His heer was by his eerys ful rownd yshorn;
His top was dokked lyk a preest byforn.
Ful longe weere hise legges and ful leene,
Ylik a staf – ther was no calf yseene.
Wel koude he keepe a gerner and a bynne;
Ther was noon auditour koude on him wynne.
Wel wiste he by the droghte and by the reyn
The yeldynge of his seed and of his greyn.
His lordes sheepe, his neet, his dayerye,
His swyn, his hors, his stoor and his pultrye
Was hoolly in this Reves governynge,
And by his covenant yaf the rekenynge
Syn that his loord was twenty yeer of age.
Ther koude no man brynge hym in arrerage.
Ther nas baillyf, ne hierde, nor oother hyne
That he ne knew his sleyghte and his covyne:
They weere adrad of hym as of the deeth.
His wonyng was ful faire upon an heeth;
With greene trees shadwed was his place.
He koude bettre than his lord purchace;
Ful riche he was astoored pryvely.
His lord wel koude he plesen subtilly,
To yeve and leene hym of his owene good
And have a thank and yet a coote and hood.

571 Always he was so sharply on the look-out in his purchasing. **572** always ahead of the game. **574** surpass. **577** skilful. **581** own wealth. **582** unless he were crazy. **585** chance to happen. **586** made fools of them all. **593** granary, grain-bin. **594** get the better of him. **597** oxen, dairy-herd. **598** horses, livestock. **602** catch him in arrears on his accounts. **603** herdsman, servant. **604** cheating. **605** afraid. **606** dwelling. **609** provided. **611** lend, his (master's) own money.

In youthe he lerned hadde a good mister:
He was a wel good wrighte, a carpenter.
This Reve sat upon a wel good stot
That was a pomely gray and highte Scot.
A long surcote of pers upon he haade
And by his syde he baar a rusty blaade.
Of Northfolk was this Reve of which I telle,
Bisyde a town men clepyn Baldeswelle.
Tukked he was as is a frere aboute
And evere he rood the hyndreste of oure route.
A SOMONOUR was ther with us in that place
That hadde a fyr-reed cherubynnes face,
For sawceflewm he was, with eyen narwe,
And hoot he was and lecherous as a sparwe,
With scaled browes blake and pyled berd.
Of his visage children weere aferd.
Ther nas quyk-silver, lytarge ne brymstoon,
Borace, ceruce, ne oille of tartre noon,
Ne oynement that wolde clense and byte,
That hym myghte helpen of his whelkes whyte
Nor of the knobbes sittynge on his chekes.
Wel loved he garlek, oynons and eek lekes
And for to drynke strong wyn, reed as blood;
Thanne wolde he speke and crye as he were wood,
And whan that he wel dronken hadde the wyn
Thanne wolde he speke no word but Latyn.
A fewe termes hadde he, two or thre,
That he hadde lerned out of som decree –
No wonder is, he herde it al the day,
And eek ye knowe wel how that a jay
Kan clepen 'Watte!' as wel as kan the pope.
But who-so koude in oother thyng hym grope,
Thanne hadde he spent al his philosophie;
Ay '*Questio quid juris*' wolde he crye.
He was a gentil harlot and a kynde;
A bettre felawe sholde men noght fynde.
He wolde suffre for a quart of wyn
A good felawe to have his concubyn
A twelf-monthe, and excusen hym at the fulle;
Ful pryvely a fynch eek koude he pulle.
And if he foond owher a good felawe
He wolde techen him to have noon awe

613 craft. **614** workman. **615** horse. **616** dappled, called. **617** grey-blue cloth. **620** Bawdswell (in Norfolk). **621** with his gown tucked up in his belt. **627** scabby, wispy. **629** lead monoxide nor sulphur. **630** borax, white lead. **632** pustules. **643** shout 'Walter!'. **647** rascal. **652** trick someone simple. **653** anywhere.

In swich caas of the ercedeknes curs,
But if a mannes soule were in his purs,
For in his purs he sholde ypunysshed be.
'Purs is the ercedeknes helle,' seyde he.
But wel I woot he lyed right indede:
Of cursyng oghte ech gilty man him drede,
For curs wol sle right as assoillyng savyth –
And also war hym of a *Significavit*.
In daunger hadde he at his owene gyse
The yonge gerles of the diocise
And knew hir conseil and was al hir reed.
A gerland hadde he set upon his heed,
As greet as it were for an ale-stake;
A bokeler hadde he maad hym of a cake.
With hym ther rood a gentil PARDONER
Of Rouncyval, his freend and his comper,
That streight was comen fro the court of Rome.
Ful loude he soong 'Com hyder, love, to me!'
This Somonour baar to hym a styf burdoun,
Was nevere trompe of half so greet a soun.
This Pardoner hadde heer as yelow as wex,
But smothe it heeng as dooth a stryke of flex;
By ounces henge his lokkes that he hadde
And therwith he his shuldres overspradde;
But thynne it lay, by colpons oon and oon.
But hood, for jolitee, wered he noon,
For it was trussed up in his walet.
Hym thoughte he rood al of the newe jet;
Dischevelee, save his cappe he rood al bare.
Swiche glarynge eyen hadde he as an hare.
A vernycle hadde he sowed upon his cappe,
His walet biforn hym in his lappe,
Bretful of pardoun comen from Rome al hoot.
A voys he hadde as smal as hath a goot.
No berd hadde he, ne nevere sholde have:
As smothe it was as it were late yshave –
I trowe he were a geldyng or a mare.
But of his craft, fro Berwik into Ware
Ne was ther swich another pardoner.
For in his male he hadde a pilwe-beer
Which hat he seyde was Oure Lady veyl;

655 archdeacon's excommunication. **661** slay, absolution. **662** let him beware of an order for imprisonment. **663** in his power, at his own pleasure. **665** secrets, their only source of advice. **667** alehouse-sign. **668** round flat loaf. **670** companion. **673** strong bass. **676** hank. **677** In thin strands. **679** in straggling separate strands. **681** tucked away, pouch. **682** in the latest fashion. **683** With hair hanging down, save for his (skull-)cap he rode all bare-headed. **687** Chock-full. **688** thin and high-pitched. **694** bag, pillow-case.

He seyde he hadde a gobet of the seyl
That Seint Peter hadde whan that he wente
Upon the see, til Jesu Crist hym hente;
He hadde a cros of latoun ful of stones
And in a glas he hadde pigges bones.
But with thise relykes, whan that he foond
A povre person dwellyng upon lond,
Upon a day he gat hym moore moneye
Than that the persoun gat in monthes tweye;
And thus with feyned flaterye and japes
He made the person and the peple his apes.
But trewely to tellen at the laste,
He was in chirche a noble ecclesiaste.
Wel koude he rede a lesson and a storie,
But alderbest he soong an offertorie;
For wel he wiste, whan that soong was songe,
He moste preche and wel affyle his tonge
To wynne silver, as he ful wel koude;
Therfore he soong the muryerly and loude.
   Now have I told you soothly, in a clause,
Th' estaat, th' array, the nombre and eek the cause
Why that assembled was this compaignye
In Southwerk at this gentil hostelrye
That highte the Tabard, faste by the Belle.
But now is tyme to yow for to telle
How that we baren us that ilke nyght,
Whan we weere in that hostelrye alyght,
And after wol I telle of oure viage
And al the remenant of oure pilgrymage.
   But first I pray yow of youre curteisye
That ye n'arette it noght my vileynye
Though that I pleynly speke in this matere,
To telle yow hir wordes and hir cheere,
Ne thogh I speke hir wordes proprely.
For this ye knowen al so wel as I:
Who-so shal telle a tale after a man
He moot reherce as neigh as evere he kan
Everich a word, if it be in his charge,
Al speke he never so rudeliche and large,
Or ellis he moot telle his tale untrewe
Or feyne thyng or fynde wordes newe.
He may noght spare, althogh he weere his brother;

696 piece. **698** took up. **699** cross, brass alloy. **702** parson, in the country. **705** tricks. **706** dupes. **710** best of all, anthem sung at the offering. **712** smooth ('file'). **715** briefly. **719** (another pub). **721** conducted ourselves. **723** journey. **726** attribute to, rudeness. **728** behaviour. **729** exactly. **732** close. **733** be his job. **734** Though he speak, broadly.

He moot as wel seye o word as another.
Crist spak hymself ful brode in holy writ –
And wel ye woot no vileynye is it.
Ek Plato seith, who-so kan hym rede,
'The wordes mote be cosyn to the dede.'
Also I pray yow to foryeve it me,
Al have I nat set folk in hir degree
Here in this tale, as that they sholde stonde:
My wit is short, ye may wel understonde.
  Greet cheere made oure Hoost us everichon
And to the souper sette he us anon.
He served us with vitaille at the beste;
Strong was the wyn, and wel to drynke us leste.
A semely man oure Hoost was withalle
For to been a marchal in an halle.
A large man he was with eyen stepe –
A fairer burgeys was ther noon in Chepe –
Boold of his speche and wys and wel ytaught,
And of manhode hym lakkede right naught.
Eke therto he was right a murye man,
And after souper pleyen he bigan
And spak of murthe amonges othere thynges
(Whan that we hadde maad oure rekenynges),
And seyde thus: 'Now, lordes, trewely,
Ye been to me right welcome, hertely;
For by my trouthe, if that I shal nat lye,
I seigh noght this yeer so murye a compaignye
Atones in this herberwe as is now.
Fayn wolde I doon yow myrthe, wiste I how,
And of a myrthe I am right now bithoght
To doon yow ese, and it shal coste noght.
  'Ye goon to Caunterbury – God yow spede,
The blisful martir quyte yow youre mede!
And wel I woot, as ye goon by the weye,
Ye shapen yow to talen and to pleye,
For trewely, confort ne murthe is noon
To ryde by the weye domb as stoon;
And therfore wol I maken yow desport,
As I seyde erst, and doon yow som confort.
And if yow liketh alle by oon assent
For to stonden at my juggement
And for to werken as I shal yow seye,
Tomorwe, whan ye ryden by the weye,

739 plainly. **744** Though I have. **747** Good cheer. **750** it pleased us. **751** suitable. **752** master of ceremonies. **753** prominent. **765** place of lodging. **768** pleasure. **770** grant, reward. **772** tell tales. **776** first.

Now, by my fader soule that is deed,
But ye be murye I wol yeve yow myn heed!
Holde up youre hondes, withouten moore speche.'
  Oure conseil was nat longe for to seche;
Us thoughte it was nat worth to make it wys
And graunted hym withouten moore avys
And bade hym seye his voirdit as hym leste.
  'Lordynges,' quod he, 'now herkneth for the beste;
But taketh it noght, I pray yow, in desdeyn.
This is the poynt, to speken short and pleyn,
That ech of yow, to shorte with oure weye,
In this viage shal tellen tales tweye –
To Caunterbury-ward, I mene it so –
And homward he shal tellen othere two,
Of aventures that whilom have bifalle.
And which of yow that bereth hym best of alle –
That is to seyn, that telleth in this cas
Tales of best sentence and moost solas –
Shal have a souper at oure aller cost
Here in this place, sittynge by this post,
Whan that we come agayn fro Caunterbury.
And for to make yow the moore mury
I wol myself goodly with yow ryde,
Right at myn owene cost, and be youre gyde;
And who-so wole my juggement withseye
Shal paye al that we spende by the weye.
And if ye vouchesauf that it be so,
Tel me anoon, withouten wordes mo,
And I wol erly shape me therfore.'
  This thyng was graunted and oure othes swore
With ful glad herte, and preyden hym also
That he wolde vouchesauf for to do so
And that he wolde been oure governour
And of oure tales juge and reportour
And sette a souper at a certeyn prys
And we wol ruled been at his devys
In heigh and logh; and thus by oon assent
We been acorded to his juggement.
And therupon the wyn was fet anoon;
We dronken, and to reste wente echon,
Withouten any lenger taryynge.
  A-morwe, whan that day bigan to sprynge,
Up roos oure Hoost and was oure aller cok

781 father's. **782** Unless. **784** seek. **785** make difficulties. **786** discussion **787** decision. **798** serious content, power of giving pleasure. **799** at the expense of all of us. **805** oppose. **807** agree. **809** prepare. **814** record-keeper. **816** wish. **817** in every respect. **819** fetched. **823** of us all.

And gadred us togydres in a flok
And forth we ryden a litel moore than pas
Unto the wateryng of Seint Thomas;
And there oure Hoost bigan his hors areste
And seyde, 'Lordes, herkneth, if yow leste.
Ye woot youre forward and it yow recorde:
If even-song and morwe-song acorde,
Lat se now who shal telle the firste tale.
As evere mote I drynke wyn or ale,
Who-so be rebel to my juggement
Shal paye for al that by the wey is spent.
Now draweth cut, er that we ferrer twynne:
He which that hath the shorteste shal bigynne.
'Sire Knyght,' quod he, 'my mayster and my lord,
Now draweth cut, for that is myn acord.
Cometh neer,' quod he, 'my lady Prioresse,
And ye, sire Clerc, lat be youre shamefastnesse,
Ne studieth noght; ley hond to, every man!'
Anoon to drawen every wight bigan,
And shortly for to tellen as it was,
Were it by aventure, or sort, or cas,
The sothe is this: the cut fil to the Knyght,
Of which ful blithe and glad was every wight,
And telle he moste his tale, as was resoun,
By forward and by composicioun,
As ye han herd; what nedeth wordes mo?
And whan this goode man saugh that it was so,
As he that wys was and obedient
To kepe his forward by his free assent,
He seyde, 'Syn I shal bigynne the game,
What, welcome be the cut, in Goddes name!
Now lat us ryde, and herkneth what I seye.'
And with that word we ryden forth oure weye
And he bigan with right a murye cheere
His tale anoon and seyde as ye may heere.

The Knight's Tale follows

The Wife of Bath's Prologue and Tale

The Wife of Bath's Prologue

'Experience, thogh noon auctoritee
Were in this world, is right ynogh for me

825 walking pace. **829** call it to your mind. **835** draw lots, go any further. **838** decision. **848** agreement. **851** Being one that. **1** written authority.

To speke of wo that is in mariage;
For lordynges, sith that I twelf yeer was of age,
Thonked be God that is eterne on lyve,
Housbondes atte chirche dore I have had fyve –
If I so ofte myghte han wedded be –
And alle were worthy men in hir degree.
But me was told, certeyn, noght longe agon is,
That sith that Crist ne wente nevere but onys
To weddyng, in the Cane of Galilee,
That by the same ensample taughte he me
That I ne sholde wedded be but ones.
   Herke eek, lo, which a sharp word for the nones,
Bisyde a welle, Jesus, God and man,
Spak in repreeve of the Samaritan:
"Thow hast yhad fyve housbondes," quod he,
"And that ilke man which that now hath thee
Is nat thyn housbonde," thus he seyde certeyn.
What that he mente therby I kan nat seyn,
But that I axe why that the fifthe man
Was noon housbonde to the Samaritan?
How manye myghte she han in mariage?
Yet herde I nevere tellen in myn age
Upon this nombre diffynycioun.
Men may dyvyne and glosen up and doun
But wel I woot, expres, withoute lye,
God bad us for to wexe and multiplye –
That gentil text kan I wel understonde.
Eek wel I woot he seyde that myn housbonde
Sholde lete fader and moder and take to me;
But of no nombre mencioun made he,
Of bigamye, or of octogamye;
Why sholde men thanne speke of it vileynye?
   Lo here the wise kyng, daun Salomon:
I trowe he hadde wyves many oon –
As wolde God it leveful were to me
To be refresshed half so ofte as he!
Which yifte of God hadde he for alle hise wyvys!
No man hath swich that in this world alyve is.
God woot, this noble kyng, as to my wit,
The firste nyght hadde many a murye fit
With ech of hem, so wel was hym on lyve.
Blessed be God that I have wedded fyve!
Of whiche I have pyked out the beste, 44[a]

5 in life (alive). **10** once. **14** what. **16** reproof. **21** Except that I ask. **26** conjecture, interpret this way or that. **27** expressly. **31** leave, cleave (Matt. 19:5). **34** bad things. **35** take note of. **37** permissible. **39** What a gift, with. **43** so happy was he to be alive.

Bothe of here nether purs and of here cheste.
Diverse scoles maken parfyt clerkes,
And diverse practyk in many sondry werkes
Maken the werkman parfyt sekirly;
Of fyve husbondes scoleiyng am I –
Welcome the sixte, whan that evere he shal.
For sith I wol nat kepe me chaast in al,
Whan myn housbonde is fro the world agon,
Som Cristen man shal wedde me anon,
For thanne th' Apostle seith that I am free
To wedde, a Goddes half, where it liketh me.
He seith that to be wedded is no synne;
Bet is to be wedded than to brynne.
What rekketh me theigh folk seye vileynye
Of shrewed Lameth and his bigamye?
I woot wel Abraham was an holy man
And Jacob eek, as fer as evere I kan,
And ech of hem hadde wyves mo than two,
And many another holy man also.
   Where kan ye seye in any maner age
That heighe God defended mariage
By expres word? I pray yow telleth me;
Or where comanded he virgynytee?
I woot as wel as ye, it is no drede,
Th' Apostle, whan he speketh of maydenhede,
He seyde that precept therof hadde he noon.
Man may conseille a womman to be oon
But conseillyng nys no comandement.
He put it in oure owene juggement;
For hadde God comanded maydenhede,
Thanne hadde he dampned weddyng with the dede,
And certes, if ther were no seed ysowe,
Virgynytee, thanne wherof sholde it growe?
Poul dorste nat comanden, at the leeste,
A thyng of which his mayster yaf noon heeste.
The dart is set up for virgynytee;
Cacche who-so may, who renneth best lat se.
   But this word is noght take of every wight,
But ther as God list yeve it of his myght.
I woot wel that th' Apostle was a mayde,
But natheless, thogh that he wroot or sayde
He wolde that every wight were swich as he,
Al nys but conseil to virgynytee.

44f schooling. **50** with God's blessing. **52** burn. **53** do I care. **54** cursed. **56** as far as I know. **60** forbade. **63** doubt. **66** single (a virgin). **70** condemned. **74** commandment. **77** applicable to. **78** pleases. **79** virgin.

And for to been a wyf he yaf me leve
Of indulgence; so nys it no repreve
To wedde me if that my make dye,
Withouten excepcioun of bigamye –
Al were it good no womman for to touche
(He mente as in his bed or in his couche,
For peril is bothe fyr and tow t' assemble:
Ye knowe what this ensample may resemble).
This al and som: he heeld virgynytee
Moore parfit than weddyng in freletee –
Freletee clepe I but if that he and she
Wolde leden al hir lyf in chastitee.
  I graunte it wel; I have noon envye,
Thogh maydenhede preferre bigamye.
It liketh hem to be clene in body and goost;
Of myn estat ne wol I make no boost,
For wel ye knowe a lord in his houshold
Ne hath nat every vessel al of gold;
Somme been of tree and doon hir lord servyse.
God clepeth folk to hym in sondry wyse,
And everich hath of God a propre yifte –
Som this, som that, as hym liketh shifte.
  Virgynytee is greet perfeccioun
And continence eek with devocioun,
But Crist, that of perfeccion is welle,
Bad nat every wight he sholde go selle
Al that he hadde and yeve it to the poore,
And in swich wise folwe hym and his foore.
He spak to hem that wol lyve parfitly –
And lordynges, by youre leve, that am nat I.
I wol bistowe the flour of al myn age
In th' actes and in fruyt of mariage.
  Telle me also, to what conclusioun
Were membres maad of generacioun,
And of so parfit wys a wight ywroght?
Trusteth right wel, they were nat maad for noght!
Glose who-so wole, and seye bothe up and doun
That they were maked for purgacioun
Of uryne, and oure bothe thynges smale
Was eek to knowe a femelle from a male
And for noon oother cause – sey ye no?
Th' experience woot wel it is noght so.

84 matter of reproach. **85** mate. **86** objection on the grounds of. **87** even though it were. **89** flax. **90** parallel, signify. **91** This is what it amounts to. **92** frailty. **93** unless. **95** resentment. **96** take precedence over, remarriage. **97** spirit. **98** way of life. **101** wood. **103** special talent. **104** as it pleases God to provide. **110** his footsteps. **115** end. **119** Interpret, in every way.

So that the clerkes be nat with me wrothe,
I sey this: that they maked been for bothe –
That is to seyn, for office and for ese
Of engendrure, ther we nat God displese.
Why sholde men ellis in hir bokes sette
That man shal yelde to his wyf hir dette?
Now wherwith sholde he make his paiement
If he ne used his sely instrument?
Thanne were they maad upon a creature
To purge uryne and eek for engendrure.
  But I seye noght that every wight is holde,
That hath swich harneys as I to yow tolde,
To goon and usen hem in engendrure;
Thanne sholde men take of chastitee no cure.
Crist was a mayde and shapen as a man
And many a seynt sith that the world bigan,
Yet lyved they evere in parfit chastitee.
I nyl envie no virgynytee:
Lat hem be breed of pured whete-seed
And lat us wyves hote barly-breed –
And yet with barly-breed, Mark telle kan,
Oure Lord Jesu refresshed many a man.
In swich estat as God hath clepyd us
I wol persevere; I nam nat precius.
In wifhode wol I use myn instrument
As frely as my Makere hath it sent.
If I be daungerous, God yeve me sorwe!
Myn housbonde shal it han bothe eve and morwe,
Whan that hym list com forth and paye his dette.
An housbonde wol I have – I wol nat lette –
Which shal be bothe my dettour and my thral
And have his tribulacion withal
Upon his flessh whil that I am his wyf.
I have the power duryng al my lyf
Upon his propre body, and nat he.
Right thus th' Apostle tolde it unto me
And bad oure housbondes for to love us wel.
Al this sentence me liketh everydel.'
  Up stirte the Pardoner, and that anon;
'Now, dame,' quod he, 'by God and by Seint John!
Ye been a noble prechour in this cas.
I was aboute to wedde a wyf: allas!
What sholde I bye it on my flessh so deere?

125 Provided that. **127** function. **128** procreation. **135** bound. **138** (if they did) then, heed. **142** resent. **144** be called. **148** fastidious. **151** play hard to get. **154** give up my right. **155** slave. **162** sound doctrine. **163** started. **167** Why, pay for it.

Yet hadde I levere wedde no wyf to-yeere!'
'Abyd!' quod she, 'my tale is nat bigonne.
Nay, thow shalt drynken of another tonne
Er that I go, shal savoure wors than ale.
And whan that I have toold thee forth my tale
Of tribulacion in maryage,
Of which I am expert in al myn age –
This is to seye, myself hath been the whippe –
Thanne maystow chese wheither that thow wolt sippe
Of thilke tonne that I shal abroche.
Be war of it er thow to neigh approche,
For I shal telle ensamples mo than ten.
"Whoso that nyle be war by othere men,
By hym shal othere men corrected be."
Thise same wordes writeth Ptholome:
Rede in his Almageste and take it there.'
'Dame, I wolde pray yow, if youre wyl it were,'
Seyde this Pardoner, 'as ye bigan,
Telle forth youre tale, spareth for no man,
And techeth us yonge men of youre praktyke.'
'Gladly,' quod she, 'syn it may yow lyke,
But that I praye to al this compaignye,
If that I speke after my fantasye,
As taketh nat agrief of that I seye,
For myn entente nys but for to pleye.
Now, sire, thanne wol I telle yow forth my tale.
As evere moot I drynke wyn or ale,
I shal seye sooth: tho housbondes that I hadde,
As three of hem were goode and two were badde.
The thre men were goode and ryche and olde;
Unnethe myghte they the statut holde
In which that they were bounden unto me –
Ye woot wel what I mene of this, pardee!
As help me God, I laughe whan I thynke
How pitously a-nyght I made hem swynke!
And by my fey, I tolde of it no stoor.
They hadde me yeven hir land and hir tresoor:
Me neded nat do lenger diligence
To wynne hir love or doon hem reverence.
They loved me so wel, by God above,
That I ne tolde no deyntee of hir love!
A wys womman wol bisye hire evere in oon
To gete hir love, ye, ther as she hath noon,

168 this year. **176** choose. **177** open up. **178** close. **180** warned. **183** find. **187** practical knowledge. **190** fancy. **191** don't take offence at. **203** faith, had no regard for it. **208** set no value on. **209** constantly.

But sith I hadde hem hoolly in myn hond,
And sith that they hadde yeven me al hir lond,
What sholde I take kepe hem for to plese
But it were for my profit and myn ese?
I sette hem so a-werk, by my fey,
That many a nyght they songen "Weylawey!"
The bacon was nat fet for hem, I trowe,
That som men han in Essex at Donmowe.
I governed hem so wel after my lawe
That ech of hem ful blisful was and fawe
To brynge me gaye thynges fro the feyre.
They were ful glad whan I spak to hem feyre,
For, God it woot, I chidde hem spitously.
  Now herkneth how I bar me proprely.
Ye wise wyves that konne understonde,
Thus sholde ye speke and bere hem wrong on honde,
For half so boldely kan ther no man
Swere and lye as a womman kan.
I sey nat this by wyves that ben wyse,
But if it be whan they hem mysavyse.
A wys womman, if that she kan hir good,
Shal bere hym an hond the cow is wood,
And take witnesse of hir owene mayde
Of hire assent. But herkneth how I sayde:
  "Sire olde kaynard, is this thyn array?
Why is my neghebores wyf so gay?
She is honoured overal ther she goth;
I sitte at hoom; I have no thrifty cloth.
What dostow at my neghebores hous?
Is she so fair? Artow so amorous?
What rowne ye with oure mayde? Benedicite!
Sire olde lechour, lat thy japes be!
And if I have a gossib or a freend,
Withouten gilt, ye chiden as a feend
If that I walke or pleye unto his hous!
Thow comest hoom as dronken as a mous
And prechest on thy bench, with yvel preef!
Thow seyst to me it is a greet mescheef
To wedde a povre womman, for costage;
And if that she be ryche, of heigh parage,
Thanne seistow that it is a tormentrye
To suffre hir pryde and hir malencolye;

211 power. **213** take trouble. **214** Unless. **216** Woe is me!. **217** fetched. **220** eager. **223** scolded. **226** accuse them wrongfully. **229** for the benefit of wives. **230** Except it be, act unadvisedly. **231** knows what's good for her. **232** deceive him into thinking. **234** Who is on her side. **235** dotard, way of behaving. **238** decent clothes. **241** whisper. **247** curse you!. **249** because of the expense. **250** high birth. **252** bad humour.

And if that she be fair, thow verray knave,
Thow seist that every holour wol hire have;
She may no while in chastitee abyde
That is assayled upon ech a syde.
"Thow seyst som folk desiren us for richesse,
Somme for oure shape and somme for oure fairnesse
And somme for she kan outher synge or daunce
And somme for gentillesse and dalyaunce,
Somme for hir handes and hir armes smale;
Thus goth al to the devel, by thy tale.
Thow seyst men may nat kepe a castel wal,
It may so longe assaylled been overal.
"And if that she be foul thow seyst that she
Coveiteth every man that she may se,
For as a spaynel she wol on hym lepe,
Til that she fynde som man hir to chepe;
Ne noon so grey goos goth ther in the lake
As, seistow, wol be withoute make,
And seyst it is an hard thyng for to wolde
A thyng that no man wole, his thankes, holde.
Thus seistow, lorel, whan thow goost to bedde,
And that no wys man nedeth for to wedde,
Ne no man that entendeth unto hevene.
With wilde thonder-dynt and firy levene
Moote thy welked nekke be to-broke!
"Thow seyst that droppyng houses and eek smoke
And chidyng wyves maken men to flee
Out of hir owene houses; a, benedicitee!
What eyleth swich an old man for to chide?
"Thow seyst we wyves wil oure vices hyde
Til we be fast, and thanne we wol hem shewe –
Wel may that be a proverbe of a shrewe!
"Thow seist that oxen, asses, hors and houndes,
They been assayed at dyverse stoundes,
Bacynes, lavours, er that men hem bye,
Spoones, stooles and al swich housbondrye,
And so be pottes, clothes and array;
But folk of wyves maken noon assay
Til they be wedded – olde dotard shrewe! –
And thanne, seistow, we wil oure vices shewe.
"Thow seist also that it displeseth me
But if that thow wolt preise my beautee

254 lecher. **261** slender. **262** according to what you say. **268** do a deal with her. **269** no goose so grey (i.e. plain). **270** mate. **271** control. **272** willingly. **273** wretch. **275** aims for. **276** lightning. **277** shrivelled, broken to bits. **278** leaking. **283** securely married. **284** malicious wretch. **286** tested, times. **287** basins, wash-bowls. **288** household equipment. **290** trial.

And but thow powre alwey upon my face
And clepe me 'faire dame' in every place,
And but thow make a feeste on thilke day
That I was born and make me fressh and gay,
And but thow do to my norice honour
And to my chambrere withinne my bour
And to my fadres folk and his allyes –
Thus seistow, olde barel-ful of lyes!
"And yet of oure apprentice Janekyn,
For his crispe heer, shynyng as gold so fyn,
And for he squyereth me bothe up and doun,
Yet hastow caught a fals suspecioun.
I wil hym nat, thogh thow were deed to-morwe!
"But tel me this: why hidestow, with sorwe,
The keyes of thy cheste awey fro me?
It is my good as wel as thyn, pardee!
What, wenestow make an ydiote of oure dame?
Now by that lord that called is Seint Jame,
Thow shalt noght bothe, thogh that thow were wood,
Be maister of my body and my good;
That oon thow shalt forgo, maugree thyne eyen.
What helpeth it of me enquere and spyen?
I trowe thow woldest lok me in thy chiste!
Thow sholdest seye, 'Wyf, go wher thee liste;
Taak youre disport; I nyl leve no talis.
I knowe yow for a trewe wyf, dame Alis.'
We love no man that taketh kepe or charge
Wher that we goon; we wol been at oure large.
"Of alle men yblessed moote he be,
The wise astrologen, Daun Ptholome,
That seith this proverbe in his Almageste:
'Of alle men his wisdom is hyeste
That rekketh nat who hath the world in honde.'
By this proverbe thow shalt understonde,
Have thow ynogh, what thar thee rekke or care
How myrily that othere folkes fare?
For certes, olde dotard, by youre leve,
Ye shal han queynte right ynogh at eve.
He is to greet a nygard that wil werne
A man to lighte a candle at his lanterne;
He shal han never the lasse light, pardee.
Have thow ynogh, thee thar nat pleyne thee.
"Thow seist also that if we make us gay

295 gaze intently. **299** nurse. **300** chambermaid, bedchamber. **301** kinsfolk. **304** curly. **308** (damn you). **311** do you think, a fool of our mistress (i.e. of me). **315** (i.e. despite all you can do). **319** believe. **321** takes too keen an interest. **322** be free. **327** cares, in his control. **329** what need. **333** refuse.

With clothyng and with precious array
That it is peril of oure chastitee;
And yet – with sorwe! – thow most enforce thee
And seye thise wordes in th' Apostles name:
'In habit maad with chastitee and shame
Ye wommen shal apparaille yow,' quod he,
'And nat in tressed heer and gay perree,
As perlys, ne with gold, ne clothes ryche.'
After thy text ne after thy rubryche
I wol nat werke as muche as is a gnat.
"Thow seydest this, that I was lyk a cat;
For who-so wolde senge a cattes skyn,
Thanne wolde the cat wel dwellen in his in;
And if the cattes skyn be slyk and gay,
She wol nat dwelle in house half a day,
But forth she wole er any day be dawed
To shewe hir skyn and goon a-caterwawed.
This is to seye, if I be gay, sire shrewe,
I wol renne out my borel for to shewe.
Sire olde fool, what helpeth thee t' espyen?
Thogh thow preye Argus with his hundred eyen
To be my warde-corps, as he kan best,
In feith he shal nat kepe me but me lest;
Yet koude I make his berd, as mote I thee!
"Thow seydest eek that ther ben thynges thre,
The whiche thynges troublen al this erthe,
And that no wight may endure the ferthe.
O leeve sire shrewe, Jesu shorte thy lyf!
Yet prechestow and seist an hateful wyf
Yrekened is for oon of thise myschaunces.
Been ther noone othere maner resemblaunces
That ye may likne youre parables to,
But if a sely wyf be oon of tho?
"Thow liknest eek wommanes love to helle,
To bareyne lond ther water may nat dwelle.
Thow liknest it also to wilde-fyr:
The moore it brenneth, the moore it hath desyr
To consumen every thyng that brent wol be.
Thow seist, right as wormes shende a tree,
Right so a wyf destroyeth hir housbonde;
This knowen they that been to wyves bonde."
Lordynges, right thus, as ye han understonde,

340 try to strengthen your case. **342** clothing. **344** jewels. **346** instruction for reading a text. **349** singe. **350** dwelling-place. **351** sleek. **354** a-caterwauling. **356** cheap clothing. **359** body-guard. **360** unless I please. **361** deceive him, as I may thrive!. **365** dear. **374** burns. **376** destroy.

Bar I stifly myne olde housbondes on honde
That thus they seyden in hir dronkenesse;
And al was fals, but that I took witnesse
On Janekyn and on my nece also.
O Lord! the pyne I dide hem and the wo,
Ful giltelees, by Goddes swete pyne!
For as an hors I koude byte and whyne.
I koude pleyne – and I was in the gilt –
Or ellis often tyme I hadde been spilt.
Whoso that first to mille comth, first grynt;
I pleyned first, so was oure werre stynt.
They were ful glad to excusen hem ful blyve
Of thyng of which they nevere agilte hir lyve.
Of wenches wolde I beren hem on honde,
Whan that for syk they myghte unnethe stonde.
Yet tikled I his herte for that he
Wende that I hadde had of hym so greet chiertee!
I swoor that al my walkyng out by nyghte
Was for to espye wenches that he dighte;
Under that colour hadde I many a myrthe.
For al swich wit is yeven us in oure birthe;
Deceite, wepyng, spynnyng God hath yeve
To wommen kyndely whil they may lyve.
And thus of o thyng I avante me:
At ende I hadde the bet in ech degree,
By sleighte or force or by som maner thyng,
As by continuel murmur or grucchyng.
Namely abedde hadden they meschaunce:
Ther wolde I chide and do hem no plesaunce.
I wolde no lenger in the bed abyde,
If that I felte his arm over my syde,
Til he hadde maad his raunceon unto me;
Thanne wolde I suffre hym do his nycetee.
And therfore every man this tale I telle:
Wynne whoso may, for al is for to selle;
With empty hond men may none haukes lure.
For wynnyng wolde I al his lust endure
And make me a feyned appetit;
And yet in bacoun hadde I nevere delit.
That made me that evere I wolde hem chyde,
For thogh the pope hadde seten hem bisyde,
I wolde noght spare hem at hir owene bord,
For by my trouthe I quytte hem word for word.

380 Deceived . . . into thinking. **384** suffering. **388** ruined. **389** grinds. **390** finished. **391** hurriedly. **392** were guilty in their lives. **394** sickness, hardly. **396** fondness. **398** was having sex with. **402** by nature. **403** boast. **404** in all respects. **406** grumbling. **411** ransom. **416** profit. **418** bacon (i.e. old dried meat). **420** sat. **421** dinner-table. **422** repaid.

As help me verray God omnipotent,
Thogh I right now sholde make my testament,
I ne owe hem nat a word that it nys quyt.
I broghte it so aboute by my wit
That they moste yeve it up, as for the beste,
Or ellis hadde we nevere been in reste;
For thogh he looked as a wood leoun,
Yet sholde he faille of his conclusioun.
  Thanne wolde I seye, "Goode lief, taak keepe
How mekely looketh Wilkyn, oure sheepe!
Com neer, my spouse, lat me ba thy cheke!
Ye sholden be al pacient and meke
And han a swete spyced conscience,
Sith ye so preche of Jobes pacience.
Suffreth alwey, syn ye so wel kan preche,
And but ye do, certeyn we shal yow teche
That it is fair to han a wyf in pees.
Oon of us two moste bowen, doutelees,
And sith a man is moore resonable
Than womman is, ye mosten been suffrable.
What eyleth yow to grucche thus and grone?
Is it for ye wolde have my queynte allone?
Wy, taak it al! Lo, have it everydel!
Peter! I shrewe yow, but ye love it wel.
For if I wolde selle my *bele chose*,
I koude walke as fressh as is a rose;
But I wol kepe it for youre owene tooth.
Ye be to blame, by God! I sey yow sooth."
  Swiche manere wordes hadde we on honde.
Now wol I speken of my ferthe housbonde.
  My ferthe housbonde was a revelour –
This is to seyn, he hadde a paramour –
And I was yong and ful of ragerye,
Stibourne and strong, and joly as a pye.
How koude I daunce to an harpe smale
And synge, ywys, as any nyghtyngale,
Whan I hadde dronke a draghte of swete wyn!
Metellyus, the foule cherl, the swyn,
That with a staf birafte his wyf hir lyf
For she drank wyn, though I hadde been his wyf
He sholde nat han daunted me fro drynke!
And after wyn on Venus moste I thynke,
For al so siker as coold engendreth hayl,
A likerous mouth moste han a likerous tayl.

427 yield. **430** purpose. **431** 'dearie'. **433** kiss. **435** scrupulous. **436** Job's. **437** Be patient. **442** patient. **446** By St Peter, damn you!. **447** fair thing. **451** on a regular basis. **455** wild wantonness. **456** Untamed, magpie. **463** frightened. **466** greedy, lecherous.

In wommen vynolent is no defence –
This knowen lechours by experience.
But – Lord Crist! – whan that it remembreth me
Upon my yowthe and on my jolytee,
It tikeleth me aboute myn herte roote.
Unto this day it dooth myn herte boote
That I have had my world as in my tyme.
But age, allas, that al wole envenyme,
Hath me biraft my beautee and my pith.
Lat go, farewel! The devel go therwith!
The flour is goon, ther is namoore to telle:
The bren as I best kan now moste I selle;
But yet to be right murye wol I fonde.
Now wol I tellen of my ferthe housbonde.
I seye, I hadde in herte gret despit
That he of any oother had delit;
But he was quyt, by God and by Seint Joce!
I made hym of the same wode a croce –
Nat of my body, in no foul manere,
But certeynly I made folk swich chiere
That in his owene grece I made hym frye
For angre and for verray jalousye.
By God, in erthe I was his purgatorie,
For which I hope his soule be in glorie.
For God it woot, he sat ful ofte and soong
Whan that his shoo ful bitterly hym wroong.
Ther was no wight, save God and he, that wiste
In many wise how soore I hym twiste.
He deyde whan I cam fro Jerusalem
And lith ygrave under the roode beem,
Al is his toumbe noght so curyus
As was the sepulcre of hym Daryus,
Which that Appellus wroghte subtilly;
It nys but wast to burye hym preciously.
Lat hym fare wel, God gyve his soule reste!
He is now in his grave and in his cheste.
Now of my fifthe housbonde wol I telle –
God lat his soule nevere come in helle!
And yet was he to me the mooste shrewe:
That feele I on my rybbes al by rewe
And evere shal unto myn endyng day.
But in oure bed he was so fressh and gay
And therwithal so wel koude he me glose,

467 drunk with wine. **472** good (a healing remedy). **474** poison. **478** bran. **479** strive. **483** paid back, St Judocus. **492** pinched. **494** tormented. **498** that Darius. **500** waste. **502** coffin. **505** greatest scoundrel. **506** one by one in a row. **509** flatter.

Whan that he wolde han my *bele chose*,
That thogh he hadde me bet on every bon
He koude wynne agayn my love anon.
I trowe I loved hym best for that he
Was of his love daungerous to me.
We wommen han, if that I shal nat lye,
In this matere a queynte fantasye:
Wayte what thyng we may nat lightly have,
Therafter wol we crye al day and crave.
Forbede us thyng, and that desiren we;
Presse on us faste, and thanne wol we fle.
With daunger oute we al oure chaffare;
Greet prees at market maketh deere ware,
And to greet cheepe is holden at litel prys:
This knoweth every womman that is wys.
My fifthe housbonde – God his soule blesse! –
Which that I took for love and no rychesse,
He somtyme was a clerk of Oxenford,
And hadde laft scole and wente at hom to bord
With my gossyb, dwellyng in oure town –
God have hir soule! Hir name was Alisoun.
She knew myn herte and eek my pryvetee
Bet than oure parysshe preest, so mote I thee!
To hire biwreyed I my conseil al,
For hadde myn housbonde pissed on a wal
Or doon a thyng that sholde have cost his lyf,
To hire and to another worthy wyf
And to my nece, which that I loved wel,
I wolde han toold his conseil everydel;
And so I dide ful often, God it woot,
That made his face often reed and hoot
For verray shame, and blamed hymself for he
Hadde toold to me so greet a pryvetee.
And so bifel that ones in a Lente –
So often tymes I to my gossyb wente,
For evere yet I lovede to be gay,
And for to walke in March, Averyll and May
From hous to hous to here sondry tales –
That Jankyn clerk and my gossyb dame Alys
And I myself into the feeldes wente.
Myn housbonde was at Londoun al that Lente:
I hadde the bettre leyser for to pleye
And for to se and eek for to be seye

510 wanted. **511** beaten. **514** coldly reserved. **516** strange and curious. **517** Look for whatever, easily. **520** Entreat us earnestly. **521** coy reserve, put out, merchandise. **522** crowd, expensive. **523** bargain, value. **531** secrets. **532** as I may thrive. **533** revealed, secret. **551** leisure. **552** seen.

Of lusty folk – what wiste I wher my grace
Was shapen for to be, or in what place?
Therfore I made my visitacions
To vigilies and to processions,
To prechyng eek and to thise pilgrymages,
To pleyes of myracles and to mariages,
And wered upon my gaye scarlet gytes.
Thise wormes ne thise mothes ne thise mytes,
Upon my peril, frete hem never a del;
And wostow why? For they were used wel.
Now wol I tellen forth what happed me.
I seye that in the feeldes walked we,
Til trewely we hadde swich daliaunce,
This clerk and I, that of my purveiaunce
I spak to hym and seyde hym how that he,
If I were wydewe, sholde wedde me.
For certeynly – I seye for no bobaunce –
Yet was I nevere withouten purveiaunce
Of mariage, n' of other thynges eek:
I holde a mouses herte noght worth a leek
That hath but oon hole for to sterte to,
And if that faille thanne is al ydo.
I bar hym on honde he hadde enchanted me –
My dame taughte me that soutiltee –
And eek I seyde I mette of hym al nyght,
He wolde han slayn me as I lay upright,
And al my bed was ful of verray blood –
But yet I hope that he shal do me good,
For blood bitokeneth gold, as me was taught.
And al was fals, I dremed of it right naught –
But I folwed ay my dames loore,
As wel of this as othere thynges moore.
But now, sire, lat me se, what shal I seyn?
A ha! by God, I have my tale ageyn.
Whan that my fourthe housbonde was a-beere
I weep, algate, and made sory cheere,
As wyves mooten, for it is usage,
And with my coverchief covered my visage;
But for that I was purveyed of a make
I wepte but smal, and that I undertake.
To chirche was myn housbonde born a-morwe
With neghebores that for hym maden sorwe,

559 had on, gowns. **561** On peril of my soul, devoured. **566** as part of my forward planning. **569** boastfulness. **573** run off to. **575** deceived him into thinking. **576** mother, subtle trick. **577** dreamed. **578** flat on my back. **587** bier. **588** I wept, anyhow. **591** provided beforehand with a mate.

And Jankyn oure clerk was oon of tho.
As help me God, whan that I saw hym go
After the beere, me thoughte he hadde a payre
Of legges and of feet so clene and fayre
That al myn herte I yaf unto his hoold.
He was, I trowe, twenty wynter oold,
And I was fourty, if I shal seye sooth –
But yet I hadde alwey a coltes tooth,
Gat-tothed I was, and that bicam me weel;
I hadde the preynte of seynte Venus seel.
As help me God, I was a lusty oon,
And fayr and ryche and yong and wel bigoon,
And trewely, as myne housbondes tolde me,
I hadde the beste *quonyam* myghte be.
For certes I am al Venerien
In feelynge, and myn herte is Marcien:
Venus me yaf my lust, my likerousnesse,
And Mars yaf me my sturdy hardynesse.
Myn ascendent was Taur, and Mars therinne –
Allas, allas! that evere love was synne!
I folwed ay myn inclinacioun
By vertu of my constellacioun;
That made me I koude noght withdrawe
My chambre of Venus from a good felawe.
Yet have I Martes mark upon my face
And also in another privee place.
For God so wys be my savacioun,
I ne loved nevere by no discrecioun
But evere folwed myn appetit,
Al were he short or long or blak or whit;
I took no kepe, so that he liked me,
How poore he was ne eek of what degree.
  What sholde I seye but at the monthes ende
This joly clerk Jankyn that was so hende
Hath wedded me with greet solempnytee
And to hym yaf I al the lond and fee
That evere was me yeven therbifore.
But afterward repented me ful sore;
He nolde suffre nothyng of my list.
By God, he smoot me ones on the lyst,
For that I rente out of his book a leef,
That of the strook myn ere weex al deef.
Stibourne I was as is a leonesse

599 keeping. **602** youthful tastes. **604** (birth)mark. **606** well set up. **608** 'whatsit' ('whatchamacallit'). **612** boldness. **619** the (birth)mark of Mars. **621** As surely as God may be. **624** dark or fair. **625** pleased. **628** courteous. **630** property. **633** allow, desire. **634** ear.

And of my tonge a verray jangleresse,
And walke I wolde as I hadde doon biforn
From hous to hous, althogh he hadde it sworn;
For which he often tymes wolde preche,
And me of olde Romayn gestes teche,
How he Symplicius Gallus lafte his wif
And hire forsook for terme of al his lif,
Noght but for open-heveded he hir say
Lokynge out at his dore upon a day.
  Another Romayn tolde he me by name
That for his wyf was at a someres game
Withouten his wityng, he forsook hire eke.
And thanne wolde he upon his Bible seke
That ilke proverbe of Ecclesiaste
Where he commandeth and forbedeth faste
Man shal nat suffre his wyf go roule aboute.
Thanne wolde he seye right thus, withouten doute:
"Whoso that buyldeth his hous al of salwes,
And priketh his blynde hors over the falwes,
And suffreth his wyf to go seken halwes,
Is worthy to been hanged on the galwes!"
But al for noght – I sette noght an hawe
Of his proverbe n' of his olde sawe,
N'I wolde nat of hym corrected be.
I hate hym that my vices telleth me,
And so doon mo, God woot, of us than I.
This made hym with me wood al outrely;
I nolde noght forbere hym in no cas.
  Now wol I seye yow sooth, by Seint Thomas,
Why that I rente out of his book a leef,
For which he smoot me so that I was deef.
  He hadde a book that gladly, nyght and day,
For his disport he wolde rede alway;
He clepyd it "Valerie and Theofraste",
At which book he logh alwey ful faste.
And eek ther was somtyme a clerk at Rome,
A cardynal that highte Seint Jerome
That made a book agayn Jovinian;
In which book eek ther was Tertulan,
Crisippus, Trotula and Helowys,
That was abbesse nat fer fro Parys,
And eek the Parables of Salomon,

638 loud chatterbox. **640** sworn to forbid it. **642** stories. **644** to the end of. **645** bare-headed. **649** knowledge. **651** (Eccles. 25:26). **652** strictly. **653** wander. **655** willow branches. **656** fallow fields. **657** pilgrimage shrines. **659** hawthorn-berry. **660** saying. **664** absolutely. **665** submit to. **672** laughed. **679** the Book of Proverbs.

Ovydes Art, and bokes many on –
And alle thise were bounden in o volume.
And every nyght and day was his custume,
Whan he hadde leyser and vacacioun
From oother worldly ocupacioun,
To reden in this book of wikked wyves.
He knew of hem mo legendes and lyves
Than been of goode wyves in the Bible.
For trusteth wel, it is an inpossible
That any clerk wol speke good of wyves,
But if it be of holy seintes lyves,
N'of noon oother womman never the mo.
Who peynted the leoun, tel me who?
By God, if wommen hadden writen stories
As clerkes han, withinne hir oratories,
They wolde han writen of men moore wikkednesse
Than al the mark of Adam may redresse.
The children of Mercurie and Venus
Been in hir wirkyng ful contrarius:
Mercurie loveth wysdam and science
And Venus loveth riot and dispence:
And for hir diverse disposicioun
Ech faileth in ootheres exaltacioun,
And thus, God woot, Mercurie is desolat
In Pisces, wher Venus is exaltat,
And Venus faileth ther Mercurie is reysed.
Therfore no womman of no clerk is preysed.
The clerk, whan he is old and may noght do
Of Venus werkes worth his olde sho,
Thanne sit he doun and writ in his dotage
That wommen kan nat kepe hir mariage.
  But now to purpos why I tolde thee
That I was beten for a book, pardee!
Upon a nyght Jankyn, that was oure sire,
Redde on his book as he sat by the fire
Of Eva first, that for hir wikkednesse
Was al mankynde broght to wrecchednesse,
For which that Jesu Crist hymself was slayn
That boghte us with his herte blood agayn.
Lo, heere expres of womman may ye fynde
That womman was the los of al mankynde.
  Tho redde he me how Sampson loste his herys:
Slepynge, his lemman kitte it with hir sherys,
Thurgh which tresoun loste he bothe his eyen.

680 many a one. **683** spare time. **696** the male sex. **699** knowledge. **713** my husband. **719** explicitly. **720** ruin. **722** lady-love, cut.

Tho redde he me, if that I shal nat lyen,
Of Hercules and of his Dianyre,
That caused hym to sette hymself afyre.
Nothyng forgat he the sorwe and wo
That Socrates hadde with his wyves two,
How Xantippa caste pisse upon his heed.
This sely man sat stille as he were deed;
He wiped his heed, namoore dorste he seyn
But "Er that thonder stynte, comth a reyn!"
Of Phasifpha, that was the queene of Crete,
For shrewednesse hym thoughte the tale swete;
Fy! spek namoore – it is a grisly thyng –
Of hire horrible lust and hir likyng.
Of Clitermystra, for hir lecherye,
That falsly made hir housbonde for to dye,
He redde it with ful good devocioun.
He tolde me eek for what occasioun
Amphiorax at Thebes loste his lyf.
Myn housbonde hadde a legende of his wyf
Eriphilem, that for an ouch of gold
Hath prively unto the Grekys told
Wher that hir housbonde hidde hym in a place,
For which he hadde at Thebes sory grace.
Of Lyvia tolde he me and of Lucie:
They bothe made hir housbondes for to dye,
That oon for love, that oother was for hate.
Lyvia hir housbonde, on an even late,
Empoysoned hath for that she was his fo;
Lucya, likerous, loved hir housbonde so
That for he sholde alwey upon hir thynke
She yaf hym swich a manere love-drynke
That he was deed er it were by the morwe.
And thus algates housbondes han sorwe.
Thanne tolde he me how that oon Latumyus
Compleyned unto his felawe Arrius
That in his gardyn growed swich a tree
On which he seyde how that hise wyves thre
Honged hemself for hertes despitus.
"O leeve brother," quod this Arrius,
"Yif me a plante of thilke blissed tree
And in my gardyn planted shal it be."
Of latter date of wyves hath he red
That somme han slayn hir housbondes in hir bed
And lete hir lechour dighte hire al the nyght

732 stops. **743** brooch. **746** sad fate. **756** always. **757** a certain. **761** out of spite. **767** have sex with.

Whan that the corps lay in the floor upryght;
And somme han dryven nayles in hir brayn
Whil that they sleepe and thus they han hem slayn;
Somme han hem yeven poysoun in hir drynke.
He spak moore harm than herte may bithynke,
And therwithal he knew of mo proverbes
Than in this world ther growen gras or herbes.
"Bet is," quod he, "thyn habitacioun
Be with a leoun or a foul dragoun
Than with a womman usyng for to chide.
Bet is," quod he, "hye in the roof abyde
Than with an angry wyf down in the hous.
They been so wikked and contrarious,
They haten that hir housbondes loveth ay."
He seyde, "A womman cast hir shame away,
Whan she cast of hir smok", and forthermo,
"A fair womman, but she be chaast also,
Is lyk a gold ryng in a sowes nose."
Who wolde wene, or who wolde suppose,
The wo that in myn herte was, and pyne?
 And whan I say he wolde nevere fyne
To reden on this cursed book al nyght,
Al sodeynly thre leves have I plyght
Out of his book, right as he radde, and eke
I with my fist so took hym on the cheke
That in oure fyr he fil bakward adown.
And he up stirte as dooth a wood leoun
And with his fest he smoot me on the heed
That in the floor I lay as I were deed.
And whan he say how stille that I lay,
He was agast and wolde have fled his way,
Til atte laste out of my swowgh I brayde:
"O! hastow slayn me, false theef?" I sayde,
"And for my land thus hastow mordred me?
Er I be deed yet wol I kisse thee."
 And neer he cam and kneled faire adown,
And seyde, "Deere suster Alisoun,
As help me God, I shal thee nevere smyte!
That I have doon it is thyself to wyte.
Foryeve it me, and that I thee biseke!"
And yet eftsoones I hitte hym on the cheke,
And seyde, "Theef, thus muchel am I wreke;
Now wol I dye, I may no lenger speke."

768 stretched out flat. **772** imagine. **781** what. **782** casts. **787** pain. **788** saw, finish. **790** snatched. **791** was reading. **799** swoon, started awake. **806** blame. **808** straightway. **809** revenged.

But at the laste, with muchel care and wo,
We fille acorded by us selven two.
He yaf me al the brydel in myn hond
To han the governance of hous and lond
And of his tonge and his hond also;
And made hym brenne his book anon right tho.
And whan that I hadde geten unto me
By maistrye al the soveraynetee,
And that he seyde, "Myn owene trewe wyf,
Do as thee lust the terme of al thy lyf;
Keepe thyn honour, and keepe eek myn estaat" –
After that day we hadden nevere debaat.
God help me so, I was to hym as kynde
As any wyf from Denmark unto Inde
And also trewe, and so was he to me.
I pray to God that sit in magestee,
So blesse his soule for his mercy deere.
Now wol I seye my tale, if ye wol heere.'
The Frere logh, whan he hadde herd al this;
'Now dame,' quod he, 'so have I joye or blys,
This is a long preamble of a tale!'
And whan the Somnour herde the Frere gale,
'Lo,' quod the Somonour, 'Goddes armes two!
A frere wol entremette hym everemo.
Loo, goode men, a flye and eek a frere
Wol falle in every dyssh and ech matere.
What spekestow of preambulacioun?
What! amble or trotte or pisse or go sit doun!
Thow lettest oure disport in this manere.'
'Ye, woltow so, sire Somnour?' quod the Frere;
'Now by my feith I shal er that I go
Telle of a somnour swich a tale or two
That al the folk shal laughen in this place.'
'Now ellis, Frere, I wol bishrewe thy face,'
Quod this Somnour, 'and I bishrewe me
But if I telle tales two or thre
Of freres er I come to Sydyngborne
That I shal make thyn herte for to morne,
For wel I woot thy pacience is gon.'
Oure Hoost cryde 'Pees! and that anon!'
And seyde, 'Lat the womman telle hir tale.
Ye fare as folk that dronken ben of ale.
Do, dame, tel forth youre tale, and that is best.'
'Al reddy, sire,' quod she, 'right as yow lest,
If I have licence of this worthy Frere?'

820 to the end. **832** exclaim thus. **834** always be meddling. **839** spoilest our fun. **844** curse. **848** mourn.

'Yis, dame,' quod he, 'tel forth, and I wol heere.'

The Wife of Bath's Tale

In th' olde dayes of the kyng Arthour,
Of which that Britons speken greet honour,
Al was this land fulfild of fairye.
The elf-queene with hir joly compaignye
Daunced ful ofte in many a grene mede;
This was the olde opynyoun, as I rede –
I speke of manye hundred yerys ago.
But now kan no man se none elves mo,
For now the grete charitee and prayeres
Of lymytours and othere holy freres,
That serchen every lond and every streem,
As thikke as motes in the sonne-beem,
Blessynge halles, chambres, kichenes, boures,
Citees, burghes, castels, hye toures,
Thropes, bernes, shipnes, dayeryes –
This maketh that ther been no fairyes.
For ther as wont to walken was an elf
Ther walketh now the lymytour hymself
In undermelys and in morwenynges,
And seith his matyns and his holy thynges
As he gooth in his lymytacioun.
Wommen may go saufly up and down:
In every bussh or under every tree
Ther is noon oother incubus but he,
And he ne wol doon hem but dishonour.
And so bifel that this kyng Arthour
Hadde in his hous a lusty bachiler,
That on a day cam ridyng fro ryver,
And happed that, allone as he was born,
He say a mayde walkynge hym biforn,
Of which mayde anoon, maugree hir hed,
By verray force he rafte hir maydenhed.
For which oppressioun was swich clamour
And swich pursuyte unto the kyng Arthour
That dampned was this knyght for to be deed
By cours of lawe and sholde han lost his heed –
Paraventure swich was the statut tho –
But that the queene and othere ladyes mo
So longe preyeden the kyng of grace
Til he his lyf hym graunted in the place

859 full of supernatural creatures. **867** find their way to. **868** specks of dust. **871** Villages, barns, stables. **875** early afternoons, mornings. **877** assigned territory. **883** young knight. **884** hawking by the riverside. **887** despite all she could do. **890** suing for justice.

And yaf hym to the queene, al at hir wille,
To chese wheither she wolde hym save or spille.
  The queene thanketh the kyng with al hir myght
And after this thus spak she to the knyght,
Whan that she saw hir tyme upon a day:
'Thow standest yet,' quod she, 'in swich array
That of thy lyf yet hastow no suretee.
I graunte thee lyf if thow kanst tellen me
What thyng is it that wommen moost desiren:
Be war, and keepe thy nekke-boon from iren!
And if thow kanst nat tellen me anon
Yet wol I yeve thee leve for to gon
A twelf-monthe and a day to seche and lere
An answere suffisant in this matere;
And seuretee wol I han, er that thow pace,
Thy body for to yelden in this place.'
  Wo was this knyght and sorwefully he siketh;
But what! he may nat doon al as hym liketh,
And atte laste he chees hym for to wende
And come agayn right at the yeres ende
With swich answere as God wolde hym purveye;
And taketh his leve, and wendeth forth his weye.
  He seketh every hous and every place
Where as he hopeth for to fynde grace
To lerne what thyng wommen love moost,
But he ne koude arryven in no coost
Where as he myghte fynde in this matere
Two creatures acordyng in-feere.
Somme seyden wommen loven best richesse,
Somme seyde honour, somme seyde jolifnesse,
Somme riche array, somme seyden lust abedde,
And ofte tyme to be widwe and wedde.
Somme seyde that oure herte is moost esed
Whan that we been yflatered and yplesed –
He gooth ful ny the sothe, I wol nat lye:
A man shal wynne us best with flaterye,
And with attendaunce and with bisynesse
Been we ylymed, bothe moore and lesse.
  And somme seyn that we loven best
For to be free and do right as us lest
And that no man repreve us of oure vice
But seye that we be wise and nothyng nyce.
For trewely ther is noon of us alle,
If any wight wolde clawe us on the galle,

898 cause to die. **902** in such a state. **906** iron (i.e. the executioner's axe). **907** straightaway. **909** search and learn. **911** depart. **912** surrender. **913** sighs. **915** chose. **917** provide. **922** region. **924** together. **934** ensnared. **938** foolish. **940** sore spot.

That we nyl kike for he seith us sooth.
Assay and he shal fynde it that so dooth;
For be we never so vicious withinne
We wol be holden wise and clene of synne.
  And somme seyn that greet delit han we
For to be holden stable and eek secree
And in o purpos stedefastly to dwelle
And nat biwreye thyng that men us telle –
But that tale is nat worth a rake-stele.
Pardee, we wommen konne nothyng hele:
Witnesse on Mida – wol ye heere the tale?
  Ovyde, amonges othere thynges smale,
Seyde Mida hadde under his longe herys,
Growynge upon his heed, two asses erys,
The whiche vice he hidde as he best myghte
Ful sotilly from every mannes sighte,
That save his wyf ther wiste of it namo.
He loved hire moost and trusted hire also;
He preyed hire that to no creature
She sholde tellen of his diffigure.
  She swoor him nay – for al this world to wynne,
She nolde do that vileynye or syn
To make hir housbonde han so foul a name;
She nolde nat telle it for hir owene shame.
But nathelees hir thoughte that she dyde
That she so longe sholde a conseil hyde;
Hir thoughte it swal so soore aboute hir herte
That nedely som word hir moste asterte;
And sith she dorste nat telle it to no man,
Doun to a marys faste by she ran –
Til she cam there hir herte was afyre –
And as a bitore bombleth in the myre
She leyde hir mouth unto the water down:
'Biwrey me nat, thow water, with thy sown,'
Quod she. 'To thee I telle it and namo:
Myn housbonde hath longe asses erys two!
Now is myn herte al hool, now is it oute.
I myghte no lenger kepe it, out of doute.'
Heere may ye se, thogh we a tyme abyde,
Yet out it moot; we kan no conseil hyde.
The remenant of the tale if ye wol heere,
Redeth Ovyde, and ther ye may it leere.
  This knyght, of which my tale is specially,

941 will not kick out. **944** wish to be considered. **946** able to keep a secret. **948** betray. **949** rake-handle. **950** hide. **955** defect. **960** disfigurement. **965** would die. **966** secret. **967** swelled. **968** of necessity, must escape. **970** marsh. **972** bittern (type of heron) booms. **982** learn.

When that he say he myghte nat come therby –
This is to seye, what wommen loven moost –
Withinne his brest ful sorweful was the goost.
But hom he gooth, he myghte nat sojorne;
The day was come that homward moste he torne.
And in his wey it happed hym to ryde
In al this care under a forest syde,
Wher as he say upon a daunce go
Of ladyes foure and twenty and yet mo;
Toward the whiche daunce he drow ful yerne
In hope that som wysdom sholde he lerne.
But certeynly er he cam fully there
Vanysshed was this daunce, he nyste where.
No creature say he that bar lyf
Save on the grene he say sittynge a wyf –
A fouler wight ther may no man devyse.
Agayn the knyght this olde wyf gan ryse,
And seyde, 'Sire knyght, heer forth ne lyth no wey.
Tel me what that ye seken, by youre fey!
Paraventure it may the bettre be;
This olde folk konne muchel thyng,' quod she.
  'My leeve moder,' quod this knyght, 'certeyn
I nam but deed but if that I kan seyn
What thyng it is that wommen moost desire.
Koude ye me wisse I wolde wel quyte youre hyre.'
  'Plight me thy trouthe here in myn hand,' quod she,
'The nexte thyng that I requere thee
Thow shalt it do, if it lye in thy myght,
And I wol telle it yow er it be nyght.'
  'Have heer my trouthe,' quod the knyght, 'I graunte.'
  'Thanne,' quod she, 'I dar me wel avaunte
Thy lyf is sauf, for I wole stonde therby;
Upon my lyf the queene wol seye as I.
Lat see which is the prouddeste of hem alle
That wereth on a coverchief or a calle
That dar seye nay of that I shal thee teche.
Lat us go forth withouten lenger speche.'
Tho rowned she a pistel in his ere
And bad hym to be glad and have no fere.
  Whan they be comen to the court, this knyght
Seyde he hadde holde his day as he had hight
And redy was his answere, as he sayde.
Ful many a noble wyf and many a mayde

986 spirit. **993** eagerly. **996** knew not. **997** was living. **1000** At the approach of. **1004** These. **1008** inform, pay you a reward. **1014** make boast. **1015** be your support. **1018** has on, decorative hairnet. **1021** whispered, message. **1024** promised.

And many a widwe – for that they ben wise –
The queene hirself sittyng as justise,
Assembled been this answere for to here,
And afterward this knyght was bode appere.
  To every wight comanded was silence
And that the knyght sholde telle in audience
What thyng that worldly wommen loven best.
This knyght ne stood nat stille as dooth a best
But to his question anon answerde
With manly voys that al the court it herde:
  'My lige lady, generally,' quod he,
'Wommen desire to have sovereyntee
As wel over hir housbonde as hir love
And for to been in maistrie hym above.
This is youre mooste desir, thogh ye me kille.
Dooth as yow list: I am here at youre wille.'
  In al the court ne was ther wyf ne mayde
Ne wydwe that contraryed that he sayde
But seyden he was worthy han his lyf.
  And with that word up stirte that olde wyf
Which that the knyght say sittyng on the grene:
'Mercy,' quod she, 'my sovereyn lady queene!
Er that youre court departe, do me right.
I taughte this answere unto the knyght,
For which he plighte me his trouthe there,
The firste thyng that I wolde hym requere
He wolde it do, if it laye in his myght.
Bifore the court thanne preye I thee, sire knyght,'
Quod she, 'that thow me take unto thy wyf,
For wel thow woost that I have kept thy lyf.
If I seye fals, sey nay, upon thy fey!'
  This knyght answerde, 'Allas and weilawey!
I woot right wel that swich was my biheste.
For Goddes love, as chees a newe requeste!
Taak al my good and lat my body go.'
  'Nay, thanne,' quod she, 'I shrewe us bothe two!
For thogh that I be foul, old and poore
I nolde for al the metal ne for oore
That under erthe is grave or lith above
But if thy wyf I were and eek thy love.'
  'My love?' quod he, 'nay, my dampnacioun!
Allas, that any of my nacioun
Sholde evere so foule disparaged be!'
But al for noght; th'ende is this, that he

1030 bidden to. **1034** beast. **1037** liege. **1059** promise. **1060** choose. **1061** wealth. **1062** curse. **1068** family. **1069** disgraced.

Constreyned was, he nedes moste hir wedde;
And taketh his olde wyf and goth to bedde.
  Now wolden som men seye, paraventure,
That for my necligence I do no cure
To tellen yow the joye and al th' array
That at the feste was that ilke day.
To which thyng shortly answere I shal:
I seye ther nas no joye ne feste at al;
Ther nas but hevynesse and muche sorwe.
For prively he wedded hire on morwe
And al day after hidde hym as an owle,
So wo was hym his wyf looked so foule.
  Greet was the wo the knyght hadde in his thoght
Whan he was with his wyf abedde ybroght;
He walweth and he turneth to and fro.
His olde wyf lay smylynge everemo,
And seyde, 'O deere housbonde, benedicite!
Fareth every knyght thus with his wyf as ye?
Is this the lawe of kyng Arthures hous?
Is every knyght of his thus daungerous?
I am youre owene love and youre wyf;
I am she which that saved hath youre lyf,
And certes yet ne dide I yow nevere unright;
Why fare ye thus with me this firste nyght?
Ye faren lyk a man hadde lost his wit.
What is my gilt? For Goddes love, tel it
And it shal ben amended, if I may.'
  'Amended?' quod this knyght, 'Allas, nay, nay!
It wol nat ben amended neveremo.
Thow art so loothly and so old also
And therto comen of so lowe a kynde
That litel wonder is thogh I walwe and wynde.
So wolde God myn herte wolde breste!'
  'Is this,' quod she, 'the cause of youre unreste?'
  'Ye, certeynly,' quod he, 'no wonder is.'
  'Now, sire,' quod she, 'I koude amende al this,
If that me liste, er it were dayes thre,
So wel ye myghte bere yow unto me.
  'But for ye speken of swich gentillesse
As is descended out of old richesse –
That therfore sholden ye be gentil men –
Swich errogaunce is nat worth an hen.
Looke who that is moost vertuous alway,
Pryvee and apert, and moost entendeth ay

1074 That it's because of my negligence that I take no trouble. **1090** of his (court). **1101** low-born. **1102** twist about. **1103** break. **1108** Provided that, behave well. **1114** In private and in public.

To do the gentil dedes that he kan:
Taak hym for the gentileste man.
Crist wol we clayme of hym oure gentilesse,
Nat of oure eldres for hir old richesse.
For thogh they yeve us al hir heritage,
For which we clayme to been of hir parage,
Yet may they nat biquethe for nothyng
To noon of us hir vertuous lyvyng,
That made hem gentil men ycalled be,
And bad us folwen hem in swich degree.
'Wel kan the wise poete of Florence,
That highte Dant, speken in this sentence.
Lo, in swich maner rym is Dantes tale:
"Ful selde up riseth by his braunches smale
Prowesse of man, for God of his goodnesse
Wole that of hym we clayme oure gentilesse".
For of oure eldres may we nothyng clayme
But temporel thyng that man may hurte and mayme.
'Eek every wight woot this as wel as I,
If gentilesse were planted naturelly
Unto a certeyn lynage doun the lyne,
Pryvee and apert, thanne wolde they nevere fyne
To doon of gentilesse the faire office –
They myghte do no vileynye or vice.
'Taak fyr and bere it in the derkeste hous
Bitwix this and the mount of Kaukasous
And lat men shette the dores and go thenne,
Yet wol the fyr as faire lye and brenne
As twenty thousand men myghte it biholde:
His office naturel ay wol it holde,
Up peril of my lyf, til that it dye.
'Here may ye se wel how that genterye
Is nat annexed to possessioun,
Sith folk ne doon hir operacioun
Alwey, as dooth the fyr, lo, in his kynde.
For God it woot men may wel often fynde
A lordes sone do shame and vileynye;
And he that wol han prys of his gentrye,
For he was born of a gentil hous
And hadde his eldres noble and vertuous,
And nyl hymselven do no gentil dedis
Ne folwen his gentil auncestre that deed is –
He nys nat gentil, be he duc or erl,

1117 wishes that. **1120** noble lineage. **1124** And (made that they) bade us. **1126** on this theme. **1128** by the branches (of his family tree). **1130** Desires. **1132** (i.e. that is transient). **1136** cease. **1140** Caucasus. **1141** thence. **1145** I stake my life on it. **1146** innate nobility. **1148** what they should do. **1149** according to its nature. **1156** who is dead.

For vileynes synful dedes maken a cherl.
For gentilesse nys but renomee
Of thyne auncestres for hir hye bountee,
Which is a straunge thyng for thy persone;
Thy gentilesse cometh fro God allone.
Thanne comth oure verray gentilesse of grace;
It was nothyng biquethe us with oure place.
'Thenketh how noble, as seith Valerius,
Was thilke Tullius Hostillius
That out of poverte roos to heigh noblesse.
Redeth Senek and redeth eek Boece:
Ther shul ye seen expres that no drede is
That he is gentil that dooth gentil dedis.
'And therfore, leve housbonde, I thus conclude:
Al were it that myne auncestres weren rude,
Yet may the hye God – and so hope I –
Graunte me grace to lyven vertuously.
Thanne am I gentil whan that I bigynne
To lyven vertuously and weyve synne.
'And ther as ye of poverte me repreve,
The hye God, on whom that we bileve,
In wilful poverte chees to lyve his lyf.
And certes every man, mayden or wyf
May understonde that Jesus, hevene kyng,
Ne wolde nat chese a vicious lyvyng.
Glad poverte is an honeste thyng, certeyn;
This wol Senek and othere clerkes seyn.
Whoso that halt hym payd of his poverte
I holde hym riche, al hadde he nat a sherte.
He that coveiteth is a povre wight
For he wolde han that is nat in his myght;
But he that noght hath, ne coveiteth have,
Is riche, althogh we holde hym but a knave.
Verray poverte, it syngeth proprely:
Juvenal seith of poverte, "Myrily
The povre man, whan he gooth by the weye,
Biforn the theves he may synge and pleye."
Poverte is hateful good and, as I gesse,
A ful greet bryngere out of bisynesse,
A greet amendere eek of sapience
To hym that taketh it in pacience.
Poverte is this, althogh it seme elenge:
Possessioun that no wight wol chalenge.

1159 the gentility you claim, renown. **1160** goodness. **1161** a thing alien to. **1169** there is no doubt. **1172** low-born. **1176** abandon. **1179** voluntary. **1183** honourable. **1185** is content with. **1190** peasant. **1191** of its own accord. **1196** Something very effective in freeing one from care. **1197** improver. **1199** wretched.

Poverte ful often, whan a man is lowe,
Maketh hymself and eek his God to knowe.
Poverte a spectacle is, as thynketh me,
Thurgh which he may his verray freendes se.
And therefore, sire, syn that I noght yow greve,
Of my poverte namoore ye me repreve.
'Now, sire, of elde ye repreve me:
And certes, sire, thogh noon auctoritee
Were in no book, ye gentils of honour
Seyn that men an old wight sholde doon favour
And clepe hym fader, for youre gentilesse:
And auctours shal I fynden, as I gesse.
'Now ther ye seye that I am foul and old –
Thanne drede yow noght to been a cokewold,
For filthe and elde, also mote I thee,
Been grete wardeyns upon chastitee.
But nathelees, syn I knowe youre delit,
I shal fulfille youre worldly appetit.
'Chees now,' quod she, 'oon of thise thynges tweye:
To han me foul and old til that I deye
And be to yow a trewe, humble wyf
And nevere yow displese in al my lyf;
Or ellis ye wol han me yong and fair
And take youre aventure of the repair
That shal be to youre hous bycause of me –
Or in som oother place, may wel be.
Now chees yourselven wheither that yow liketh.'
This knyght avyseth hym and soore siketh,
But atte laste he seyde in this manere:
'My lady and my love, and wyf so deere,
I putte me in youre wise governaunce:
Cheseth yourself which that may be moost plesaunce
And moost honour to yow and me also.
I do no fors the wheither of the two,
For as yow liketh it suffiseth me.'
'Thanne have I gete of yow maistrye,' quod she,
'Syn I may chese and governe as me lest?'
'Ye, certes, wyf,' quod he, 'I holde it best.'
'Kys me,' quod she, 'we be no lenger wrothe,
For by my trouthe I wol be to yow bothe –
This is to seyn, ye, bothe fair and good.
I prey to God that I mote sterven wood

1202 Enables him. **1203** eyeglass. **1209** gentlemen. **1212** authoritative writers (to support this). **1214** cuckold. **1215** age. **1216** guardians. **1217** what you take pleasure in. **1224** chance, resort (visits). **1227** whichever of the two. **1228** considers carefully. **1234** I do not care. **1242** may die insane.

But I to yow be also good and trewe
As evere was wyf syn that the world was newe.
And but I be to-morn as fair to sene
As any lady, emperice or queene
That is bitwix the est and eek the west,
Do with my lyf and deth right as yow lest.
Cast up the curtyn, looke how that it is.'
   And whan the knyght say verraily al this,
That she so fair was and so yong therto,
For joye he hente hire in his armes two,
His herte bathed in a bath of blisse.
A thousand tyme a-rewe he gan hir kisse
And she obeyed hym in every thyng
That myghte do hym plesance or likyng.
   And thus they lyve unto hir lyves ende
In parfit joye; and Jesu Crist us sende
Housbondes meke, yonge and fressh abedde –
And grace t' overbyde hem that we wedde;
And eek I praye Jesu shorte hir lyves
That noght wol be governed by hir wyves;
And olde and angry nygardes of dispence,
God sende hem soone verray pestilence!

The Friar's Prologue follows

The Pardoner's Prologue and Tale

The Introduction

The Host is much moved by the Physician's Tale, of how the Roman lord Virginius slew his daughter Virginia to save her from the lust of the judge Appius. He moralizes upon the Tale and misses the point in a characteristic way. He then calls upon the Pardoner to tell his tale; the two tales together form what is usually called Fragment VI of the *Tales*, the line-numbering of which is followed here.

Oure Hoost gan to swere as he were wood:
'Harrow!' quod he, 'by nayles and by blood!
This was a fals cherl and a fals justise.
As shameful deeth as herte may devyse
Come to thise juges and hire advocatz!
Algate this sely mayde is slayn, allas!
Allas, to deere boghte she beautee!
Wherfore I seye al day that men may se
That yiftes of Fortune and of Nature

1243 as good. **1245** in the morning. **1249** curtain (round the bed). **1254** in succession. **1260** outlive. **1263** expenditure. **288** Alas!. **292** All the same, innocent. **295** gifts.

Been cause of deeth to many a creature.
Hir beaute was hir deth, I dar wel sayn.
Allas, so pitously as she was slayn!
Of bothe yiftes that I speke of now
Men han ful ofte moore for harm than prow.
But trewely, myn owene maister deere,
This is a pitous tale for to heere.
But nathelees, passe over, is no fors.
I pray to God so save thy gentil cors,
And eek thyne urynals and thy jurdones,
Thyn ypocras, and eek thy galiones,
And every boyste ful of thy letuarie –
God blesse hem, and oure lady Seinte Marie!
So mote I then, thow art a propre man,
And lyk a prelat, by Seint Ronyan!
Seyde I nat wel? I kan nat speke in terme,
But wel I woot thow doost myn herte to erme,
That I almoost have caught a cardynacle.
By corpus bones! but if I have triacle,
Or ellis a draghte of moyste and corny ale,
Or but I heere anon a murye tale,
Myn herte is lost for pitee of this mayde.
Thow *beel amy*, thow Pardoner,' he sayde,
'Tel us som myrthe or japes right anon.'
'It shal be doon,' quod he, 'by Seint Ronyon!
But first,' quod he, 'heere at this ale-stake
I wol bothe drynke and eten of a cake.'
And right anon thise gentils gonne to crye,
'Nay, lat hym telle us of no ribawdye!
Telle us som moral thyng, that we may leere
Som wit, and thanne wol we gladly heere.'
'I graunte, ywis,' quod he, 'but I moot thynke
Upon som honeste thyng whil that I drynke.'

The Pardoner's Prologue

'Lordynges,' quod he, 'in chirches whan I preche
I peyne me to han an hauteyn speche
And rynge it out as round as gooth a belle,
For I kan al by rote that I telle.
My theme is alwey oon, and evere was –

300 benefit. **303** it's no matter. **304** body. **305** (medical vessels). **306** (medicines). **307** box, medicine. **309** as I may thrive. **310** Ronan. **311** technical language. **312** makest, grieve. **314** medicine. **315** fresh and malty. **318** fair friend (perhaps mockingly). **319** funny stories. **323** gentlefolk. **324** filthiness. **325** learn. **326** wisdom. **330** lofty and resonant. **333** sermon-text, one and the same.

Radix malorum est cupiditas.
'First I pronounce whennes that I come
And thanne my bulles shewe I, alle and some.
Oure lige lordes seel on my patente,
That shewe I first, my body to warente,
That no man be so boold, ne preest ne clerk,
Me to destourbe of Cristes holy werk.
And after that thanne telle I forth my tales;
Bulles of popes and of cardynales,
Of patriarkes and bisshopes I shewe,
And in Latyn I speke a wordes fewe
To saffron with my predicacioun
And for to stire hem to devocioun.
Thanne shewe I forth my longe cristal stones,
Ycrammed ful of cloutes and of bones –
Relikes been they, as wenen they echon.
Thanne have I in a latoun a shulder-bon
Which that was of an holy Jewes sheepe.
"Goode men," I seye, "tak of my wordes keepe:
If that this boon be wasshe in any welle,
If cow or calf or sheepe or oxe swelle
That any worm hath ete or worm ystonge,
Taak water of that welle and wassh his tonge,
And it is hool anoon; and forthermoor,
Of pokkes and of scabbe and every soor
Shal every sheepe be hool that of this welle
Drynketh a draughte. Taak kepe eek what I telle:
If that the goode-man that the bestes oweth
Wol every wike, er that the cok hym croweth,
Fastynge, drynken of this welle a draghte,
As thilke holy Jew oure eldres taghte,
Hise bestes and his stoor shal multiplie.
'"And, sire, also it heeleth jalousie:
For thogh a man be falle in jalous rage,
Lat maken with this water his potage
And nevere shal he moore his wyf mystriste,
Thogh he the soothe of hir defaute wiste,
Al hadde she taken preestes two or thre.
'"Heere is a miteyn eek that ye may se:
He that his hand wol putte in this mitayn,
He shal have multiplyyng of his grayn
Whan he hath sowen, be it whete or otes,
So that he offre pens or ellis grotes.

336 one and all. **338** protect. **345** add spice to. **347** glass cases. **348** rags. **349** think. **350** latten (brass alloy). **355** snake. **357** whole. **361** householder, owns. **362** week. **365** stock. **368** soup. **369** mistrust. **370** misdeed. **372** mitten (glove for sowing seed). **376** pence, groats (worth fourpence).

'"Goode men and wommen, o thyng warne I yow:
If any wight be in this chirche now
That hath doon synne horrible, that he
Dar nat for shame of it yshryven be,
Or any womman, be she yong or old,
That hath ymaked hir housbond cokewold,
Swich folk shal have no power ne no grace
To offren to my relikes in this place.
And whoso fyndeth hym out of swich blame
He wol come up and offre a Goddes name
And I assoille him by the auctoritee
Which that by bulle ygraunted was to me."
'By this gaude have I wonne, yeer by yeer,
An hundred mark sith I was pardoner.
I stonde lyk a clerk in my pulpet
And whan that lewed peple is doun yset
I preche so as ye han herd bifore
And telle an hundred false japes more.
Thanne peyne I me to strecche forth the nekke
And est and west upon the peple I bekke
As dooth a dowve sittyng on a berne.
Myne handes and my tonge goon so yerne
That it is joye to se my bisynesse.
'Of avarice and of swich cursednesse
Is al my prechyng, for to make hem free
To yeven hir pens, and namely unto me.
For myn entente is nat but for to wynne
And nothyng for correccioun of synne.
I rekke nevere, whan that they been beryed,
Thogh that hir soules goon a-blakeberyed!
For certes many a predicacioun
Comth ofte tyme of yvel entencioun:
Som for plesance of folk and flaterye,
To been avanced by ypocrisie,
And som for veyne glorie and som for hate.
For whan I dar noon oother weyes debate,
Thanne wol I stynge hym with my tonge smerte
In prechyng, so that he shal nat asterte
To been diffamed falsly, if that he
Hath trespased to my bretheren or to me.
For though I telle noght his propre name,
Men shal wel knowe that it is the same
By signes and by othere circumstances.

380 confessed. **386** in God's name. **387** absolve. **389** trick. **390** (a mark is two-thirds of a pound). **392** ignorant. **396** nod my head. **397** barn-roof. **398** briskly. **403** obtain money. **406** a-blackberrying. **412** argue against someone. **413** sharply. **414** escape. **416** fellow-pardoners.

Thus quyte I folk that doon us displesances;
Thus spete I out my venym under hewe
Of holynesse, to seme holy and trewe.
'But shortly myn entente I wol devyse:
I preche of nothyng but for coveitise.
Therfore my theme is yet and evere was
Radix malorum est cupiditas.
Thus kan I preche agayn that same vice
Which that I use, and that is avarice.
But though myself be gilty in that synne,
Yet kan I maken oother folk to twynne
From avarice and soore to repente –
But that is nat my principal entente:
I preche nothyng but for coveitise.
Of this matere it oghte ynow suffise.
'Thanne telle I hem ensamples many oon
Of olde stories longe tyme agoon,
For lewed peple loven tales olde –
Swiche thynges kan they wel reporte and holde.
What, trowe ye that whiles I may preche
And wynne gold and silver for I teche,
That I wol lyve in poverte wilfully?
Nay, nay, I thoghte it nevere, trewely!
For I wol preche and begge in sondry landes;
I wol nat do no labour with myne handes
Ne make baskettes and lyve therby,
Bycause I wol nat beggen ydelly.
I wol none of the apostles countrefete;
I wol have moneye, wolle, chese and whete,
Al were it yeven of the poverest page
Or of the povereste widwe in a village,
Al sholde hir children sterve for famyne.
Nay, I wol drynke licour of the vyne
And have a joly wenche in every toun.
'But herkneth, lordynges, in conclusioun:
Youre likyng is that I shal telle a tale;
Now have I dronke a draghte of corny ale,
By God, I hope I shal yow telle a thyng
That shal by resoun been at youre likyng.
For thogh myself be a ful vicious man,
A moral tale yet I yow telle kan
Which I am wont to preche for to wynne.
Now holde youre pees! My tale I wol bigynne.'

420 pay back. **421** spit, colour (pretence). **423** describe. **427** against. **430** turn away. **435** exemplary stories. **440** because of how. **441** in voluntary poverty. **442** had it in mind. **446** without making a profit. **448** wool(len clothes). **449** lad.

The Pardoner's Tale

'In Flandres whilom was a compaignye
Of yonge folk that haunteden folye,
As riot, hasard, stewes and tavernes,
Where as with harpes, lutes, and gyternes
They daunce and pleyen at dees bothe day and nyght
And ete also and drynke over hir myght,
Thurgh which they doon the devel sacrifise
Withinne that develes temple in cursed wise
By superfluytee abhomynable.
Hir othes been so grete and so dampnable
That it is grisly for to heere hem swere.
Oure blissed Lordes body they to-tere –
Hem thoughte that Jewes rente hym noght ynough –
And eech of hem at otheres synne lough.
And right anon thanne coomen tombesteres
Fetys and smale, and yonge frutesteres,
Syngeris with harpes, baudes, waufereres,
Whiche been the verray develes officers
To kyndle and blowe the fyr of lecherye,
That is annexed unto glotonye.
The holy writ take I to my witnesse
That luxure is in wyn and dronkenesse.
  Lo, how that dronken Loth unkyndely
Lay by his doghtres two, unwityngly:
So dronke he was he nyste what he wroghte.
  Herodes, whoso wel the stories soghte,
Whan he of wyn was replet at his feste,
Right at his owene table he yaf his heste
To sleen the Baptist John, ful giltelees.
  Senec seith a good word doutelees:
He seith he kan no difference fynde
Bitwix a man that is out of his mynde
And a man which that is dronkelewe,
But that woodnesse, yfallen in a sherewe,
Persevereth lenger than dooth dronkenesse.
O glotonye, ful of cursednesse!
O cause first of oure confusioun!
O original of oure dampnacioun,
Til Crist hadde boght us with his blood agayn!
Lo, how deere, shortly for to sayn,
Aboght was thilke cursed vileynye!

464 lived a life of. **465** debauchery, gambling, brothels. **466** guitars. **467** dice. **474** tear in pieces. **477** dancing-girls. **478** shapely and slender, fruit-girls. **479** cake-sellers. **484** lechery. **485** against nature. **490** command. **495** habitually drunk. **496** bad man. **499** ruin.

Corrupt was al this world for glotonye.
  Adam oure fader and his wyf also
Fro Paradys to labour and to wo
Were dryven for that vice, it is no drede.
For whil that Adam fasted, as I rede,
He was in Paradys, and whan that he
Eet of the frut defended on a tree,
Anon he was out cast to wo and peyne.
O glotonye, on thee wel oghte us pleyne!
O, wiste a man how manye maladies
Folwen of excesse and of glotonyes,
He wolde been the moore mesurable
Of his diete, sittyng at his table.
Allas, the shorte throte, the tendre mouth,
Maketh that est and west and north and south,
In erthe, in eyr, in water, men to swynke
To gete a gloton deyntee mete and drynke!
Of this matere, O Paul, wel kanstow trete:
"Mete unto wombe, and wombe eek unto mete,
Shal God destroyen bothe," as Paulus seith.
Allas, a foul thyng is it, by my feith,
To seye this word, and fouler is the dede,
Whan man so drynketh of the white and rede
That of his throte he maketh his pryvee
Thurgh thilke cursed superfluite.
  The Apostle wepyng seith ful pitously,
"Ther walken manye of whiche yow toold have I –
I seye it now wepyng with pitous voys –
Ther been enemys of Cristes croys,
Of whiche the ende is deth; wombe is hir god!"
O wombe! O bely! O stynkyng cod,
Fulfilled of dong and of corrupcioun!
At either ende of thee foul is the soun.
How greet labour and cost is thee to fynde!
Thise cokes, how they stampe and streyne and grynde
And turnen substance into accident
To fulfillen al thy likerous talent!
Out of the harde bones knokke they
The mary, for they caste nat awey
That may go thurgh the golet softe and soote.
Of spicerie of lief and bark and roote
Shal been his sauce ymaked by delit,
To make hym yet a newer appetit.

510 forbidden. **522** belly. **526** (wines). **532** cross. **534** bag of guts. **537** it is to provide food for you. **540** gluttonous inclination. **542** marrow. **543** (Anything) that, sweetly. **545** for his pleasure.

But certes he that haunteth swiche delices
Is deed, whil that he lyveth in tho vices.
   A lecherous thyng is wyn, and dronkenesse
Is ful of stryvyng and of wrecchednesse.
O dronke man, disfigured is thy face,
Sour is thy breeth, foul artow to embrace,
And thurgh thy dronke nose semeth the soun
As thogh thou seydest ay "Sampsoun, Sampsoun!"
And yet, God woot, Sampson drank nevere no wyn.
Thou fallest as it were a stiked swyn;
Thy tonge is lost and al thyn honest cure,
For dronkenesse is verray sepulture
Of mannes wit and his discrecioun.
In whom that drynke hath domynacioun
He kan no conseil kepe, it is no drede.
Now kepe yow fro the white and fro the rede
And namely fro the white wyn of Lepe
That is to selle in Fissh-strete or in Chepe:
This wyn of Spaigne crepeth subtilly
In othere wynes growynge faste by,
Of which ther riseth swich fumositee
That whan a man hath dronken draghtes thre
And weneth that he be at hom in Chepe,
He is in Spaigne, right at the toune of Lepe –
Nat at the Rochel, ne at Burdeux toun –
And thanne wol he seyn "Sampson, Sampsoun!"

{The Pardoner continues with further examples against drunkenness and then goes on to gambling and swearing.}

But, sires, now wol I telle forth my tale.
   Thise riotoures thre of whiche I telle,
Longe erst er pryme ronge of any belle,
Were set hem in a taverne to drynke,
And as they sat they herde a belle klynke
Biforn a cors, was caryed to his grave.
That oon of hem gan callen to his knave:
"Go bet," quod he, "and axe redily
What cors is this that passeth heer forby,
And looke that thow reporte his name wel."
   "Sire," quod this boy, "it nedeth never-a-del;
It was me told er ye cam heer two houres.
He was, pardee, an old felawe of youres
And sodeynly he was yslayn to-nyght,
Fordronke, as he sat on his bench upright.

547 delights. **550** strife. **556** stuck pig. **557** care for decency. **561** secret. **666** servant. **667** Go quickly. **668** goes past by here. **670** lad. **674** Blind drunk.

Ther cam a privee theef men clepeth Deeth
That in this contree al the peple sleeth
And with his spere he smoot his herte a-two
And wente his wey withouten wordes mo.
He hath a thousand slayn this pestilence,
And, maister, er ye come in his presence,
Me thynketh that it were necessarie
For to be war of swich an adversarie.
Beeth redy for to meete hym everemoore:
Thus taughte me my dame; I sey namoore."
"By seinte Marie!" seyde this taverner,
"The child seith sooth, for he hath slayn this yer,
Henne over a myle, withinne a greet village,
Bothe man and womman, child and hyne and page:
I trowe his habitacioun be there.
To been avysed greet wisdom it were,
Er that he dide a man a dishonour."
"Ye, Goddes armes!" quod this riotour,
"Is it swich peril with hym for to meete?
I shal hym seke by wey and eek by strete,
I make avow to Goddes digne bones!
Herkneth, felawes, we thre been al ones:
Lat ech of us holde up his hand to oother
And ech of us bicomen ootheres brother
And we wol sleen this false traytour Deeth.
He shal be slayn, he that so manye sleeth,
By Goddes dignytee, er it be nyght!"
Togidres han thise thre hir trouthes plyght
To lyve and dyen ech of hem with oother,
As thogh he were his owene ybore brother.
And up they stirte, al dronken in this rage,
And forth they goon towardes that village
Of which the taverner hadde spoke biforn,
And many a grisly ooth thanne han they sworn
And Cristes blessed body they to-rente –
Deeth shal be deed if that they may hym hente!
Whan they had goon nat fully half a myle,
Right as they wolde han treden over a style,
An old man and a povre with hem mette.
This olde man ful mekely hem grette
And seyde thus, "Now, lordes, God yow se!"
The proudeste of thise riotoures thre
Answerde agayn, "What, carl, with sory grace!
Why artow al forwrapped save thy face?

684 mother. **686** young lad. **687** From here. **688** farm-worker and serving boy. **690** wary. **694** (everywhere). **695** worthy. **696** all of one mind. **704** brother by birth. **709** tore to pieces. **710** seize. **714** greeted. **717** in reply, churl, damn you. **718** completely wrapped up.

Why lyvestow so longe in so greet age?"
  This olde man gan looke in his visage
And seyde thus: "For I ne kan nat fynde
A man, thogh that I walked into Inde,
Neither in citee ne in no village,
That wolde chaunge his youthe for myn age;
And therfore moot I han myn age stille,
As longe tyme as it is Goddes wille.
Ne Deeth, allas, ne wol nat have my lyf.
Thus walke I lyk a restelees caytyf
And on the ground, which is my modres gate,
I knokke with my staf bothe erly and late
And seye, 'Leeve moder, leet me in!
Lo how I vanysshe, flessh and blood and skyn!
Allas, whan shal my bones been at reste?
Moder, with yow wolde I chaunge my cheste
That in my chambre longe tyme hath be,
Ye, for an heyre clowt to wrappe me!'
But yet to me she wol nat do that grace,
For which ful pale and welked is my face.
  "But, sires, to yow it is no curteisye
To speken to an old man vileynye
But he trespase in word or ellis in dede.
In holy writ ye may yourself wel rede:
'Agayns an old man, hoor upon his heed,
Ye shal arise'; wherfore I yeve yow reed,
Ne dooth unto an old man noon harm now
Namoore than that ye wolde men dide to yow
In age – if that ye so longe abyde.
And God be with yow wher ye go or ryde!
I moot go thider as I have to go."
  "Nay, olde cherl, by God, thow shalt nat so,"
Seyde this oother hasardour anon;
"Thow partest nat so lightly, by Seint John!
Thow speeke right now of thilke traytour Deeth
That in this contree alle oure freendes sleeth;
Have heer my trouthe, as thow art his espye,
Tel wher he is or thow shalt it abye,
By God and by the holy sacrament!
For soothly thow art oon of his assent
To sleen us yonge folk, thow false theef!"
  "Now, sires," quod he, "if that yow be so leef
To fynde Deeth, turn up this croked wey,

728 captive wretch. **731** Dear. **734** treasure-chest. **736** haircloth (shroud). **738** withered. **740** offensive words. **741** Unless. **743** In the presence of, grey-haired. **744** stand up (in respect), advice. **748** wherever you walk. **755** spy. **756** pay for it. **758** in league with him. **760** desirous.

For in that grove I lafte hym, by my fey,
Under a tree, and there he wol abyde;
Nat for youre boost he wol hym nothyng hyde.
Se ye that ook? Right ther ye shal hym fynde.
God save yow that boghte agayn mankynde,
And yow amende!" Thus seyde this olde man.
  And everich of thise riotoures ran
Til he cam to that tree, and ther they founde
Of floryns fyne of gold ycoyned rounde
Wel-ny an eighte busshels, as hem thoughte:
No lenger thanne after Deeth they soughte.
But ech of hem so glad was of the sighte,
For that the floryns been so faire and brighte,
That doun they sette hem by this precious hoord.
The worste of hem, he spak the firste word.
  "Bretheren," quod he, "taak kepe what that I seye:
My wit is greet, thogh that I bourde and pleye.
This tresor hath Fortune unto us yeven
In myrthe and jolitee oure lyf to lyven,
And lightly as it cometh so wol we spende.
Ey, Goddes precious dignytee! Who wende
Today that we sholde han so fair a grace?
But myghte this gold be caried fro this place
Hoom to myn hous, or ellis unto youres –
For wel ye woot that al this gold is oures –
Thanne were we in heigh felicitee.
But trewely, by daye it may nat be:
Men wolde seyn that we were theves stronge
And for oure owene tresor doon us honge.
This tresor moste ycaried be by nyghte
As wisly and as sleyly as it myghte.
Therfore I rede that cut amonges us alle
Be drawe and lat se wher the cut wol falle,
And he that hath the cut with herte blithe
Shal renne to the towne, and that ful swithe,
And brynge us breed and wyn ful prively.
And two of us shal kepen subtilly
This tresor wel; and if he wol nat tarye,
Whan it is nyght we wol this tresor carye
By oon assent wher as us thynketh best."
That oon of hem the cut broghte in his fest
And bad hem drawe and looke wher it wol falle;
And it fel on the yongeste of hem alle
And forth toward the town he wente anon.

778 jest. **782** would have thought. **789** arrant thieves. **790** have us hanged. **793** advise, lots be drawn. **796** very quickly. **802** fist.

And also soone as that he was agon
That oon of hem spak thus unto that oother:
"Thow knowest wel thow art my sworn brother;
Thy profit wol I telle thee anon.
Thow woost wel that oure felawe is agon,
And heere is gold, and that ful greet plentee,
That shal departed been among us thre.
But nathelees, if I kan shape it so
That it departed were among us two,
Hadde I nat doon a freendes torn to thee?"
   That oother answerde, "I noot how that may be:
He woot how that the gold is with us tweye.
What shal we doon? What shal we to hym seye?"
   "Shal it be conseil?" seyde the firste shrewe,
"And I shal tellen in a wordes fewe
What we shul doon and brynge it wel aboute."
   "I graunte," quod that oother, "out of doute,
That by my trouthe I wol thee nat biwreye."
   "Now," quod the firste, "thow woost wel we be tweye
And two of us shul strenger be than oon.
Looke whan that he is set, that right anon
Arys as though thow woldest with hym pleye
And I shal ryve hym thurgh the sydes tweye
Whil that thow strogelest with hym as in game
And with thy daggere looke thow do the same;
And thanne shal al this gold departed be,
My deere freend, bitwixe thee and me.
Thanne may we bothe oure lustes al fulfille
And pleye at dees right at oure owene wille."
And thus acorded been thise sherewes tweye
To sleen the thridde, as ye han herd me seye.
   This yongeste, which that wente to the toun,
Ful ofte in herte he rolleth up and doun
The beautee of thise floryns newe and brighte.
"O Lord!" quod he, "if so were that I myghte
Have al this tresor to myself allone,
Ther is no man that lyveth under the trone
Of God that sholde lyve so myrie as I!"
And at the laste the feend, oure enemy,
Putte in his thoght that he sholde poyson beye
With which he myghte sleen his felawes tweye –
For-why the feend foond hym in swich lyvynge
That he hadde leve hym to sorwe brynge.
For this was outrely his ful entente,

812 divided. **819** a secret, villain. **823** betray. **826** sat down. **827** (have some horse-play). **828** stab. **842** throne. **845** buy. **847** The reason being that, state of life. **848** permission (from God). **849** plainly.

To sleen hem bothe and nevere to repente.
  And forth he goth – no lenger wolde he tarye –
Into the toun unto a pothecarye,
And preyed hym that he hym wolde selle
Som poysoun that he myghte his rattes quelle;
And eek ther was a polcat in his hawe
That as he seyde his capons hadde yslawe,
And fayn he wolde wreke hym, if he myghte,
On vermyn that destroyed hym by nyghte.
  The pothecarie answerde, "And thow shalt have
A thyng that, also God my soule save,
In al this world ther is no creature
That ete or dronke hath of this confiture
Nat but the montaunce of a corn of whete
That he ne shal his lyf anoon forlete –
Ye, sterve he shal, and that in lasse while
Than thow wolt goon a-paas nat but a myle,
The poyson is so strong and violent."
  This cursed man hath in his hand yhent
This poyson in a box and sith he ran
Into the nexte strete unto a man
And borwed hym large botels thre
And in the two his poison poured he;
The thridde he kepte clene for his drynke,
For al the nyght he shoope hym for to swynke
In cariyng of the gold out of that place.
And whan this riotour, with sory grace,
Hadde filled with wyn hise grete botels thre,
To hise felawes agayn repaireth he.
  What nedeth it to sarmone of it moore?
For right as they hadde cast his deeth bifore,
Right so they han hym slayn and that anon.
And whan that this was doon, thus spak that oon:
"Now lat us sitte and drynke and make us merye
And afterward we wol his body berye."
And with that word it happed hym, *par cas*,
To take the botel ther the poyson was,
And drank, and yaf his felawe drynke also,
For which anon they storven bothe two.
  But certes, I suppose that Avycen
Wroot nevere in no canon ne in no *fen*
Mo wonder signes of empoysonyng
Than hadde thise wrecches two er hir endyng.
Thus ended been thise homicides two

854 kill. **855** yard. **857** avenge himself. **862** mixture. **863** amount. **864** lose. **865** die. **866** at a walking pace. **868** seized. **874** planned. **876** accursed may he be. **878** returns. **879** preach. **880** planned. **885** by chance. **888** died. **890** set of rules, chapter of treatise.

And eek the false empoysonere also.
O cursed synne of alle cursednesse!
O traytours homicide, O wikkednesse!
O glotonye, luxure, and hasardrye!
Thou blasphemour of Crist with vileynye
And othes grete of usage and of pryde!
Allas, mankynde, how may it bityde
That to thy Creatour which that thee wroghte
And with his precious herte-blood the boghte
Thow art so fals and so unkynde, allas!
Now, goode men, God foryeve yow youre trespas
And ware yow fro the synne of avarice!
Myn holy pardoun may yow alle warisse,
So that ye offre nobles or starlynges,
Or ellis silver broches, spones, rynges.
Boweth youre heed under this holy bulle!
Cometh up, ye wyves, offreth of youre wolle!
Youre name I entre here in my rolle anon:
Into the blisse of hevene shul ye gon.
I yow assoille, by myn heighe power,
Ye that wol offre, as clene and eek as cler
As ye were born. – And lo, sires, thus I preche.
And Jesu Crist, that is oure soules leche,
So graunte yow his pardoun to receyve,
For that is best – I wol yow nat deceyve.
But sires, o word forgat I in my tale:
I have relikes and pardon in my male
As faire as any man in Engelond,
Whiche were me yeven by the popes hond.
If any of yow wol of devocion
Offren and han myn absolucioun,
Com forth anon and kneleth here adoun
And mekely receyveth my pardoun;
Or ellis taketh pardoun as ye wende
Al newe and fressh at every myles ende,
So that ye offren, alwey newe and newe,
Nobles or pens whiche that been goode and trewe.
It is an honour to everich that is heer
That ye mowe have a suffisant pardoner
T' assoille yow in contree as ye ryde
For aventures whiche that may bityde.
Paraventure ther may falle oon or two
Doun of his hors and breke his nekke a-two:

896 treacherous. **897** lechery. **899** oaths, habit. **902** redeemed thee. **905** guard. **906** save. **907** Provided, gold coins, silver pennies. **910** wool. **913** absolve. **916** physician. **920** bag. **932** competent. **934** chances, befall.

Looke which a seuretee is it to yow alle
That I am in youre felaweship yfalle
That may assoille yow, bothe moore and lasse,
Whan that the soule shal fro the body passe.
I rede that oure Hoost heere shal bigynne,
For he is moost envoluped in synne.
Com forth, sire Hoost, and offre first anon
And thow shalt kisse the relikes everychon,
Ye, for a grote! Unbokele anon thy purs.'
'Nay, nay!' quod he, 'thanne have I Cristes curs!
Lat be,' quod he, 'it shal nat be, so thee ich!
Thow woldest make me kisse thyn olde breech
And swere it were a relyk of a seint,
Thogh it were with thy fondement depeynt!
But, by the croys which that Seint Eleyne foond,
I wold I hadde thy coylons in myn hond.
Instide of relikes or of seintuarie
Lat cutte hem of, I wol thee helpe hem carie:
They shul be shryned in an hogges toord!'
This Pardoner answerde nat a word:
So wrooth he was, no word ne wolde he seye.
'Now,' quod oure Hoost, 'I wol no lenger pleye
With thee, ne with noon oother angry man.'
But right anon the worthy Knyght bigan,
Whan that he saugh that al the peple lough,
'Namoore of this, for it is right ynough!
Sire Pardoner, be glad and murye of cheere;
And ye, sire Hoost, that been to me so deere,
I pray yow that ye kisse the Pardoner.
And Pardoner, I pray thee, drawe thee neer,
And as we diden lat us lawe and pleye.'
Anon they kiste, and ryden forth hir weye.

937 what an excellent form of insurance. **941** suggest. **945** even if you only give a groat. **946** may I be damned first!. **947** as I may thrive (I swear). **948** drawers (under-breeches). **950** arse-hole. **952** testicles. **953** Instead of, a sainted relic. **954** Let's have them cut off. **955** turd. **967** laugh. **968** rode.

William Langland (fl. 1375–1380)

From the Vision of Piers Plowman (C-text)

Prologue, 1–94, 139–233 (end): The Field Full of Folk

In a somur sesoun whan softe was the sonne
I shope me into shroudes as I a shep were –
In abite as an heremite unholy of werkes
Wente forth in the world wondres to here,
And say many sellies and selkouthe thynges.
Ac on a May mornyng on Malverne hulles
Me biful for to slepe, for werynesse of-walked;
And in a launde as I lay, lened I and slepte,
And merveylousliche me mette, as I may telle.
Al the welthe of the world and the wo bothe
Wynkyng, as hit were, witterliche I seigh hit;
Of treuthe and tricherye, tresoun and gyle,
Al I say slepynge, as I shal telle.
  Estward I beheld aftir the sonne
And say a tour – as I trowed, Treuthe was there-ynne;
  Westward I waytede in a while aftir
And seigh a depe dale – Deth, as I leue,
Woned in tho wones, and wikkede spirites.
A fair feld ful of folk fond I ther bytwene
Of alle manere men, the mene and the pore,
Worchyng and wandryng as this world asketh.
  Somme putte hem to the plogh, playde ful selde,
In settynge and in sowynge swonken ful harde
And wonne that this wastors with glotony destrueth.
And summe putte hem to pruyde and parayled hem ther-aftir
In continance of clothyng in many kyne gyse.
In preiers and penaunces putten hem mony,
Al for love of oure lord lyveden swythe harde

2 dressed, rough woollen garments. **3** Dressed in the habit of a hermit, but not one dedicated to holy works. **5** marvels, extraordinary. **7** exhausted with walking. **8** grassy clearing, reclined. **9** I dreamed. **11** truly. **14** in the direction of. **16** looked. **17** believe. **18** dwelt, regions. **23** worked. **24** what. **25** dressed accordingly. **26** outward show, kinds of way.

In hope to have a good ende and hevenriche blisse,
As ankeres and eremites that holdeth hem in here selles,
Coveyten noght in contreys to cayren aboute
For no likerous liflode here lycame to plese.
And summe chesen chaffare – thei cheveth the bettre,
As it semeth to oure sighte that suche men ythryveth;
And summe murthes to make as mynstrels conneth,
Wolleth neyther swynke ne swete, bote sweren grete othes,
Fyndeth out foule fantasyes and foles hem maketh
And hath wytt at wille to worche yf thei wolde.
That Poule prechede of hem preve hit I myhte:
Qui turpiloquium loquitur is Luciferes knave.
Bidders and beggers fast aboute yede
Til here bagge and here bely was bretful ycrammed,
Fayteden for here fode and foughten at the ale.
In glotonye tho gomes goth thei to bedde
And ryseth with rybaudrye tho Robardes knaves;
Slep and also slewthe sueth suche ever.
Pilgrymes and palmers plighten hem togyderes
To seke seynt Jame and seyntes of Rome,
Wenten forth on here way with many wyse tales
And hadde leve to lye aftir, al here lyf-tyme.
Eremites on an hep with hokede staves
Wenten to Walsyngham, and here wenches aftir;
Grete lobies and longe that loth were to swynke
Clothed hem in copis to be knowe fram othere
And made hemself heremites, here ese to have.
I fonde ther of freris alle the foure ordres,
Prechyng the peple for profyt of the wombe,
And glosede the gospel as hem good likede;
For coveytise of copis contraryed somme doctours.
Mony of thise maistres of mendenant freres
Here moneye and marchandise marchen togyderes.
Ac sith charite hath be chapman and chief to shryve lordes
Mony ferlyes han falle in a fewe yeres,
And but holi chirche and charite choppe adoun suche shryvars
The moste meschief on molde mounteth up faste.
Ther prechede a pardoner as he a prest were
And brought forth a bulle with bischopis selys,
Sayde that hymself myhte assoylen hem alle
Of falsnesses of fastynges, of vowes ybrokene.
Lewed men leved hym wel and lykede his wordes

30 anchorites. **31** wander. **32** dainty living, body. **33** choose trade. **35** know how to. **37** behave like fools. **38** at their command. **41** Beggars. **42** brimful. **43** Begged falsely. **45** robbers (a cant term, 'Bob's lads'). **46** attend upon. **47** bound. **53** lazy hulking fellows. **54** long gowns, known (as different). **59** doctors of theology. **62** merchant. **63** marvels. **64** unless.

And comen and knelede to kyssen his bulles;
He bounchede hem with his bulles and blered here yes
And raughte with his rageman rynges and broches.
 Thus ye gyve youre gold glotons to helpe
And leneth hit lorelles that lecherye haunten!
Were the bischop yblessed and worth bothe his eres
His seel sholde nought be ysent in deseyte of the people.
Ac it is nought by the bischop, I leve, that the boy precheth
For the parsche prest and the pardoner parten the selver
That the peple in parsches sholde have, yf thei ne were.
 Persones and parsche prestis pleyned to the bischop
That here parsches were pore sithe this pestelence tyme,
To have a licence and a leve in Londoun to dwelle
And synge ther for symonye while selver is so swete.
 Bischopes and bachelers, bothe maystres and doctours,
That han cure under Crist and crownyng in tokene –
Ben charged with holy chirche charite to tylie,
That is lele love and lyfe among lered and lewed –
Leyen in Londoun in lenton and elles.
Summe serven the kynge and his silver tellen,
In the Cheker and in the Chancerye chalengen his dettes
Of wardes and of wardemotis, wayves and strayves;
And summe aren as seneschalles and serven other lordes
And ben in stede of stewardes and sitten and demen.

{Conscience has an intervention here condemning worldly priests before the poem turns to the question of authority in this field full of folk, this turbulent commonwealth: by what right does the king rule?}

Thenne cam ther a kyng, knyghthede hym ladde,
Myght of tho men made hym to regne.
And thenne cam Kynde Wytt and clerkes he made
For to counseillen the kyng and the commune save
And Conscience and Kynde Wit and knyghthed togedres
Caste that the comunes sholde here comunes fynde.
Kynde Wytt and the commune contreved alle craftes
And for most profitable to the peple a plogh gonne thei make,
With lele labour to lyve while lif on londe lasteth.
 Thenne Kynde Witt to the kynge and to the comune saide,
'Crist kepe the, kynge, and thy kyneriche
And leve the lede so thy londe that Lewte the lovye

72 tapped them on the head. **73** raked in, roll of papal parchment. **75** give, lazy rascals. **76** truly blessed (in his vocation) and "worth his salt". **78** according to the bishop's will. **79** divide. **81** Parsons. **85** bachelors of divinity. **86** cure of souls, tonsure. **87** cultivate. **88** true. **90** count. **91** Exchequer, make formal demand of. **94** pass judgement. **141** 'Natural Intelligence'. **144** Made a plea that the commons should provide food for the whole community. **145** devised. **149** kingdom. **150** grant.

And for thy rightful ruylynge be rewardid in hevene.'
  Conscience to clergie and to the kynge sayde,
'"*Sum Rex, sum princeps*" – *neutrum fortasse deinceps!*
O qui jura regis christi specialia regis,
Hoc ut agas melius, justus es, esto pius.
Nudum jus a te vestiri vult pietate.
Qualia vis metere talia grana sere.
Si seritur pietas de pietate metas.'
  Conscience and the kynge into court wente
Where hoved an hundrid in hoves of selke,
Serjantz it semede that serveth at the barre,
Plededen for penyes and poundes be lawe
And nat for love of oure lord unlose here lyppes ones.
Thow myghtest betre meten myst on Malverne hilles
Than gete a mum of here mouth ar moneye were hem shewed!
  Then ran ther a route of ratones as hit were
And smale muys with hem, mo then a thousend,
Comen til a conseyl for here comune profyt.
For a cat of a court cam whan hym likede
And overlep hem lightliche and laghte hem alle at wille
And playde with somme perilously and putte hem ther hym lykede.
'And yf we groche of his game he wol greve us sore,
To his clees clawe us and in his cloches us halde
That us lotheth the lyf ar he lette us passe.
Myghte we with eny wyt his wille with-sytte
We myhte be lordes a-lofte and lyve as us luste.'
  A ratoun of renown moste resonable of tonge
Sayde, 'I have seyen grete syres in cytees and in townes
Bere beyes of bryghte gold al aboute here nekkes
And colers of crafty werk, bothe knyghtes and squieres.
Wer ther a belle on here beygh, by Jesu, as me thynketh,
Men myghte ywete where thei wente and here way roume.
Ryght so,' quath the raton, 'reison me shewith
A belle to byggen of bras other of bryghte sylver
And knytten hit on a coler for oure comune profyt
And hongen hit aboute the cattes halse, thanne here we mowe
Wher he rit othere reste or rometh to pleye;
And yf hym lust for to layke than loke we mowe
And apere in his presence the while hym pleye lyketh
And yf hym wratheth ben we war and his way roume.'

153 (You say) "I am king, I am prince" – but neither perhaps one day! You who administer the supreme laws of Christ the king, that you may do it better, be merciful, as you are just. Naked justice should be clothed by you in mercy. Sow as you would reap. If mercy is sown, may you reap mercy. **160** lawyers' caps. **161** serjeants-at-law (barristers). **164** measure. **166** crowd. **170** pounced on, seized. **172** grumble. **173** claws. **175** withstand. **182** know, leave clear. **184** buy. **187** rides. **188** play (be in a good mood). **190** And if he is in a bad mood we can be wary and get out of his way.

Alle thise route of ratones to this resoun thei assentide,
Ac tho the belle was ybrought and on the beygh hangid
Ther ne was no raton of al the route for al the reame of Fraunce
That derste have ybounde the belle aboute the kattes nekke
Ne have hanged it aboute his hals al Yngelond to wynne;
And leten here labour ylost and al here longe study.
A mous that moche good couthe, as me tho thoughte,
Strok forth sturnely and stod byfore hem alle
And to the route of ratones rehersede thise wordes:
'Thogh we hadde ykuld the cat yut shulde ther come another
To crache us and alle oure kynde thogh we crope under benches.
Forthy I conseile for oure comune profit lat the cat yworthe
And be nevere so bold the belle hym to shewe.
For I herde my syre sayn, sevene yer ypassed,
"Ther the cat is but a kytoun the court is ful elynge."
Wyttenesse at holy wryt, who-so kan rede:
Ve terre ubi puer est Rex!
I seye it for me,' quod the mous, 'I se so muche aftur,
Shal never the cat ne kytoun be my conseil be greved
Ne carpen of here colers that costede me nevere.
And thogh hit costed my catel, byknowen I ne wolde
But soffre and sey nought and that is the beste
Til that meschief amende hem that many man chasteth.
For many mannys malt we muys wolde distruye
And the route of ratones of reste men awake
Ne were the cat of the court and yonge kitones toward;
For hadde ye ratones youre reik, ye couthe nat reule yow-selven.'
(What this meteles bymeneth, ye men that ben merye,
Devyne ye, for I ne dar, by dere god almyhten.)
Yut mette me more of mene and of riche,
As barones and burgeys and bondemen of thorpes,
Al I say slepynge as ye shal here heraftur:
Bothe bakeres and breweres, bochers and other,
Webbesteres and walkeres and wynners with handes,
As taylers and tanners and tulyers of the erthe,
As dykers and delvers that doth here dedis ylle
And dryveth forth here days with '*Dew vous save, dame Emme.*'
Cokes and here knaves cryede, 'Hote pyes, hote!
Goode gees and grys! Ga we dyne, ga we!'
Taverners til hem tolde the same:
'Whit wyn of Oseye and wyn of Gascoyne,
Of the Reule and of the Rochele the roost to defye!'
Al this I say sleping and sevyn sythes more.

196 considered. **198** Stepped quickly. **202** be. **207** Woe to the land where a child is king (cf. Eccl. 10:16). **210** speak. **213** misfortune, chastens. **216** ready at hand. **217** free run. **218** dream. **221** important city men, villages. **224** Women-weavers, cloth-fullers. **226** ditchers. **229** piglets. **230** cried their wares. **231** Alsace. **233** times.

{In Passus I, the lady Holy Church explains Will's vision to him, shows him how a right use of worldly goods would be in accord with God's Law, and answers his urgent entreaty, How may I save my soul? (I.80), which in a sense initiates the whole movement of the poem, with a preliminary outline of the doctrine of Charity. But Will wishes to understand more of the ways of the world, and is presented in Passus II–IV with the vision of maiden Meed, an allegorical portrayal of the corruption of every estate and activity of society through the influence of money. Meed is on the brink of marriage to Falsehood, or, as it might be, the incentive of financial gain (not in itself wicked) is to become an institutionalized form of corruption; but Theology insists that Meed is already betrothed to Truth, and the king, as her guardian, must adjudicate. So all must go to the king's court at Westminster.}

Passus III. 1–67: Meed at Westminster

Now is Mede the mayde and namo of hem alle
Thorw bedeles and baylifs ybrouhte byfor the kyng.
The kyng callede a clerke – I can nat his name –
To take Mede the mayde and maken here at ese.
'I shal asaye here mysulve and sothliche appose
What man of this world that here levest hadde,
And yf she worche wysely and by wys men consayl
I wol forgyve here alle gultes, so me God helpe.'
  Cortesliche the clerk thenne, as the kyng hyhte,
Took Mede by the myddel and myldeliche here brouhte
Into boure with blisse and by here gan sitte.
Ac there was myrthe and mynstracie Mede to plese;
That wendeth to Westmynstre worschipede here monye.
Genteliche with joye the justices somme
Boskede hem to the bour ther this buyrde dwelte
And confortede here as they couthe, by the clerkes leve,
And sayden, 'Mourne nat, Mede, ne make thow no sorwe
For we wol wisse the kyng and thy way shape
For to wedde at thy wille where the leef liketh
For al Consciences cast and craft, as y trowe.'
  Myldeliche Mede thenne mercyede hem alle
Of here grete goodnesse and gaf hem uchone
Coupes of clene gold, coppes of sylver,
Rynges with rubees and othere riche yeftes,
The leste man of here mayne a motoun of gold.
  Whenne they hadde lauhte here leve at this lady Mede
Thenne come clerkes to conforte here the same
And beden here be blythe, 'For we beth thyn owene
For to worche thy wille the while thou myhte dure.'

5 ask. **9** commanded. **13** Those many who. **14** some of them. **15** Hastened, maiden. **18** advise. **19** gladly. **20** contrivance. **21** thanked. **23** Bowls. **25** (Give) the humblest of her followers a gold coin (stamped with a sheep). **26** taken. **28** bade.

And Mede hendeliche behyhte hem the same,
To lovye hem leeliche and lordes to make,
'And purchace yow provendres while youre panes lasteth
And bygge yow benefices, pluralite to have,
And in the constorie at court do calle youre names.
Shal no lewedenesse lette the clerk that I lovye
That he ne worth furste vaunsed, for I am byknowe
There connynge clerkes shal clokke byhynde.'
  Thenne come ther a confessour ycoped as a frere,
To Mede the mayde myldeliche he sayde:
'Thogh lewed men and lered men haved layn by the bothe,
And Falshede yfonde the al this fourty wyntur,
I shal assoyle the mysulve for a seem whete
And yut be thy bedman and brynge adoun Conscience
Amonge kynges and knyhtes and clerkes and the lyke.'
  Thenne Mede for here mysdedes to this man knelede,
Shrofe here of here synne, shameles, I leve,
Tolde hym a tale and toke hym a noble
For to ben here bedman and to bere wel here ernde
Among knyhtes and clerkes, Conscience to turne.
  And he assoilede here sone and sethen he sayde:
'We han a wyndowe a-worchynge wol stande us ful heye;
Wolde ye glase that gable and grave ther youre name
In masse and in matynes for Mede we shal synge
Solempneliche and softlyche as for a suster of oure ordre.'
  Loveliche that lady laghynge sayde:
'I shal be youre frende, frere, and fayle yow nevere
The whiles ye lovyen this lordes that lecherye haunteth
And lacketh nat this ladyes that lovyeth the same.
Hit is but frelete of fleysche, ye fyndeth wel by bokes,
And a cours of kynde wherof we comen alle.
Ho may askape the sclaundre, the skathe myhte sone be mended;
Hit is synne as of sevene noon sonner relesed.
Haveth mercy,' quod Mede, 'on men that hit haunteth
And I shal cuvere youre kyrke and youre cloistre make,
Bothe wyndowes and wowes I wol amende and glase
And peynten and purtrayen ho payede for the makyng
That every seg shal se I am a sustre of youre ordre.'

[A long debate on the legitimacy of Meed ends with Conscience distinguishing carefully between improper reward (graft) and 'mesurable hyre'; a new age, with the king under the guidance of Conscience and Reason, seems about to begin. But first the conscience of

30 graciously. **31** truly. **32** pence. **33** buy. **35** ignorance hinder. **36** promoted, acknowledged. **37** hobble. **40** both slept with thee. **41** provided for. **42** horse-load of. **47** gave, gold coin. **48** message. **49** do down. **50** then. **51** cost. **58** blame. **59** frailty. **60** process of nature. **61** harm. **62** none more easily forgiven. **64** roof. **65** walls. **67** man.

the body politic must be purged by confession, and Will, in a passage new in C, makes first his own 'confession'. Whether autobiographically accurate in every detail or not, it places the author's 'life' squarely at the centre of the poem's meaning. It combines contrition with pugnacious self-justification in a characteristic way.}

Passus V. 1–104: Will's 'apologia pro vita sua'

Thus I awakede, wot God, whan I wonede in Cornehull,
Kytte and I in a cote, yclothed as a lollare,
And lytel ylet by, leveth me for sothe,
Amonges lollares of Londone and lewede ermytes,
For I made of tho men as resoun me tauhte.
  For as I cam by Conscience with Resoun I mette
In an hot hervest whenne I hadde myn hele
And lymes to labory with and lovede wel fare
And no dede to do but to drynke and to slepe.
In hele and in inwitt oon me apposede;
Romynge in remembraunce, thus Resoun me aratede.
  'Can thow serven,' he sayde, 'or syngen in a churche,
Or koke for my cokeres or to the cart piche,
Mowen or mywen or make bond to sheves,
Repe or been a rype-reve and aryse erly,
Or have an horn and be hayward and lygge theroute nyhtes
And kepe my corn in my croft fro pykares and theves?
Or shap shon or cloth, or shep and kyne kepe,
Heggen or harwen, or swyn or gees dryve,
Or eny other kynes craft that to the comune nedeth,
That thou betere therby that byleve the fynden?'
  'Sertes,' I sayde, 'and so me god helpe,
I am to wayke to worche with sykel or with sythe
And to long, lef me, lowe to stoupe,
To wurche as a werkeman eny while to duyren.'
  'Thenne hastow londes to lyve by,' quod Resoun, 'or lynage ryche
That fynde the thy fode? For an ydel man thow semest,
A spendour that spene mot or a spille-tyme,
Or beggest thy bylyve aboute at men hacches
Or faytest uppon Frydayes or feste-dayes in churches,
The whiche is lollarne lyf, that lytel is preysed
There ryhtfulnesse rewardeth ryht as men deserveth.

1 lived in Cornhill (a district of London). **2** little cottage. **3** esteemed, believe. **5** composed verses about. **7** health. **8** to live well. **10** questioned. **12** assist in the service. **13** pile hay, haycock-makers. **14** Mow, or stack the mown swathes, or make straw-binding for sheaves. **15** head-reaper. **16** hedge-ward. **17** field, pilferers. **20** kind of. **21** That you might improve thereby the life of those that provide for you. **23** weak. **28** must spend. **29** food, men's. **30** begs falsely. **31** idlers'.

Reddet unicuique iuxta opera sua.
Or thow art broke, so may be, in body or in membre
Or ymaymed thorw som myshap, whereby thow myhte be excused?'
'When I yong was, many yer hennes,
My fader and my frendes fonde me to scole,
Tyl I wyste witterly what holy writ menede
And what is beste for the body, as the bok telleth,
And sykerest for the soule, by so I wol contenue.
And fond I nere, in fayth, seth my frendes deyede,
Lyf that me lykede but in this longe clothes.
And yf I be labour sholde lyven and lyflode deserven,
That laboure that I lerned beste therwith lyven I sholde.
In eadem vocacione in qua vocati estis.
And so I lyve yn London and opelond bothe;
The lomes that I labore with and lyflode deserve
Is *pater-noster* and my prymer, *placebo* and *dirige*,
And my sauter som tyme and my sevene psalmes.
This I segge for here soules of suche as me helpeth,
And tho that fynden me my fode fouchen-saf, I trowe,
To be welcome when I come, other-while in a monthe,
Now with hym, now with here; on this wyse I begge
Withoute bagge or botel but my wombe one.
'And also moreover me thynketh, syre Resoun,
Me sholde constrayne no clerc to no knaves werkes,
For by the lawe of Levyticy that oure lord ordeynede,
Clerkes ycrouned, of kynde understondynge,
Sholde nother swynke ne swete ne swerien at enquestes
Ne fyhte in no faumewarde ne his foe greve.
Non reddas malum pro malo.
For hit ben eyres of hevene, alle that ben ycrouned,
And in quoer and in kyrkes Cristes mynistres.
Dominus pars hereditatis mee. Et alibi: Clemencia non constringit.
Hit bycometh for clerkes Crist for to serve
And knaves uncrounede to carte and to worche.
For sholde no clerke be crouned but yf he come were
Of frankeleynes and fre men and of folke ywedded.
Bondemen and bastardes and beggares children,
Thyse bylongeth to labory, and lordes kyn to serve
God and good men, as here degre asketh,
Somme to synge masses or sitten and wryten,
Reden and resceyven that resoun ouhte to spene.
'Ac sythe bondemen barnes han be mad bisshopes

37 truly. **39** provided that I persevere. **40** never. **44** up in the country. **45** tools. **48** These I say. **49** vouchsafe. **50** from time to time. **52** stomach alone. **54** Men, low-born men's. **55** (Leviticus 21). **56** tonsured, it stands to reason. **58** vanguard of an army. **59** they are the heirs. **60** choir. **67** rank requires. **69** Advise. **70** children.

And barnes bastardes han be erchedekenes
And soutares and here sones for sulver han be knyhtes
And lordes sones here laboreres and leyde here rentes to wedde,
For the ryhte of this reume ryden ayeyn oure enemyes
In confort of the comune and the kynges worschipe,
'And monkes and moniales, that mendenantes sholde fynde,
Imade here kyn knyhtes and knyhtes-fees ypurchased,
Popes and patrones pore gentel blood refused
And taken Symondes sones seyntwarie to kepe,
Lyf-holynesse and love hath be longe hennes,
And wol, til hit be wered out, or otherwyse ychaunged.
'Forthy rebuke me ryhte nauhte, Resoun, I yow praye,
For in my conscience I knowe what Crist wolde I wrouhte.
Preyeres of a parfit man and penaunce discret
Is the levest labour that oure lord pleseth.
Non de solo,' I sayde, 'for sothe *vivit homo*,
Nec in pane et in pabulo, the pater-noster wittenesseth;
Fiat voluntas dei – that fynt us alle thynges.'
Quod Conscience, 'By Crist, I can nat se this lyeth;
Ac it semeth no sad parfitnesse in citees to begge,
But he be obediencer to prior or to mynistre.'
'That is soth,' I saide, 'and so I beknowe –
That I have ytynt tyme and tyme myspened;
Ac yut, I hope, as he that ofte hath ychaffared
And ay loste and loste, and at the laste hym happed
He bouhte suche a bargayn he was the bet evere,
And sette al his los at a leef at the laste ende,
Suche a wynnyng hym warth thorw wordes of grace.
Simile est regnum celorum thesauro abscondito in agro.
Mulier que inuenit dragmam, etc.
So hope I to have of hym that is almyghty
A gobet of his grace, and bigynne a tyme
That alle tymes of my tyme to profit shal turne.'
'I rede the,' quod Resoun tho, 'rape the to bigynne
The lyf that is louable and leele to thy soule' –
'Ye, and contynue!' quod Conscience; and to the kyrke I wente.

[Reason now preaches a sermon before the king, calling upon the people to amend their lives and to seek Saint Truth. The confessions of the Seven Deadly Sins follow. Langland personifies the Sins as individuals, and draws for their portrayal on a rich repertoire of sermon-material, a mass of vivid and circumstantial detail of urban and rural life, and a variety of dramatic, pictorial and iconographic techniques. Much goes beyond the possible experience of a single individual, and the Sins are not self-standing satirical

72 shoemakers. **73** mortgaged their estates. **76** nuns, beggars. **77** knights' estates. **79** sanctuary. **85** most precious. **88** provides us with. **90** steadfast. **91** Unless he be someone licensed to beg by a prior or church official. **92** acknowledge. **93** wasted. **94** made business deals. **97** at nothing. **98** came to him. **102** hasten.

'characters' but individualized versions of different characteristic types of homiletic treatment of the vices in question. Pride leads off, followed by Envy and then Wrath.}

Passus VI. 103–69, 196–238, 350–441 (end): The Confession of the People

Thenne awakede Wrathe, with two whyte eyes
And with a nivilynge nose, nippynge his lippes.
'I am Wrothe' quod that weye, 'wol gladliche smyte
Bothe with stoon and with staf, and stele uppon myn enemye;
To sle hym sleyliche sleythes I bythenke.
Thogh I sitte this sevene yer I sholde nat wel telle
The harm that I have do with hand and with tonge;
Inpacient in alle penaunces, and pleyned as hit were,
On God, when me greved auht, and grochede of his sonde,
As som tyme in somur and also in hervest,
But I hadde weder at my wille, I witte God the cause
In alle manere angres that I hadde or felede.
'Amonges alle manere men my dwellyng is som tyme,
With lewed and lered that leef ben to here
Harm of eny man, byhynde or bifore.
Freres folewen my fore fele tyme and ofte
And preven inparfit prelates of holy churche;
And prelates pleyneth on hem for they here parschiens shryuen
Withoute licence and leve – and herby lyveth wrathe.
Thus thei speke and dispute that uchon dispiseth other.
Thus beggares and barones at debat aren ofte
Til I, Wrathe, wexe an hey and walke with hem bothe.
Or til they bothe be beggares and by spiritualte libbe
Or alle riche and ryde, reste shal I nat, Wrathe,
That I ne mot folowe this folk – my fortune is non other.
'I have an aunte to nonne and an abbesse;
Here were lever swowe or swelte then soffre eny payne.
I have be cok in here kychene and the covent served,
Mony monthes with hem and with monkes bothe.
I was the prioresse potager and other pore ladies,
And made hem joutes of jangelynge: "Dame Jone was a bastard,
And dame Clarice a knyhtes douhter, a cokewolde was here syre,
And dame Purnele a prestis fyle – prioresse worth she nevere;
For she hadde childe in the chapun-cote she worth chalenged at the eleccioun."

103 praiseworthy. **104** running with mucus. **105** man. **107** cunning plots, think up. **111** grumbled, what he sends. **113** blamed. **116** glad. **117** behind his back or in his presence. **118** lead. **120** parishioners. **124** grow strong. **125** Either, live. **126** grow rich. **128** who is a nun. **129** swoon or die. **132** vegetable-cook. **133** soups of squabbling. **135** filly (concubine), will be. **136** hen-house, accused.

Thus sytte they, tho sustres, sum tyme, and disputen
Til "thow lixt" and "thow lixt" be lady over hem alle;
And thenne awake I, Wrathe, and wolde be avenged.
And thenne I crye and crache with my kene nayles,
Byte and bete and brynge forth suche thewes
That alle ladyes me lotheth that lovyeth eny worschipe.
'Amonges wyves and wydewes I am woned to sitte
Yparroked in pues; the persone hit knoweth
How lytel I lovye Letyse-at-the-style;
For she had haly-bred ar I, my herte gan change.
Aftur mete aftirward she and she chydde
And I, Wrath, was war, and wrathe on hem bothe,
Tyl ayther clepede other "hore" and on with the clawes
Til bothe here hedes were bar and blody here chekes.
'Amonges monkes I myhte be, ac mony tyme I spare,
For there aren many felle frekes myne aferes to aspye,
That is, priour and suppriour and oure *pater abbas.*
And yf I telle eny tales they taken hem togyderes
And don me faste Fridayes to bred and to water.
Yut am I chalenged in oure chapitre-hous as I a childe were
And balayshed on the bare ers and no brech bytwene.
I have no luste, lef me, to longe amonges monkes,
For I ete more fysch then flesche there, and feble ale drynke.
Ac other-while when wyn cometh and when I drynke late at even
I have a flux of a foul mouth wel fyve daies aftur,
And al that I wiste wykked by eny of oure covent
I cough hit up in oure cloystre, that al the covent wot hit.'
'Now repente,' quod Repentaunce, 'and reherce nevere
Consayl that thow knowest, by continaunce ne by speche.
And drynke nat overdelycatly no to depe neyther,
That thy wil ne thy wit to wrathe myhte turne.
Esto sobrius,' he saide, and assoiled hym aftur,
And bad hym bid to god, be his help to amende.

{Lechery makes a brief appearance, then Covetousness.}

Thenne cam Covetyse – I can hym nat descreve,
So hungrily and holow sire Hervy hym lokede.
He was bitelbrowed and baburlippid, with two blered eyes,
And as a letherne pors lollede his chekes,
Wel sydere then his chyn ycheveled for elde;
And as a bondemannes bacoun his berd was yshave,

138 liest. **141** shows of behaviour. **144** Enclosed in pews. **147** the one woman and the other. **148** stirred them to anger. **151** don't bother. **152** stern, doings. **154** consult. **157** caned. **158** dwell long. **164** repeat. **165** Secret. **168** Be sober (1 Pet. 5:8). **169** pray, to be. **196** describe. **198** thick-lipped. **199** purse. **200** lower, wobbled.

With his hood on his heved and his hat bothe,
In a tore tabard of twelve wynter age –
But yf a lous couthe lepe, I leve and I trowe,
He ne sholde wandre uppon that walch, so was hit thredbare.
'I have be covetous,' quod this kaytif, 'I biknowe hit here.
For som tyme I served Symme-at-the-style
And was his prentis yplyht, his profit to wayte.
Furste I lerned to lye a leef other tweye;
Wykkedliche to waye was my furste lessoun.
To Wy and to Wynchestre I wente to the fayre
With many manere marchandise, as my maister hyhte;
Ne hadde the grace of gyle go among my ware,
Hit hadde be unsold this sevene yer, so me god helpe!
'Thenne drow I me amonge drapers, my donet to lere,
To drawe the lyst along, the lenger hit semede.
Amonges the ryche rayes I rendrede a lessoun,
To brochen hem with a bat-nelde and bande hem togyderes,
Putte hem in pressoures and pynne hem ther-ynne,
Til ten yerde other twelve tolde out threttene.
'My wyf was a webbe and wollene cloth made;
Sche spak to the spynnesteres to spynnen it oute.
The pound that she payede hem by peysed a quarter more
Then myn owene auncel, when I wayed treuthe.
'I bouhte here barly, she brew hit to sulle;
Peny-ale and poddyng-ale she poured togederes,
For laboreres and for louh folke that lay by hymsulve.
Ac the beste ale lay in my bour and in my bedchaunbre
And ho-so bommede thereof he bouhte hit theraftur
A galon for a grote – and yut no grayth mesure
When hit cam in coppe-mele; this crafte my wyf usede.
Rose the regrater was here ryhte name;
Sche hadde holde hokkerye this elevene wynter.'
'Repentedestow nevere?' quod Repentaunce, 'ne restitucioun madest?'
'Yus, ones I was herberwed,' quod he, 'with an heep of chapmen;
I ros and ryflede here males when they a-reste were.'
'That was a ruful restitucioun,' quod Repentaunce, 'for sothe;
Thow wolt be hanged heye therfore, here other in helle!'

[The interrogation of Covetousness continues at some length. The account of Gluttony that follows is unique in being presented, up to l. 421, as a continuous narrative.]

203 torn jerkin. **204** believe. **205** cheap Welsh flannel. **206** wretch, confess. **208** bound, see to. **209** pageful or two. **210** weigh. **211** Weyhill (in Hampshire). **212** commanded. **215** to learn my grammar. **216** stretch the edge of the cloth. **217** striped cloths. **220** reckoned out at. **221** weaver. **222** spin out the yarn loosely (to make it go further). **223** weighed. **224** scales. **225** brewed, sell. **226** thin ale (penny a gallon), thick. **229** tasted. **230** (fourpence), true. **231** cupfuls (inexact measures). **232** retailer. **233** carried on fraudulent retail-dealing. **235** lodged. **236** bags.

Now bygynneth Glotoun for to go to shryfte
And kayres hym to kyrke-ward, his conpte to shewe.
Fastyng on a Friday forth gan he wende
By Betene hous the brewestere, that bad hym good morwen,
And whodeward he wolde the breuh-wyf hym askede.
'To holy churche,' quod he, 'for to here masse,
And sennes sitte and be shryve and synege no more.'
'I have good ale, gossip Glotoun, woltow assaye?'
'Hastow,' quod he, 'eny hote spyces?'
'I have pepur and pyonie and a pound of garlek,
A ferthyng-worth fenkelsedes, for fastyng-dayes I bouhte hit.'
Thenne goth Glotoun in and Grete Othes aftur.
Sesse the souteres sat on the benche,
Watte the wernare and his wyf dronke,
Tymme the tynekare and tweyne of his knaves,
Hicke the hackenayman and Hewe the nedlare,
Claryce of Cockes-lane and the clerc of the churche,
Syre Peres of Prydie and Purnele of Flaundres,
An hayward, an heremyte, the hangeman of Tybourne,
Dawe the dikere, with a doseyne harlotes
Of portours and of pikeporses and of pilede toth-draweres,
A rybibour and a ratoner, a rakeare and his knave,
A ropere and a redyng-kynge and Rose the disshere,
Godefray the garlek-monger and Gryffyth the Walshe,
And of uphalderes an heep, herly by the morwe
Geven Glotoun with glad chere good ale to hansull.
Clement the coblere cast of his cloke
And to the newe fayre nempnede hit forth to sull.
Hicke the hackenayman hit his hod aftur
And bade Bitte the bochere ben on his syde.
There were chapmen ychose this chaffare to preyse,
That ho-so hadde the hood sholde nat have the cloke,
And that the bettere thyng, be arbitreres, bote sholde the worse.
Tho rysen up rapliche and rouned togyderes
And preisede this peniworths apart by hemsulve,
And there were othes an heep, for on sholde have the worse.
They couthe nat by here conscience acorden for treuthe
Til Robyn the ropere aryse they bisouhte
And nempned hym for a noumper, that no debat were.
Hicke the hostiler hadde the cloke,

351 goes, reckoning (of sin). **353** Betty's. **354** whither. **356** then, sin. **357** have a taste. **359** peony(-seeds). **362** Cissy the shoemaker-woman. **363** Walt the warren-keeper. **365** horse-hirer. **366** (a street of brothels). **367** Prunella. **368** hedge-warden. **369** Davy the ditch-digger. **370** bald-headed. **371** A rubible-player and a ratcatcher, a street-sweeper and his lad. **372** master reed-thatcher, dish-seller. **374** second-hand clothes dealers. **375** as a gift ('the first round'). **377** nominated, sell. **378** threw in. **380** deal, appraise. **382** arbitrators, compensate. **383** quickly, whispered. **388** nominated, umpire, so that there should be. **389** ostler.

In covenaunt that Clement sholde the coppe fulle,
And have Hickes hood the hostiler and holde hym yserved;
And ho-so repentede hym rathest sholde aryse aftur
And grete syre Glotoun with a galon of ale.
  There was leyhing and louryng and 'lat go the coppe!'
Bargaynes and bevereges bygan tho to awake,
And seten so til evensong, and songen umbywhile,
Til Glotoun hadde yglobbed a galoun and a gylle.
His gottes gan to gothly as two grydy sowes;
He pissede a potel in a pater-noster whyle,
He blew his rownd ruet at his rygebones ende,
That alle that herde the horne helde here nose aftur
And wesched hit hadde be wasche with a weps of breres.
He myhte nother steppe ne stande til he a staf hadde,
And thenne gan he go lyke a glemans byche,
Sum tyme asyde and sum tyme arere,
As ho-so layth lynes for to lacche foules.
  And when he drow to the dore, thenne dymmede his yes,
And thromblede at the thresfold and threw to the erthe,
And Clement the coblere cauhte hym by the myddel
And for to lyfte hym aloft leyde hym on his knees.
Ac Gloton was a greet cherl and greved in the luftynge
And cowed up a caudel in Clementis lappe;
Ys none so hungry hound in Hertfordshyre
Durste lape of that lyvynge, so unlovely hit smauhte.
  With alle the wo of this world his wyf and his wenche
Baren hym to his bed and brouhten hym ther-ynne,
And aftur al this exces he hadde an accidie aftur;
He sleep Saturday and Sonenday til the sonne yede to reste.
Then gan he wake wel wanne and wolde have ydronke;
The furste word that he spake was 'Who halt the bolle?'
His wif and his inwit edwitede hym of his synne;
He wax ashamed, that shrewe, and shrofe hym as swythe
To Repentaunce ryht thus: 'Have reuthe on me,' he saide,
'Thow lord that aloft art and alle lyves shope!
  'To the, God, I, Glotoun, gulty I me yelde
Of that I have trespased with tonge, I can nat telle how ofte,
Sworn "Godes soule and his sides!" and "So helpe me, God almyhty!"
There no nede ne was, many sythe falsly;
And over-sopped at my soper and som tyme at nones
More then my kynde myhte deffye,
And as an hound that eet gras so gan I to brake

392 soonest. **394** laughing and scowling. **395** start up anew. **396** from time to time. **398** rumble. **399** potful. **400** little trumpet, backbone's. **402** wished, sprig of briars. **405** backwards. **406** catch birds. **408** stumbled. **411** gave a lot of trouble. **412** coughed, mess. **414** leaving, smelt. **417** fit of sloth (hangover). **420** Who's got the bowl. **421** conscience, reproached. **424** created. **428** a time. **429** noon. **430** digest. **431** retch.

And spilde that I aspele myhte – I kan nat speke for shame
The vilony of my foule mouthe and of my foule mawe –
And fastyng-dayes bifore none fedde me with ale
Out of resoun, among rybaudes, here rybaudrye to here.
'Herof, gode God, graunte me foryevenesse
Of all my luyther lyf in al my lyf-tyme
For I vowe to verray God, for eny hungur or furste,
Shal nevere fysch in the Fryday defyen in my wombe
Til Abstinence myn aunte have yeve me leve –
And yut have I hated here al my lyf-tyme.'

432 what I might have kept in. **437** wicked.

The Gawain Poet (fl.1390)

Sir Gawain and the Green Knight

{A very large and fearsome knight, all green, arrives at Arthur's court at Camelot in the midst of the New Year's Day feast, and demands that the Round Table show its prowess by nominating a knight to engage with him in a Christmas 'game'. The game is that one of Arthur's knights shall strike a blow at the Green Knight with the great axe that he carries, and come a twelve-month later to the Green Chapel to receive a similar blow. Fear of the strange challenger, if not of the apparently ridiculous terms of the challenge, strikes the court dumb and Arthur has to step forward himself to take up the axe, but Gawain saves everyone further embarrassment by volunteering himself, with the utmost courtesy, to strike the first blow. His head having been struck off, the Green Knight, to everyone's dismay, picks it up and rides forth, reminding Gawain of his promise. Fit 2 (the poem is divided into four fits, or units of narration) describes Gawain's preparations to depart on the following All Soul's Day (30 November), with especial emphasis on his carrying of a pentangle on his shield and coat-armour symbolic of devotion to Christ and the Virgin. He rides off into the wilderness, apparently in the direction of the Peak District in northern England, but finds himself nowhere near his destination as Christmas Day dawns. He comes suddenly upon a marvellously beautiful castle, where he is warmly welcomed by the lord of the castle, his beautiful young wife, and an ancient crone who keeps her company. He is invited to stay over the Christmas holiday, and the lord will supply a guide to take him to the Green Chapel, which is nearby, on the appointed day. Meanwhile, he is to enjoy a game with his host on the last three days of the holiday: the lord will go out hunting each day, Gawain will stay at home and keep his wife company, and at the end of each day they will exchange whatever they have won during the day.}

Fit 3

Ful erly bifore the day the folk up rysen;
Gestes that go wolde hor gromes thay calden,
And thay busken up bilyve blonkkes to sadel,
Tyffen her takles, trussen her males,
Richen hem the rychest, to ryde alle arayde,
Lepen up lyghtly, lachen her brydeles,
Uche wyye on his way ther hym wel lyked.
The leve lorde of the londe was not the last

1128 hurry, quickly, horses. **1129** Prepare, pack their bags. **1130** Get themselves ready. **1131** take hold of. **1132** man. **1133** well-loved.

Arayed for the rydyng, with renkkes ful mony;
Ete a sop hastyly, when he had herde masse,
With bugle to bent-felde he buskes bylyve.
By that any daylyght lemed upon erthe,
He with his hatheles on hyghe horsses weren.
Thenne thise cacheres that couthe cowpled hor houndes,
Unclosed the kenel dore and calde hem theroute,
Blwe bygly in bugles thre bare mote;
Braches bayed therfore and breme noyse maked,
And thay chastysed and charred on chasyng that went,
A hundreth of hunteres, as I haf herde telle,
Of the best.
To trystors vewters yod,
Couples huntes of kest;
Ther ros for blastes gode
Gret rurd in that forest.

At the first quethe of the quest quaked the wylde;
Der drof in the dale, doted for drede,
Hiyed to the hyghe, bot heterly thay were
Restayed with the stablye, that stoutly ascryed.
Thay let the herttes haf the gate, with the hyghe hedes,
The breme bukkes also with hor brode paumes,
For the fre lorde hade defende in fermysoun tyme
That ther schulde no man meve to the male dere.
The hindes were halden in with 'hay!' and 'war!'
The does dryven with gret dyn to the depe slades.
Ther myght mon se, as thay slypte, slentyng of arwes;
At uche wende under wande wapped a flone,
That bigly bote on the broun with ful brode hedes.
What! thay brayen and bleden, bi bonkkes thay deyen,
And ay raches in a res radly hem folwes,
Hunteres with hyghe horne hasted hem after,
Wyth such a crakkande kry as klyffes haden brusten.
What wylde so atwaped wyyes that schotten
Was al to-raced and rent at the resayt,
Bi thay were tened at the hyghe and taysed to the wattres –

1134 men. **1135** He ate. **1136** open field. **1137** By the time that, gleamed. **1139** huntsmen, who knew their job, leashed in pairs. **1141** three single notes. **1142** Hounds, loud. **1143** turned back those that went chasing off. **1146** The keepers of the hounds went to their hunting-stations, and the huntsmen threw off the leashes. **1148** because of. **1149** noise. **1150** sound. **1151** fled, went frantic. **1152** high ground, promptly. **1153** Checked by the beaters, shouted out. **1154** way. **1155** fierce, antlers. **1156** forbidden in the close season. **1157** chase after. **1159** valleys. **1160** were released, the slanting flight. **1161** turn in the wood, flew an arrow. **1162** bit deeply into, brown (hide). **1164** hounds, rush, quickly. **1165** loud. **1167** escaped. **1168** receiving-station. **1169** After being barassed from, driven.

The ledes were so lerned at the lowe trysteres,
And the grehoundes so grete, that geten hem bylyve
And hem to-fylched as fast as frekes myght loke,
Ther ryght,
The lorde for blys abloy
Ful oft con launce and lyght,
And drof that day wyth joy
Thus to the derk nyght.

Thus laykes this lorde by lynde-wodes eves,
And Gawayn the god mon in gay bed lyges,
Lurkkes quyl the daylyght lemed on the wowes,
Under covertour ful clere, cortyned aboute.
And as in slomeryng he slode, sleyly he herde
A litel dyn at his dor, and derfly open;
And he heves up his hed out of the clothes,
A corner of the cortyn he caght up a lyttel,
And waytes warly thiderwarde quat hit be myght.
Hit was the ladi, loflyest to beholde,
That drow the dor after hir ful dernly and stylle,
And bowed towarde the bed; and the burne schamed
And layde hym doun lystyly and let as he slepte.
And ho stepped stilly and stel to his bedde,
Kest up the cortyn and creped withinne,
And set hir ful softly on the bed-syde
And lenged there selly longe, to loke quen he wakened.
The lede lay lurked a ful longe quyle,
Compast in his concience to quat that cace myght
Meve other amount – to mervayle hym thoght.
Bot yet he sayde in hymself: 'More semly hit were
To aspye with my spelle in space quat ho wolde.'
Then he wakenede and wroth and to-hir-warde torned
And unlouked his yye-lyddes and let as hym wondered
And sayned hym, as bi his sawe the saver to worthe,
With hande.
Wyth chynne and cheke ful swete,
Bothe quit and red in blande,
Ful lufly con ho lete,
Wyth lyppes smal laghande.

1171 seized. **1172** pulled down. **1173** Right there. **1174** carried away. **1175** galloped and dismounted. **1176** passed. **1178** enjoys sport, forest edge. **1179** lies. **1180** gleamed, walls. **1181** canopy. **1182** dozed. **1183** quickly. **1186** looks warily. **1188** stealthily. **1189** went, man. **1190** craftily, let on. **1191** she, stole. **1194** surprisingly. **1196** Turned over in his mind. **1197** Be tending or. **1199** through the course of conversation. **1200** turned. **1202** And crossed himself, as if by his prayer to be the safer. **1205** blend. **1206** speak.

'God moroun, sir Gawayn,' sayde that gay lady,
'Ye ar a sleper unslyye, that mon may slyde hider.
Now ar ye tan astyt bot true us may schape,
I schal bynde yow in your bedde, that be ye trayst.'
Al laghande the lady lauced tho bourdes.
'Goud moroun, gay,' quoth Gawayn the blythe,
'Me schal worthe at your wille, and that me wel lykes,
For I yelde me yederly and yeye after grace;
And that is the best, be my dome, for me byhoves nede.'
And thus he bourded ayayn with mony a blythe laghter.
'Bot wolde ye, lady lovely, then leve me grante,
And deprece your prysoun and pray hym to ryse,
I wolde bowe of this bed and busk me better,
I schulde kever the more comfort to karp yow wyth.'
'Nay, for sothe, beau sir,' sayd that swete,
'Ye schal not rise of your bedde, I rych yow better:
I schal happe yow here that other half als,
And sythen karp wyth my knyght that I kaght have;
For I wene wel, iwysse, sir Wowen ye are,
That alle the worlde worchipes, quere-so ye ride.
Your honour, your hendelayk is hendely praysed
With lordes, wyth ladyes, with alle that lyf bere.
And now ye ar here, iwysse, and we bot oure one;
My lorde and his ledes ar on lenthe faren,
Other burnes in her bedde, and my burdes als,
The dor drawen and dit with a derf haspe.
And sythen I have in this hous hym that al lykes,
I schal ware my whyle wel quyl hit lastes,
With tale.
Ye ar welcum to my cors,
Yowre awen won to wale;
Me behoves of fyne force
Your servaunt be, and schale.'

'In god fayth,' quoth Gawayn, 'gayn hit me thynkkes,
Thagh I be not now he that ye of speken;
To reche to such reverence as ye reherce here
I am wyye unworthy, I wot wel myselven.
Bi God, I were glad and yow god thoght

1209 careless, anyone. **1210** captured in a trice, unless we can arrange a truce. **1211** sure. **1212** uttered those jesting words. **1214** It shall be with me. **1215** promptly, cry for mercy. **1216** in my opinion. **1217** jested in return. **1219** release, prisoner. **1220** dress myself. **1221** acquire, talk. **1223** have plans for you. **1224** pin you down, side. **1228** courtesy. **1229** By lords. **1230** on our own. **1231** men, gone far away. **1232** my ladies. **1233** fastened, strong. **1235** use my time. **1236** In conversation. **1237** body. **1238** pleasure, take. **1239** sheer necessity. **1241** a better thing. **1245** if you thought fit.

At sawe other at servyce that I sette myght
To the plesaunce of your prys – hit were a pure joye.'
'In god fayth, sir Gawayn,' quoth the gay lady,
'The prys and the prowes that pleses al other,
If I hit lakked other set at lyght, hit were littel dayntye;
Bot hit ar ladyes innoghe that lever wer nowthe
Haf the, hende, in hor holde, as I the habbe here,
To daly with derely your dayntye wordes,
Kever hem comfort and colen her cares,
Then much of the garysoun other gold that thay haven.
But I louve that ilk lorde that the lyfte haldes,
I haf hit holly in my honde that al desyres,
Thurghe grace.'
Scho made hym so gret chere,
That was so fayr of face;
The knyght with speches skere
Answared to uche a cace.

'Madame,' quoth the myry mon, 'Mary yow yelde,
For I haf founden, in god fayth, yowre fraunchis nobele.
And other ful much of other folk fongen for hor dedes,
Bot the dayntye that thay delen for my disert nysen –
Hit is the worchyp of yourself that noght bot wel connes.'
'Bi Mary,' quoth the menskful, 'me thynk hit another;
For were I worth al the wone of wymmen alyve,
And al the wele of the worlde were in my honde,
And I schulde chepen and chose to cheve me a lorde,
For the costes that I haf knowen upon the, knyght, here,
Of bewte and debonerte and blythe semblaunt –
And that I haf er herkkened and halde hit here trwe –
Ther schulde no freke upon folde bifore yow be chosen.'
'Iwysse, worthy,' quoth the wyye, 'ye haf waled wel better;
Bot I am proude of the prys that ye put on me,
And soberly your servaunt, my soverayn I holde yow,
And yowre knyght I becom, and Kryst yow foryelde!'
Thus thay meled of muchquat til mydmorn paste,
And ay the lady let lyk as ho hym loved mych;
The freke ferde with defence, and feted ful fayre.

1246 In word or deed. **1247** Your honoured self. **1249** excellence. **1250** disparaged, courtesy. **1251** there are, in plenty, rather, now. **1252** courteous lord. **1254** Obtain, assuage. **1255** treasure. **1256** I give praise to, rules the heavens. **1261** pure. **1262** each. **1263** reward. **1264** generosity. **1265** And others receive plenty of praise from other folk. **1266** kind things they say are not at all to my deserving. **1267** It reflects honour upon yourself, that know only how to behave generously. **1268** noble (lady). **1269** multitude. **1270** wealth. **1271** negotiate, obtain. **1272** qualities. **1273** courtesy. **1276** chosen (i.e. your husband). **1279** reward. **1280** chatted, many things. **1281** behaved as if she. **1282** conducted himself, behaved.

'Thagh I were burde bryghtest,' the burde in mynde hade,
'The lasse luf in his lode' – for lur that he soght
Boute hone,
The dunte that schulde hym deve,
And nedes hit most be done.
The lady thenn spek of leve,
He granted hir ful sone.

Thenne ho gef hym god day, and wyth a glent laghed,
And as ho stod ho stonyed hym wyth ful stor wordes:
'Now he that spedes uche spech this disport yelde yow!
Bot that ye be Gawen, hit gos in mynde.'
'Querfore?' quoth the freke, and freschly he askes,
Ferde lest he hade fayled in fourme of his costes.
Bot the burde hym blessed, and bi this skyl sayde:
'So god as Gawayn gaynly is halden,
And cortaysye is closed so clene in hymselven,
Couth not lyghtly haf lenged so long wyth a lady,
Bot he had craved a cosse bi his courtaysye,
Bi sum towch of summe tryfle at sum tales ende.'
Then quoth Wowen: 'Iwysse, worthe as yow lykes;
I schal kysse at your comaundement, as a knyght falles,
And firre, lest he displese yow, so plede hit no more.'
Ho comes nerre wyth that, and caches hym in armes,
Loutes luflych adoun and the leude kysses.
Thay comly bykennen to Kryst ayther other;
Ho dos hir forth at the dore withouten dyn more;
And he ryches hym to ryse and rapes hym sone,
Clepes to his chamberlayn, choses his wede,
Bowes forth, quen he was boun, blythely to masse.
And thenne he meved to his mete that menskly hym keped,
And made myry al day til the mone rysed,
With game.
Was never freke fayrer fonge
Bitwene two so dyngne dame,
The alder and the yonge;
Much solace set thay same.

And ay the lorde of the londe is lent on his gamnes,
To hunt in holtes and hethe at hyndes barayne.

1283 lady. **1284** mind, grievous harm. **1285** Without delay. **1286** blow, strike down. **1290** glance. **1291** stunned, severe. **1292** makes prosper. **1293** causes some thought. **1295** manners. **1296** form of reasoning. **1297** rightly. **1300** kiss. **1301** hint, trifling remark. **1302** let it be. **1303** befits. **1304** as a further reason. **1306** bends. **1307** commend, each other. **1309** prepares, hastens. **1310** clothes. **1311** ready. **1312** awaited. **1315** received. **1318** together. **1319** gone, sports.

Such a sowme he ther slowe bi that the sunne heldet,
Of dos and of other dere, to deme were wonder.
Thenne fersly thay flokked in, folk at the laste,
And quykly of the quelled dere a querrye thay maked.
The best bowed therto with burnes innoghe,
Gedered the grattest of gres that ther were,
And didden hem derely undo as the dede askes.
Serched hem at the asay summe that ther were,
Two fyngeres thay fonde of the fowlest of alle.
Sythen thay slyt the slot, sesed the erber,
Schaved wyth a scharp knyf, and the schyre knitten.
Sythen rytte thay the foure lymmes and rent of the hyde,
Then brek thay the baly, the boweles out token
Lystily, for laucyng the lere of the knot.
Thay gryped to the gargulun, and graythely departed
The wesaunt fro the wynt-hole and walt out the guttes.
Then scher thay out the schulderes with her scharp knyves,
Haled hem by a lyttel hole, to have hole sydes.
Sithen britned thay the brest and brayden hit in twynne.
And eft at the gargulun bigynes on thenne,
Ryves hit up radly ryght to the byght,
Voydes out the avanters, and verayly therafter
Alle the rymes by the rybbes radly thay lauce.
So ryde thay of by resoun bi the rygge-bones
Evenden to the haunche, that henged alle samen,
And heven hit up al hole and hwen hit of there –
And that thay neme for the noumbles bi nome, as I trowe,
Bi kynde.
Bi the byght al of the thyghes
The lappes thay lauce bihynde;
To hewe hit in two thay hyyes,
Bi the bakbon to unbynde.

Bothe the hede and the hals thay hwen of thenne,
And sythen sunder thay the sydes swyft fro the chyne,
And the corbeles fee thay kest in a greve.
Thenn thurled thay ayther thik syde thurgh bi the rybbe,
And henged thenne ayther bi hoghes of the fourches,

1321 quantity, had set. **1322** assess. **1324** killed, heap. **1326** fat. **1327** meticulously. **1328** formal testing of quality. **1329** (thickness of flesh), worst. **1330** slit the hollow at the base of the throat and took hold of the first stomach. **1331** Cut it clear, tied up the organ. **1332** cut off. **1333** belly. **1334** Carefully. **1335** throat, expertly separated. **1336** gullet, tossed. **1337** cut. **1338** Pulled them out. **1339** cut open, pulled it apart. **1341** Cuts it up swiftly right to the fork of the back legs. **1342** neck-offal. **1343** membranes, loosen. **1344** (the membranes) along the backbone. **1345** Right down, together. **1347** designate. **1348** Properly. **1350** flaps (of loose flesh), loosen. **1353** neck. **1354** backbone. **1356** pierced. **1357** hocks (upper parts), haunches.

Uche freke for his fee as falles for to have.
Upon a felle of the fayre best fede thay thayr houndes
Wyth the lyver and the lyghtes, the lether of the paunches,
And bred bathed in blod blende ther-amonges.
Baldely thay blw prys, bayed thayr raches;
Sythen fonge thay her flesch folden to home,
Strakande ful stoutly mony stif motes.
Bi that the daylyght was done the douthe was al wonen
Into the comly castel, ther the knyght bides
Ful stille.
Wyth blys and bryght fyr bette,
The lorde is comen ther-tylle;
When Gawayn wyth hym mette,
Ther was bot wele at wylle.

Thenne comaunded the lorde in that sale to samen alle the meny,
Bothe the ladyes on loghe to lyght with her burdes.
Bifore alle the folk on the flette frekes he beddes
Verayly his venysoun to fech hym byforne;
And al godly in gomen Gawayn he called,
Teches hym to the tayles of ful tayt bestes,
Schewes hym the schyre grece schorne upon rybbes.
'How payes yow this playe? Haf I prys wonnen?
Have I thryvandely thonk thurgh my craft served?'
'Ye, iwysse,' quoth that other wyye, 'here is wayth fayrest
That I sey this seven yere in sesoun of wynter.'
'And al I gif yow, Gawayn,' quoth the gome thenne,
'For by acorde of covenaunt ye crave hit as your awen.'
'This is soth,' quoth the segge, 'I say yow that ilke;
That I haf worthyly wonnen this wones wythinne,
Iwysse with as god wylle hit worthes to youres.'
He hasppes his fayre hals his armes wythinne,
And kysses hym as comlyly as he couthe avyse;
'Tas yow there my chevicaunce, I cheved no more;
I vowche hit saf fynly, thagh feler hit were.'
'Hit is god,' quoth the god mon, 'grant mercy therfore.
Hit may be such hit is the better and ye me breve wolde
Where ye wan this ilk wele bi wytte of yorselven.'
'That was not forward,' quoth he, 'frayst me no more;

1358 to have his due portion. **1359** skin. **1360** lining. **1362** Vigorously. **1363** took, all packed up. **1364** Sounding, loud notes. **1365** By the time that, company, come. **1368** kindled. **1371** nothing but happiness. **1372** hall, gather, household. **1373** come downstairs. **1374** hall-floor, men, commands. **1376** merry mood. **1377** tallies (tails), fine-grown. **1378** fine fat flesh. **1379** pleases, praise. **1380** thoroughly, deserved. **1381** spoils. **1384** may claim. **1386** dwelling. **1387** becomes. **1389** devise. **1390** Take, winnings, got. **1391** bestow it freely, more. **1392** lord of the house, many thanks. **1393** if you would tell me. **1394** good fortune. **1395** the agreement, ask.

For ye haf tan that yow tydes, trawe ye non other
Ye mowe.'
Thay laghed and made hem blythe
Wyth lotes that were to lowe;
To soper thay yede asswythe,
Wyth dayntyes nwe innowe.

And sythen by the chymnee in chamber thay seten,
Wyyes the walle wyn weghed to hem oft,
And efte in her bourdyng thay baythen in the morn
To fylle the same forwardes that thay byfore maden:
What chaunce so bytydes, hor chevysaunce to chaunge,
What nwes so thay nome, at naght quen thay metten.
Thay acorded of the covenauntes byfore the court alle –
The beverage was broght forth in bourde at that tyme –
Thenne thay lovelych leghten leve at the last,
Uche burne to his bedde busked bylyve.
Bi that the coke hade crowen and cakled bot thryse,
The lorde was lopen of his bedde, the leudes uchone,
So that the mete and the masse was metely delyvered,
The douthe dressed to the wod, er any day sprenged,
To chace.
Hegh with hunte and hornes
Thurgh playnes thay passe in space,
Uncoupled among tho thornes
Raches that ran on race.

Sone thay calle of a quest in a ker syde,
The hunt rehayted the houndes that hit fyrst mynged,
Wylde wordes hym warp wyth a wrast noyce.
The howndes that hit herde hastid thider swythe,
And fellen as fast to the fuyt, fourty at ones.
Thenne such a glaver ande glam of gedered raches
Ros that the rocheres rungen aboute.
Hunteres hem hardened with horne and wyth muthe;
Then al in a semblee sweyed togeder
Bitwene a flosche in that fryth and a foo cragge.
In a knot bi a clyffe at the kerre syde,
Ther as the rogh rocher unrydely was fallen,

1396 Since, taken what is due to you. **1399** words, to be praised. **1400** immediately. **1403** choice, brought. **1404** jesting, agree. **1405** fulfil, agreement. **1406** winnings. **1407** new things, obtained, night. **1409** with jesting. **1410** took. **1411** hastened. **1413** leapt. **1414** quickly despatched. **1415** company. **1417** Loud, huntsmen. **1418** in due course. **1420** Hounds, (like mad). **1421** marsh. **1422** huntsman urged on, scented. **1423** uttered, loud. **1425** trail. **1426** racket and din. **1427** rocky hillsides. **1428** urged on. **1429** pack rushed. **1430** pool, forest, fearsome. **1431** wooded knoll. **1432** rocky hillside confusedly.

Thay ferden to the fyndyng, and frekes hem after.
Thay umbekesten the knarre and the knot bothe,
Wyyes, whyl thay wysten wel wythinne hem hit were,
The best that ther breved was wyth the blodhoundes.
Thenne thay beten on the buskes and bede hym up ryse,
And he unsoundyly out soght, segges overthwert –
On the sellokest swyn swenged out there,
Long sythen fro the sounder that synglere for olde.
For he was borelych and brode, bor alther-grattest,
Ful grymme quen he gronyed – thenne greved mony,
For thre at the fyrst thrast he thryght to the erthe,
And sparred forth good sped boute spyt more.
Thise other halowed 'hyghe!' ful hyghe, and 'hay! hay!' cryed,
Haden hornes to mouthe, heterly rechated.
Mony was the miry mouthe of men and of houndes
That buskkes after this bor with bost and wyth noyse,
To quelle.
Ful oft he bydes the baye
And maymes the mute in-melle;
He hurtes of the houndes, and thay
Ful yomerly yaule and yelle.

Schalkes to schote at hym schowen to thenne,
Haled to hym of her arewes, hitten hym ofte;
Bot the poyntes payred at the pyth that pyght in his sheldes,
And the barbes of his browe bite non wolde,
Thagh the schaven schaft schyndered in peces,
The hede hypped ayayn were-so-ever hit hitte.
Bot quen the dyntes hym dered of her dryye strokes,
Then braynwod for bate on burnes he rases,
Hurtes hem ful heterly ther he forth hyyes,
And mony arwed therat and on lyte drowen.
Bot the lorde on a lyght horce launces hym after,
As burne bolde upon bent his bugle he blowes,
He rechated and rode thurgh rones ful thyk,
Suande this wylde swyn til the sunne schafted.

1433 went on. **1434** surrounded the crag. **1435** until. **1436** was declared to be there. **1438** fiercely came dashing out against the men across his path. **1439** most marvellous, rushed. **1440** herd, solitary beast because of age. **1441** big, greatest of all. **1442** grunted. **1443** rush, dashed. **1444** charged, without injuring more. **1446** quickly sounded the recall. **1449** kill. **1450** stands at bay. **1451** pack, in their midst. **1453** piteously. **1454** Men, press forward. **1455** Loosed at. **1456** But the points were blunted at the toughness that was in his flanks. **1457** bristles. **1458** smooth-shaven, shattered. **1459** bounced back. **1460** hurt, unceasing. **1461** Then frenzied by the persistent attack he rushes on the men. **1462** cruelly. **1463** were afraid, drew hesitantly back. **1464** gallops. **1465** battlefield. **1466** thickets. **1467** Pursuing, slanted down.

This day wyth this ilk dede thay dryven on this wyse,
Whyle oure luflych lede lys in his bedde,
Gawayne graythely at home in geres ful ryche
Of hewe.
The lady noght foryate,
Com to hym to salue;
Ful erly ho was hym ate
His mode for to remwe.

Ho commes to the cortyn and at the knyght totes,
Sir Wawen her welcumed worthy on fyrst,
And ho hym yeldes ayayn ful yerne of hir wordes,
Settes hir sofly by his syde, and swythely ho laghes,
And wyth a luflych loke ho layde hym thyse wordes:
'Sir, yif ye be Wawen, wonder me thynkkes,
Wyye that is so wel wrast alway to god,
And connes not of compaynye the costes undertake,
And if mon kennes yow hom to knowe, ye kest hom of your mynde.
Thou has foryeten yederly that yisterday I taght te
Bi alder-truest token of talk that I cowthe.'
'What is that?' quoth the wyghe. 'Iwysse, I wot never.
If hit be sothe that ye breve, the blame is myn awen.'
'Yet I kende yow of kyssyng,' quoth the clere thenne,
'Quere-so countenaunce is couthe, quikly to clayme;
That bicumes uche a knyght that cortaysy uses.'
'Do way,' quoth that derf mon, 'my dere, that speche,
For that durst I not do, lest I devayed were;
If I were werned, I were wrang, iwysse, yif I profered.'
'Ma fay,' quoth the mery wyf, 'ye may not be werned;
Ye ar stif innoghe to constrayne wyth strenkthe, if yow lykes,
Yif any were so vilanous that yow devaye wolde.'
'Ye, be God,' quoth Gawayn, 'good is your speche,
But threte is unthryvande in thede ther I lende,
And uche gift that is geven not with goud wylle.
I am at your comaundement, to kysse quen yow lykes;
Ye may lach quen yow lyst, and leve quen yow thynkkes,
In space.'
The lady loutes adoun
And comlyly kysses his face;
Much speche thay ther expoun
Of druryes greme and grace.

1468 pass. **1470** properly, bedclothes. **1473** greet. **1475** change. **1476** peeps. **1478** eagerly. **1480** delivered. **1482** disposed **1483** manners, appreciate. **1484** one teaches, them. **1485** quickly, taught thee. **1486** truest of all teaching. **1488** declare. **1489** taught, fair lady. **1490** good reception is anticipated. **1492** brave. **1493** refused. **1494** denied. **1495** By my faith. **1499** not thought well of, land, live. **1502** take, abstain, think fit. **1503** In due course. **1504** bends. **1507** love's grief.

'I wolde wyt at yow, wyye,' that worthy ther sayde,
'And yow wrathed not therwyth, what were the skylle
That so yong and so yepe as ye at this tyme,
So cortayse, so knyghtyly, as ye are knowen oute –
And of alle chevalry to chose, the chef thyng alosed
Is the lel layk of luf, the lettrure of armes;
For to telle of this tevelyng of this trwe knyghtes,
Hit is the tytelet token and tyxt of her werkkes,
How ledes for her lele luf hor lyves han auntered,
Endured for her drury dulful stoundes,
And after venged with her valour and voyded her care,
And broght blysse into boure with bountees hor awen –
And ye ar knyght comlokest kyd of your elde,
Your worde and your worchip walkes ayquere,
And I haf seten by yourself here sere twyes,
Yet herde I never of your hed helde no wordes
That ever longed to luf, lasse ne more.
And ye, that ar so cortays and coynt of your hetes,
Oghe to a yonke thynk yern to schewe
And teche sum tokenes of trwe-luf craftes.
Why! ar ye lewed, that alle the los weldes,
Other elles ye demen me to dille your dalyaunce to herken?
For schame!
I com hider sengel and sitte
To lerne at yow sum game;
Dos teches me of your wytte,
Whil my lorde is fro hame.'

'In goud faythe,' quoth Gawayn, 'God yow foryelde!
Gret is the gode gle and gomen to me huge
That so worthy as ye wolde wynne hidere,
And pyne yow with so pover a mon, as play wyth your knyght
With anys-kynnes countenaunce – hit keveres me ese.
Bot to take the torvayle to myself to trw-luf expoun,
And towche the temes of tyxt and tales of armes
To yow that, I wot wel, weldes more slyght
Of that art, bi the half, or a hundreth of seche
As I am other ever schal, in erde ther I leve –

1509 If, annoyed, reason. **1510** fresh. **1511** far and wide. **1512** praised. **1513** true game, doctrine. **1514** striving. **1515** title-heading, text. **1516** ventured. **1517** love, times of trial. **1518** taken revenge. **1519** (lady's) bower, their own virtues. **1520** known as comeliest, age. **1521** fame, honour, everywhere. **1522** on two separate occasions. **1523** proceed. **1524** belonged. **1525** knowledgeable, obligations. **1526** young, eagerly. **1528** ignorant, renown, enjoys. **1529** stupid. **1531** alone. **1533** Do teach. **1534** away from home. **1535** reward. **1536** pleasure. **1537** make your way. **1538** bother. **1539** favour of any kind, gives. **1540** task. **1541** touch on, themes. **1542** skill. **1543** such. **1544** on earth.

Hit were a foly felefolde, my fre, by my trawthe.
I wolde yowre wylnyng worche at my myght,
As I am hyghly bihalden, and evermore wylle
Be servaunt to yourselven, so save me Dryghtyn!'
Thus hym frayned that fre and fondet hym ofte,
For to haf wonnen hym to woghe, what-so scho thoght elles;
Bot he defended hym so fayr that no faut semed,
Ne non evel on nawther halve, nawther thay wysten
Bot blysse.
Thay laghed and layked longe;
At the last scho con hym kysse,
Hir leve fayre con scho fonge,
And went hir waye, iwysse.

Then ruthes hym the renk and ryses to the masse,
And sithen hor diner was dyght and derely served.
The lede with the ladyes layked alle day,
Bot the lorde over the londes launced ful ofte,
Swes his uncely swyn, that swynges bi the bonkkes
And bote the best of his braches the bakkes in sunder
Ther he bode in his bay, tel bawemen hit breken,
And made hym, mawgref his hed, for to mwe utter,
So felle flones ther flete when the folk gedered.
Bot yet the styffest to start bi stoundes he made,
Til at the last he was so mat he myght no more renne,
Bot in the hast that he myght he to a hole wynnes
Of a rasse, bi a rokk ther rennes the boerne.
He gete the bonk at his bak, bigynes to scrape,
The frothe femed at his mouth unfayre bi the wykes,
Whettes his whyte tusches. With hym then irked
Alle the burnes so bolde that hym by stoden
To nye hym on-ferum, bot nyghe hym non durst
For wothe.
He hade hurt so mony byforne
That al thught thenne ful lothe
Be more wyth his tusches torne,
That breme was and braynwod bothe.

Til the knyght com hymself, kachande his blonk,
Sygh hym byde at the bay, his burnes bysyde.

1545 folly manifold, noble lady. **1546** I would wish to do what you want to the extent of my power. **1547** obliged. **1548** the Lord. **1549** questioned, tempted. **1550** evil-doing. **1551** was to be seen. **1554** played. **1556** take. **1558** bestirs. **1559** prepared. **1561** galloped. **1562** Pursues, ill-fated, slopes. **1563** bit. **1564** stood at bay, broke (his stand). **1565** in spite of all he could do, to move out into the open. **1566** fiercely, arrows, flew. **1567** start aside, at times. **1568** exhausted. **1570** river-bank, stream. **1572** at the corners. **1573** grew tired. **1575** harass him from afar. **1576** danger. **1580** frenzied. **1581** urging on his horse.

He lyghtes luflych adoun, leves his corsour,
Braydes out a bryght bront and bigly forth strydes,
Foundes fast thurgh the forth ther the felle bydes.
The wylde was war of the wyye with weppen in honde,
Hef hyghly the here, so hetterly he fnast
That fele ferde for the freke, lest felle hym the worre.
The swyn settes hym out on the segge even,
That the burne and the bor were bothe upon hepes
In the wyghtest of the water. The worre hade that other,
For the mon merkkes hym wel, as thay mette fyrst,
Set sadly the scharp in the slot even,
Hit hym up to the hult, that the hert schyndered,
And he yarrande hym yelde, and yedoun the water
Ful tyt.
A hundreth houndes hym hent,
That bremely con hym bite;
Burnes him broght to bent
And dogges to dethe endite.

There was blawyng of prys in mony breme horne,
Heghe halowyng on highe wyth hatheles that myght;
Brachetes bayeden that best, as bidden the maysteres,
Of that chargeaunt chace that were chef huntes.
Thenne a wyye that was wys upon wodcraftes
To unlace this bor lufly bigynnes:
Fyrst he hewes of his hed and on highe settes,
And sythen rendes hym al roghe bi the rygge after,
Braydes out the boweles, brennes hom on glede,
With bred blent therwith his braches rewardes,
Sythen he britnes out the brawen in bryght brode sheldes,
And has out the hastlettes, as hightly bisemes;
And yet hem halches al hole the halves togeder,
And sythen on a stif stange stoutly hem henges.
Now with this ilk swyn thay swengen to home;
The bores hed was borne bifore the burnes selven,
That him forferde in the forthe thurgh forse of his honde
So stronge.
Til he sey sir Gawayne
In halle hym thoght ful longe;

1584 Pulls. **1585** Goes, stream, fierce (beast). **1587** Bristled up, ferociously, snorted. **1588** many, worse. **1589** straight at the man. **1591** swiftest. **1592** measures his aim. **1593** Set firmly the sharp (sword) straight in the hollow at the base of the throat. **1594** hilt. **1595** snarlingly, went down. **1596** quickly. **1597** seized. **1599** bank. **1600** do (him). **1601** 'prize' (see 1362). **1603** Hounds bayed at that beast. **1604** strenuous. **1606** meticulously. **1608** roughly, along the backbone. **1609** red-hot coals. **1611** slices up, slabs. **1612** entrails, properly. **1613** also, fastens. **1614** pole. **1617** put paid to, stream. **1620** the time seemed long to him.

He calde, and he com gayn
His fees ther for to fonge.

The lorde ful lowde with lote laghed myry
When he seye sir Gawayn; with solace he spekes.
The goude ladyes were geten, and gedered the meyny;
He schewes hem the scheldes and schapes hem the tale
Of the largesse and the lenthe, the lithernes alse,
Of the were of the wylde swyn in wod ther he fled.
That other knyght ful comly comended his dedes,
And praysed hit as gret prys that he proved hade;
For suche a brawne of a best, the bolde burne sayde,
Ne such sydes of a swyn segh he never are.
Thenne hondeled thay the hoge hed, the hende mon hit praysed,
And let lodly therat, the lorde for to here.
'Now, Gawayn,' quoth the godmon, 'this gomen is your awen
Bi fyn forwarde and faste, faythely ye knowe.'
'Hit is sothe,' quoth the segge, 'and as siker trwe
Alle my get I schal yow gif agayn, bi my trawthe.'
He hent the hathel aboute the halse and hendely hym kysses,
And eftersones of the same he served hym there.
'Now ar we even,' quoth the hathel, 'in this eventide,
Of alle the covenauntes that we knyt sythen I com hider,
Bi lawe.'
The lorde sayde: 'Bi saynt Gile,
Ye ar the best that I knowe;
Ye ben ryche in a whyle,
Such chaffer and ye drowe.'

Thenne thay teldet tables trestes alofte,
Kesten clothes upon; clere lyght thenne
Wakned bi wowes, waxen torches;
Segges sette and served in sale al aboute.
Much glam and gle glent up therinne
Aboute the fyre upon flet, and on fele wyse
At the soper and after, mony athel songes,
As coundutes of Krystmasse and caroles newe,
With alle the manerly merthe that mon may of telle,
And ever oure luflych knyght the lady bisyde.
Such semblaunt to that segge semly ho made,

1621 promptly. **1622** dues. **1623** noise. **1624** in high good humour. **1625** household. **1626** slabs of flesh. **1627** ferocity. **1628** fighting defence. **1630** excellence. **1632** never before. **1634** And behaved with a show of horror thereat, that the lord might hear. **1635** game (catch). **1636** By completed and binding agreement. **1638** gains. **1640** once again. **1646** You will be. **1647** If you carry on such trade. **1648** set up, upon trestles. **1650** walls. **1651** hall. **1652** noisy merriment, sprang. **1653** hearth-floor, many. **1654** fine. **1655** part-songs, dance-songs. **1658** demonstration of affection.

Wyth stille stollen countenaunce, that stalworth to plese,
That al forwondered was the wyye, and wroth with hymselven;
Bot he nolde not for his nurture nurne here ayaynes,
Bot dalt with hir al in dayntye, how-se-ever the dede turned
Towrast.
Quen thay hade played in halle
As longe as hor wylle hom last,
To chambre he con hym calle,
And to the chemnee thay past.

Ande ther thay dronken and dalten, and demed eft nwe
To norne on the same note on Nwe Yeres even;
Bot the knyght craved leve to kayre on the morn,
For hit was negh at the terme that he to schulde.
The lorde hym letted of that, to lenge hym resteyed,
And sayde, 'As I am trwe segge, I siker my trawthe
Thou schal cheve to the grene chapel thy charres to make,
Leude, on Nwe Yeres lyght, longe bifore pryme.
Forthy thow lye in thy loft and lach thyn ese,
And I schal hunt in this holt and halde the towches,
Chaunge wyth the chevisaunce, bi that I charre hider;
For I haf fraysted the twys, and faythful I fynde the.
Now "thrid tyme, throwe best" thenk on the morne;
Make we mery quyl we may and mynne upon joye,
For the lur may mon lach when-so mon lykes.'
This was graythely graunted and Gawayn is lenged;
Blithe broght was hym drynk and thay to bedde yeden
With light.
Sir Gawayn lis and slepes
Ful stille and softe al night;
The lorde that his craftes kepes
Ful erly he was dight.

After messe a morsel he and his men token;
Miry was the mornyng, his mounture he askes.
Alle the hatheles that on horse schulde helden hym after
Were boun busked on hor blonkkes bifore the halle yates.
Ferly fayre was the folde, for the forst clenged,

1659 secret stolen glances. **1660** astonished. **1661** But he would not, because of his good breeding, repulse her advances openly. **1662** with delicacy. **1663** might be misinterpreted. **1665** them lasted. **1668** chatted, renewed the decision again. **1669** do the same thing. **1671** appointed time, should go. **1672** dissuaded, prevailed on him to stay. **1673** give my word. **1674** get, business. **1675** Sir, first light, (9 a.m.). **1676** take. **1677** covenant. **1678** thee winnings, when, return. **1679** tested thee. **1681** think. **1682** unhappiness, obtain. **1683** readily, is to stay. **1688** attends to. **1689** prepared. **1690** mass. **1691** mount. **1692** follow. **1693** ready prepared, horses. **1694** Wonderfully, earth, frost.

In rede rudede upon rak rises the sunne,
And ful clere castes the clowdes of the welkyn.
Hunteres unhardeled bi a holt syde,
Rocheres roungen bi rys for rurde of her hornes.
Summe fel in the fute ther the fox bade,
Trayles ofte a-traveres bi traunt of her wyles.
A kenet kryes therof, the hunt on hym calles;
His felawes fallen hym to, that fnasted ful thike,
Runnen forth in a rabel in his ryght fare,
And he fyskes hem bifore; thay founden hym sone,
And quen thay seghe hym with syght thay sued hym fast,
Wreyande hym ful weterly with a wroth noyse;
And he trantes and tornayees thurgh mony tene greve,
Havilounes and herkenes bi hegges ful ofte.
At the last bi a littel dich he lepes over a spenny
Steles out ful stilly bi a strothe rande,
Went haf wylt of the wode wyth wyles fro the houndes.
Thenne was he went, er he wyst, to a wale tryster,
Ther thre thro at a thrich thrat hym at ones,
Al graye.
He blenched ayayn bilyve
And stifly start onstray;
With alle the wo on lyve
To the wod he went away.

Thenne was hit list upon lif to lythen the houndes,
When alle the mute hade hym met, menged togeder.
Suche a sorwe at that syght thay sette on his hede
As alle the clamberande clyffes hade clatered on hepes.
Here he was halawed when hatheles hym metten,
Loude he was yayned with yarande speche;
Ther he was threted and ofte thef called,
And ay the titleres at his tayl, that tary he ne myght.
Ofte he was runnen at when he out rayked,
And ofte reled in ayayn, so Reniarde was wyly.
And ye! he lad hem bi lag-mon, the lorde and his meyny,
On this maner bi the mountes quyle myd-over-under,
Whyle the hende knyght at home holsumly slepes

1695 made ruddy, rack of cloud. **1696** dispels, sky. **1697** unleashed (the bounds), forest. **1698** in the woods, noise. **1699** trail, was lurking. **1700** to and fro across, cunning practice. **1701** small hound. **1702** panted. **1703** very track. **1704** scampers. **1705** pursued. **1706** Barking, furiously. **1707** twists and turns, rough thicket. **1708** Doubles back, listens out. **1709** little hedge. **1710** at the edge of a wooded marsh. **1711** Thought to have escaped. **1712** gone, fine hunting-station. **1713** fierce ones, rush, threatened. **1715** drew back. **1716** sharply, darted aside. **1717** on earth. **1719** joy (for anyone) alive, listen to. **1720** pack, mingled. **1721** grievous clamour. **1724** greeted, snarling. **1726** hounds. **1727** broke cover. **1728** turned, Reynard. **1729** in a procession. **1730** until mid-morning.

Withinne the comly cortynes, on the colde morne.
Bot the lady for luf let not to slepe
Ne the purpose to payre that pyght in hir hert,
Bot ros hir up radly, rayked hir theder
In a mery mantyle, mete to the erthe,
That was furred ful fyne wyth felles wel pured;
No hwef goud on hir hede, bot the hagher stones
Trased aboute hir tressour be twenty in clusteres;
Hir thryven face and hir throte throwen al naked,
Hir brest bare bifore, and bihinde eke.
Ho comes withinne the chambre dore and closes hit hir after,
Wayves up a wyndow and on the wyye calles
And radly thus rehayted hym with hir riche wordes,
With chere:
'A! mon, how may thou slepe?
This morning is so clere.'
He was in drowping depe,
Bot thenne he con hir here.

In drey droupyng of dreme draveled that noble,
As mon that was in mornyng of mony thro thoghtes,
How that destinee schulde that day dele hym his wyrde
At the grene chapel when he the gome metes
And bihoves his buffet abide withoute debate more.
Bot quen that comly com he kevered his wyttes,
Swenges out of the swevenes and swares with hast.
The lady luflych com, laghande swete,
Felle over his fayre face and fetly hym kyssed.
He welcumes hir worthily with a wale chere;
He sey hir so glorious and gayly atyred,
So fautles of hir fetures and of so fyne hewes,
Wight wallande joye warmed his hert.
With smothe smylyng and smolt thay smeten into merthe,
That al was blis and bonchef that breke hem bitwene,
And wynne.
Thay lauced wordes gode,
Much wele then was therinne;
Gret perile bitwene hem stode,
Nif Mary of hir knyght mynne.

1733 allowed herself. **1734** become blunted, was fixed. **1735** briskly, made her way. **1736** reaching. **1737** skins. **1738** fine coif (cap). **1739** Adorned, hair-net. **1740** blooming. **1743** Throws open. **1744** briskly, jokingly reproached. **1748** slumber. **1750** deep, muttered. **1751** troubled with, oppressive. **1752** on the appointed day, fate. **1753** man. **1755** recovered. **1756** dreams, answers. **1758** sweetly. **1759** courteous. **1762** Ardent welling-up. **1763** gentle, fell. **1764** happiness. **1765** joy. **1766** uttered. **1769** If, have not in mind.

For that prynces of pris depresed hym so thikke,
Nurned hym so neghe the thred, that nede hym bihoved
Other lach ther hir luf other lodly refuse.
He cared for his cortaysye, lest crathayn he were,
And more for his meschef yif he schulde make synne
And be traytor to that tolke that that telde aght.
'God schylde,' quoth the schalk. 'That schal not befalle!'
With luf-laghyng a lyt he layd hym bysyde
Alle the speches of specialtee that sprange of her mouthe.
Quoth that burde to the burne, 'Blame ye disserve,
Yif ye luf not that lyf that ye lye nexte,
Bifore alle the wyyes in the worlde wounded in hert,
Bot if ye haf a lemman, a lever, that yow lykes better,
And folden fayth to that fre, festned so harde
That yow lausen ne lyst – and that I leve nouthe,
And that ye telle me that now trwly, I pray yow;
For alle the lufes upon lyve, layne not the sothe
For gile.'
The knyght sayde, 'Be sayn Jon,'
And smethely con he smyle,
'In fayth I welde right non,
Ne non wil welde the quile.'

'That is a worde,' quoth that wyght, 'that worst is of alle;
Bot I am swared for sothe, that sore me thinkkes.
Kysse me now comly, and I schal cach hethen;
I may bot mourne upon molde, as may that much lovyes.'
Sykande ho sweye doun and semly hym kyssed,
And sithen ho severes hym fro and says as ho stondes:
'Now, dere, at this departyng do me this ese,
Gif me sumquat of thy gifte, thi glove if hit were,
That I may mynne on the, mon, my mournyng to lassen.'
'Now iwysse,' quoth that wyye, 'I wolde I hade here
The levest thing for thy luf that I in londe welde,
For ye haf deserved, for sothe, sellyly ofte
More rewarde bi resoun then I reche myght;
But to dele yow for drurye, that dawed bot neked.
Hit is not your honour to haf at this tyme
A glove for a garysoun of Gawaynes giftes;
And I am here an erande in erdes uncouthe,

1770 noble, pressed, hard. **1771** Urged, limit. **1772** accept, boorishly. **1773** a churl. **1774** the harm to himself. **1775** man, dwelling, owned. **1777** little, deflected. **1780** person. **1782** Unless, sweetheart, dearer. **1783** plighted, noble lady. **1784** break, wish, believe now. **1786** conceal. **1789** gently. **1790** possess. **1791** at present. **1793** answered, seems sad to me. **1794** go hence. **1795** mourn, woman. **1796** Sighing, stooped. **1800** think of. **1802** most precious. **1803** wonderfully. **1804** give. **1805** But to give you something as a love-token, that would avail but little (not be a good idea). **1807** keepsake. **1808** on a quest, unfamiliar lands.

And have no men wyth no males with menskful thinges.
That mislykes me, lady, for luf at this tyme;
Iche tolke mon do as he is tan, tas to non ille
Ne pine.'
'Nay, hende, of hyghe honours,'
Quoth that lufsum under lyne,
'Thagh I nade oght of youres,
Yet schulde ye have of myne.'

Ho raght hym a riche rynk of red golde werkes,
Wyth a starande ston stondande alofte,
That bere blusschande bemes as the bryght sunne;
Wyt ye wel, hit was worth wele ful hoge.
Bot the renk hit renayed, and redyly he sayde:
'I wil no giftes, for Gode, my gay, at this tyme;
I haf none yow to norne ne noght wyl I take.'
Ho bede hit hym ful bysily, and he hir bode wernes,
And swere swyfte by his sothe that he hit sese nolde;
And ho sory that he forsoke, and sayde therafter:
'If ye renay my rynk, to ryche for hit semes,
Ye wolde not so hyghly halden be to me,
I schal gif yow my girdel, that gaynes yow lasse.'
He laght a lace lyghtly that leke umbe hir sydes,
Knit upon hir kyrtel under the clere mantyle –
Gered hit was with grene sylke and with golde schaped,
Noght bot arounde brayden, beten with fyngres –
And that ho bede to the burne, and blythely bisoght,
Thagh hit unworthi were, that he hit take wolde,
And he nay that he nolde neghe in no wyse
Nauther golde ne garysoun, er God hym grace sende
To acheve to the chaunce that he hade chosen there.
'And therfore I pray yow displese yow noght,
And lettes be your bisinesse, for I baythe hit yow never
To graunte.
I am derely to yow biholde
Bicause of your sembelaunt,
And ever in hot and colde
To be your trwe servaunt.'

1809 bags, valuable. **1810** upsets, for love's sake. **1811** Each man must do as things fall out for him, don't take it amiss. **1812** Nor be distressed. **1814** lovesome under linen (i.e. lady). **1817** offered, ring. **1818** glittering. **1819** shining. **1820** wealth. **1821** refused. **1822** want, before God (i.e. by God). **1823** offer. **1824** pressed it on, offer refuses. **1825** take. **1826** refused. **1828** obliged. **1829** belt, profits. **1830** took hold of, was fastened around. **1831** Tied over. **1832** Made, trimmed. **1833** Embroidered and decorated by hand only around the edges. **1836** refused, accept. **1838** accomplish, mission. **1840** efforts, consent. **1843** kind behaviour. **1844** in all eventualities.

'Now forsake ye this silke,' sayde the burde thenne,
'For hit is symple in hitself? And so hit wel semes.
Lo! so hit is littel, and lasse hit is worthy.
Bot who-so knew the costes that knit ar therinne,
He wolde hit prayse at more prys, paraventure;
For quat gome so is gorde with this grene lace,
While he hit hade hemely halched aboute
Ther is no hathel under heven to-hewe hym that myght,
For he myght not be slayn for slyght upon erthe.'
Then kest the knyght, and hit come to his hert
Hit were a juel for the jopardy that hym jugged were
When he acheved to the chapel, his chek for to fech,
Myght he haf slypped to be unslayn, the sleght were noble.
Thenne he thulged with hir threpe and tholed hir to speke,
And ho bere on hym the belt and bede hit hym swythe,
And he granted, and ho hym gafe with a goud wylle,
And bisoght hym for hir sake discever hit never
Bot to lelly layne fro hir lorde. The leude hym acordes
That never wyye schulde hit wyt, iwysse, bot thay twayne,
For noghte.
He thonkked hir oft ful swythe,
Ful thro with hert and thoght.
Bi that on thrynne sythe
Ho has kyst the knyght so toght.

Thenne laches ho hir leve and leves hym there,
For more myrthe of that mon moght ho not gete.
When ho was gon, sir Gawayn geres hym sone,
Rises and riches hym in araye noble,
Lays up the luf-lace the lady hym raght,
Hid hit ful holdely ther he hit eft fonde.
Sythen chevely to the chapel choses he the waye,
Prevely aproched to a prest and prayed hym there
That he wolde lyste his lyf and lern hym better
How his sawle schulde be saved when he schuld seye hethen.
There he schrof hym schyrly and schewed his mysdedes
Of the more and the mynne, and merci beseches,
And of absolucioun he on the segge calles;
And he asoyled hym surely and sette hym so clene
As domesday schulde haf ben dight on the morn.
And sythen he mace hym as mery among the fre ladyes,

1846 refuse. **1849** properties. **1850** value. **1851** girt. **1852** closely fastened around. **1854** by any stratagem. **1855** pondered. **1856** assigned. **1857** arrived at, doom, receive. **1859** bore patiently with her importunity, and allowed. **1860** pressed. **1862** reveal. **1867** earnestly. **1868** three times. **1869** hardy. **1872** attires. **1873** dresses. **1874** Puts away, gave. **1875** carefully. **1876** briskly, takes. **1878** hear his confession. **1879** go hence. **1880** confessed, fully, revealed. **1881** lesser (i.e. venial). **1884** As if, appointed. **1885** makes.

With comlych caroles and alle kynnes joye,
As never he did bot that daye, to the derk nyght,
With blys.
Uche mon hade dayntye thare
Of hym, and sayde, 'Iwysse,
Thus myry he was never are,
Syn he com hider, er this.'

Now hym lenge in that lee, ther luf hym bityde!
Yet is the lorde on the launde, ledande his gomnes:
He has forfaren this fox that he folwed longe.
As he sprent over a spenny to spye the schrewe,
Ther as he herd the howndes that hasted hym swythe,
Renaud com richande thurgh a roghe greve,
And alle the rabel in a res ryght at his heles.
The wyye was war of the wylde and warly abides
And braydes out the bryght bronde and at the best castes.
And he schunt for the scharp and schulde haf arered;
A rach rapes hym to, ryght er he myght,
And ryght bifore the hors fete thay fel on hym alle
And woried me this wyly with a wroth noyse.
The lorde lyghtes bilyve and laches hym sone,
Rased hym ful radly out of the rach mouthes,
Haldes heghe over his hede, halowes faste,
And ther bayen hym mony brath houndes.
Huntes hyyed hem theder with hornes ful mony,
Ay rechatande aryght til thay the renk seyen.
Bi that was comen his compeyny noble,
Alle that ever ber bugle blowed at ones
And alle thise other halowed that hade no hornes.
Hit was the myriest mute that ever mon herde,
The rich rurd that ther was raysed for Renaude saule
With lote.
Hor houndes thay ther rewarde,
Her hedes thay fawne and frote;
And sythen thay tan Reynarde
And tyrven of his cote.

And thenne thay helden to home, for hit was niegh nyght,
Strakande ful stoutly in hor store hornes.

1889 courteous treatment. **1893** let him stay, place of comfort. **1894** engaged in his sports. **1895** headed off. **1896** jumped, rascal. **1898** running, thicket. **1899** rush. **1900** wild creature. **1901** thrusts. **1902** flinched, was about to go back. **1903** dog rushes. **1907** quickly. **1909** fierce. **1911** sounding the recall. **1912** By the time that. **1915** cry. **1916** uproar. **1918** clamour. **1919** fondle, rub. **1920** take. **1921** strip off. **1922** made for. **1923** Blowing, strong.

The lorde is lyght at the laste at hys lef home,
Fyndes fire upon flet, the freke ther-byside,
Sir Gawayn the gode, that glad was withalle:
Among the ladies for luf he ladde much joye.
He were a bleaunt of blwe that bradde to the erthe;
His surkot semed hym wel, that softe was forred,
And his hode of that ilke henged on his schulder;
Blande al of blaunner were bothe al aboute.
He metes me this godmon inmyddes the flore,
And al with gomen he hym gret and goudly he sayde:
'I schal fylle upon fyrst oure forwardes nouthe,
That we spedly han spoken ther spared was no drynk.'
Then acoles he the knyght and kysses hym thryes
As saverly and sadly as he hem sette couthe.
'Bi Kryst,' quoth that other knyght, 'ye cach much sele
In chevisaunce of this chaffer, yif ye hade goud chepes.'
'Ye, of the chepe no charge,' quoth chefly that other,
'As is pertly payed the chepes that I aghte.'
'Mary,' quoth that other mon, 'myn is bihynde,
For I haf hunted al this day and noght haf I geten
Bot this foule fox felle – the fende haf the godes!-
And that is ful pore for to pay for suche prys thinges
As ye haf thryght me here thro, suche thre cosses
So gode.'
'Inogh,' quoth sir Gawayn,
'I thonk yow, bi the rode,'
And how the fox was slayn
He tolde hym as they stode.

With merthe and mynstralsye, wyth metes at hor wylle,
Thay maden as mery as any men moghten.
With laghyng of ladies, with lotes of bordes,
Gawayn and the godemon so glad were thay bothe,
Bot if the douthe had doted other dronken ben other.
Bothe the mon and the meyny maden mony japes,
Til the sesoun was seyen that thay sever moste;
Burnes to hor bedde behoved at the laste.
Thenne lowly his leve at the lorde fyrst
Foches this fre mon, and fayre he hym thonkkes
'Of such a selly sojorne as I haf hade here;

1924 alighted, dear. **1928** wore, reached. **1931** Trimmed, ermine. **1933** good humour. **1934** fulfil, agreement now. **1935** gladly. **1936** embraces. **1937** With as much relish and vigour. **1938** happiness. **1939** acquisition, goods, bargain. **1940** no matter, briskly. **1941** openly, owed. **1945** valuable. **1946** given, earnestly. **1949** cross. **1954** words, jests. **1956** (Could not be more so) unless the company had gone crazy or been drunk. **1958** come. **1961** Takes. **1962** wonderful.

Your honour at this hyghe fest the hyghe kyng yow yelde!
I yef yow me for on of youres, if yowreself lykes;
For I mot nedes, as ye wot, meve to-morne,
And ye me take sum tolke to teche, as ye hyght,
The gate to the grene chapel, as God wyl me suffer
To dele on Nw Yeres day the dome of my wyrdes.'
'In god faythe,' quoth the godmon, 'wyth a goud wylle
Al that ever I yow hyght halde schal I redy.'
Ther asyngnes he a servaunt to sett hym in the waye
And coundue hym by the downes, that he no drech had,
For to ferk thurgh the fryth and fare at the gaynest
Bi greve.
The lorde Gawayn con thonk,
Such worchip he wolde hym weve.
Then at tho ladyes wlonk
The knyght has tan his leve,

With care and wyth kyssyng he carppes hem tille,
And fele thryvande thonkkes he thrat hom to have,
And thay yelden hym ayayn yeply that ilk.
Thay bikende hym to Kryst with ful colde sykynges.
Sythen fro the meyny he menskly departes;
Uche mon that he mette, he made hem a thonke
For his servyse and his solace and his sere pyne
That thay wyth busynes had ben aboute hym to serve;
And uche segge as sory to sever with hym there
As thay hade wonde worthyly with that wlonk ever.
Then with ledes and lyght he was ladde to his chambre
And blythely broght to his bedde to be at his rest.
Yif he ne slepe soundyly, say ne dar I,
For he hade muche on the morn to mynne, yif he wolde,
In thoght.
Let hym lyye there stille,
He has nere that he soght;
And ye wyl a whyle be stylle,
I schal telle yow how thay wroght.

1965 get going. **1966** If you provide me, promised. **1967** way. **1968** be dealt, judgement, destiny. **1972** conduct, delay. **1973** travel, wood, by the shortest route. **1974** thicket. **1976** show. **1977** noble. **1980** hearty, pressed. **1981** eagerly. **1982** sighs. **1985** special trouble. **1986** with busy care. **1988** As if, dwelt, noble knight. **1992** think about. **1995** nearly what.

Robert Henryson (c.1430–c.1505)

The Testament of Cresseid

Ane doolie sessoun to ane cairful dyte
Suld correspond and be equivalent:
Richt sa it wes quhen I began to wryte
This tragedie – the wedder richt fervent,
Quhen Aries in middis of the Lent
Schouris of haill gart fra the north discend,
That scantlie fra the cauld I micht defend.

Yit nevertheles within myne oratur
I stude, quhen Titan had his bemis bricht
Withdrawin doun and sylit under cure,
And fair Venus, the bewtie of the nicht,
Uprais and set unto the west full richt
Hir goldin face, in oppositioun
Of God Phebus, direct discending doun.

Throwout the glas hir bemis brast sa fair
That I micht se on everie syde me by:
The northin wind had purifyit the air
And sched the mistie cloudis fra the sky;
The froist freisit, the blastis bitterly
Fra Pole Artick come quhisling loud and schill
And causit me remufe aganis my will.

For I traistit that Venus, luifis quene,
To quhome sumtyme I hecht obedience,
My faidit hart of lufe scho wald mak grene,
And therupon with humbill reverence
I thocht to pray hir hie magnificence –
Bot for greit cald as than I lattit was
And in my chalmer to the fyre can pas.

4 intense(ly cold). **6** caused. **9** (the sun). **10** hidden under cover. **15** burst. **18** scattered **21** remove. **22** trusted, love's. **23** promised. **27** prevented.

Thocht lufe be hait, yit in ane man of age
It kendillis nocht sa sone as in youtheid,
Of quhome the blude is flowing in ane rage;
And in the auld the curage doif and deid
Of quhilk the fyre outward is best remeid:
To help be phisike quhair that nature faillit
I am expert, for baith I have assaillit.

I mend the fyre and beikit me about,
Than tuik ane drink, my spreitis to comfort,
And armit me weill fra tha cauld thairout.
To cut the winter nicht and mak it schort
I tuik ane quair – and left all uther sport –
Writtin be worthie Chaucer glorious
Of fair Cresseid and worthie Troylus.

And thair I fand, efter that Diomeid
Ressavit had that lady bricht of hew,
How Troilus neir out of wit abraid
And weipit soir with visage paill of hew;
For quhilk wanhope his teiris can renew,
Quhill esperance rejoisit him agane.
Thus quhyle in joy he levit, quhyle in pane.

Of hir behest he had greit comforting,
Traisting to Troy that scho suld mak retour,
Quhilk he desyrit maist of eirdly thing,
Forquhy scho was his only paramour.
Bot quhen he saw passit baith day and hour
Of hir ganecome, than sorrow can oppres
His wofull hart in cair and hevines.

Of his distres me neidis nocht reheirs,
For worthie Chauceir in the samin buik,
In gudelie termis and in joly veirs,
Compylit hes his cairis, quha will luik.
To brek my sleip ane uther quair I tuik,
In quhilk I fand the fatall destenie
Of fair Cresseid, that endit wretchitlie.

Quha wait gif all that Chauceir wrait was trew?
Nor I wait nocht gif this narratioun

29 Though love be hot. **32** sexual desire (is) dull. **33** remedy. **34** medicine (e.g. aphrodisiacs). **35** both, tried. **36** mended, basked in its warmth. **40** little book. **44** Taken (as his mistress). **45** went. **47** Because of which despair. **48** Until hope. **49** one time . . . (another time), lived. **50** promise. **53** Because. **55** return. **60** whoever. **61** keep myself awake (serving Venus).

Be authoreist, or fenyeit of the new
Be sum poeit throw his inventioun,
Maid to report the lamentatioun
And wofull end of this lustie Creisseid,
And quhat distres scho thoillit, and quhat deid.

Quhen Diomeid had all his appetyte,
And mair, fulfillit of this fair ladie,
Upon ane uther he set his haill delyte
And send to hir ane lybell of repudie
And hir excludit fra his companie.
Than desolait scho walkit up and doun,
And sum men sayis, into the court, commoun.

O fair Cresseid, the flour and A *per se*
Of Troy and Grece, how was thow fortunait
To change in filth all thy feminitie
And be with fleschelie lust sa maculait
And go amang the Greikis air and lait,
So giglotlike takand thy foull plesance!
I have pietie thow suld fall sic mischance!

Yit nevertheles, quhatever men deme or say
In scornefull langage of thy brukkilnes,
I sall excuse als far furth as I may
Thy womanheid, thy wisdome and fairnes,
The quhilk Fortoun hes put to sic distres
As hir pleisit, and nathing throw the gilt
Of the – throw wickit langage to be spilt!

This fair lady, in this wyse destitute
Of all comfort and consolatioun,
Richt privelie, but fellowschip, on fute,
Disagysit passit far out of the toun
Ane myle or twa, unto ane mansioun
Beildit full gay, quhair hir father Calchas
Quhilk than amang the Greikis dwelland was.

Quhen he hir saw, the caus he can inquyre
Of hir cumming; scho said, siching full soir:
'Fra Diomeid had gottin his desyre
He wox werie and wald of me no moir.'
Quod Calchas, 'Douchter, weip thow not thairfoir:

66 authoritative, made up. **70** suffered, death. **73** whole. **74** formal letter of divorce. **77** openly promiscuous. **79** destined by fortune. **81** spotted. **82** early and late. **83** harlot-like. **86** frailty. **89** such. **91** malicious talk, ruined. **97** where (was). **100** sighing. **101** After.

Peraventure all cummis for the best.
Welcum to me: thow art full deir ane gest!'

This auld Calchas, efter the law was tho,
Wes keiper of the tempill as ane preist
In quhilk Venus and hir sone Cupido
War honourit, and his chalmer was thame neist,
To quhilk Cresseid, with baill aneuch in breist,
Usit to pas, hir prayeris for to say,
Quhill at the last, upon ane solempne day,

As custome was, the pepill far and neir
Befoir the none unto the tempill went
With sacrifice, devoit in thair maneir.
Bot still Cresseid, hevie in hir intent,
Into the kirk wald not hirself present,
For giving of the pepill ony deming
Of hir expuls fra Diomeid the king,

Bot past into ane secreit orature,
Quhair scho micht weip hir wofull desteny.
Behind hir bak scho cloisit fast the dure
And on hir kneis bair fell doun in hy.
Upon Venus and Cupide angerly
Scho cryit out, and said on this same wyse:
'Allace, that ever I maid yow sacrifice!

'Ye gave me anis ane devine responsaill
That I suld be the flour of luif in Troy;
Now I am maid ane unworthie outwaill
And all in cair translatit is my joy.
Quha sall me gyde? Quha sall me now convoy,
Sen I fra Diomeid and nobill Troylus
Am clene excludit, as abject odious?

'O fals Cupide, is nane to wyte bot thow
And thy mother, of lufe the blind goddes!
Ye causit me alwayis understand and trow
The seid of lufe was sawin in my face,
And ay grew grene throw your supplie and grace;
But now, allace, that seid with froist is slane,
And I fra luifferis left and all forlane!'

106 according as, then. **109** dwelling, nearest to them. **110** sorrow enough. **112** Until, feast-day. **115** devout. **116** dejected, mind. **123** haste. **127** once, response. **129** outcast **131** look after. **133** one cast out. **134** blame. **137** sown. **138** assistance. **140** abandoned.

Quhen this was said, doun in ane extasie,
Ravischit in spreit, intill ane dreame scho fell,
And be apperance hard, quhair scho did ly,
Cupide the king ringand ane silver bell,
Quhilk men micht heir fra hevin unto hell;
At quhais sound befoir Cupide appeiris
The sevin planetis, discending fra thair spheiris,

Quhilk hes power of all thing generabill,
To reull and steir be thair greit influence
Wedder and wind, and coursis variabill.
And first of all Saturne gave his sentence,
Quhilk gave to Cupide litill reverence,
Bot as ane busteous churle on his maneir
Come crabitlie with auster luik and cheir.

His face fronsit, his lyre was lyke the leid,
His teith chatterit and cheverit with the chin,
His ene drowpit, how sonkin in his heid,
Out of his nois the meldrop fast can rin,
With lippis bla and cheikis leine and thin;
The ice-schoklis that fra his hair doun hang
Was wonder greit and as ane speir als lang.

Atovir his belt his lyart lokkis lay
Felterit unfair, ovirfret with froistis hoir,
His garmound and his gyte full gay of gray,
His widderit weid fra him the wind out woir.
Ane busteous bow within his hand he boir,
Under his girdill ane flasche of felloun flanis
Fedderit with ice and heidit with hailstanis.

Than Juppiter, richt fair and amiabill,
God of the starnis in the firmament
And nureis to all thing generabill –
Fra his father Saturne far different,
With burelie face and browis bricht and brent,
Upon his heid ane garland wonder gay
Of flouris fair, as it had bene in May.

His voice was cleir, as cristall wer his ene,
As goldin wyre sa glitterand was his hair,

143 heard. **146** whose. **148** able to be generated. **149** steer. **150** (i.e. not the fixed stars). **151** judgement. **153** rough. **154** ill-naturedly. **155** wrinkled, complexion, lead. **156** shivered **157** eyes, hollow sunken. **158** mucus. **159** blue. **160** icicles. **162** Down over, grey-streaked. **163** Matted, sprinkled, hoar-frost. **164** cloak and gown. **165** threadbare, caused to billow out. **167** sheaf, deadly arrows. **168** tipped. **170** stars. **171** nourisher **173** handsome, forehead, smooth.

His garmound and his gyte full gay of grene
With goldin listis gilt on everie gair;
Ane burelie brand about his middil bair,
In his richt hand he had ane groundin speir,
Of his father the wraith fra us to weir.

Nixt efter him come Mars, the god of ire,
Of strife, debait and all dissensioun,
To chide and fecht als feirs as ony fyre,
In hard harnes, hewmound and habirgeoun,
And on his hanche a roustie fell fachioun,
And in his hand he had ane roustie sword,
Wrything his face with mony angrie word.

Schaikand his sword befoir Cupide he come,
With reid visage and grislie glowrand ene,
And at his mouth ane bullar stude of fome,
Lyke to ane bair quhetting his tuskis kene,
Richt tuilyeour-lyke but temperance in tene.
Ane horne he blew with mony bosteous brag,
Quhilk all this warld with weir hes maid to wag.

Than fair Phebus, lanterne and lamp of licht,
Of man and beist, baith frute and flourisching,
Tender nureis, and banischer of nicht;
And of the warld causing, be his moving
And influence, lyfe in all eirdlie thing,
Without comfort of quhome of force to nocht
Must all ga die that in this warld is wrocht.

As king royall he raid upon his chair,
The quhilk Phaeton gydit sum tyme unricht.
The brichtnes of his face quhen it was bair
Nane micht behald for peirsing of his sicht.
This goldin cart with fyrie bemis bricht
Four yokkit steidis full different of hew
But bait or tyring throw the spheiris drew.

The first was soyr, with mane als reid as rois,
Callit Eoye, into the orient;
The secund steid to name hecht Ethios,
Quhitlie and paill, and sumdeill ascendent;
The thrid Peros, richt hait and richt fervent;

179 hems, gore (cloth-panel). **180** (he) bore. **181** sharp-ground. **182** ward off. **186** armour, helmet and coat of mail. **187** blood-rusted savage broad-sword. **189** Contorting. **192** bubble stood. **193** boar. **194** brawler-like, without, anger. **195** violent blast. **196** war, shake. **198** (of) both, blossom. **202** perforce. **204** rode, chariot. **206** bare. **210** feeding-stop or wearying through. **211** sorrel-red. **213** was called. **215** intense(ly hot).

The feird was blak, callit Phlegonie,
Quhilk rollis Phebus doun into the sey.

Venus was thair present, that goddes gay,
Hir sonnis querrell for to defend, and mak
Hir awin complaint, cled in ane nyce array,
The ane half grene, the uther half sabill-blak,
With hair as gold kemmit and sched abak.
Bot in hir face semit greit variance,
Quhyles perfyte treuth and quhyles inconstance.

Under smyling scho was dissimulait,
Provocative with blenkis amorous,
And suddanely changit and alterait,
Angrie as ony serpent vennemous,
Richt pungitive with wordis odious.
Thus variant scho was, quha list tak keip,
With ane eye lauch and with the uther weip,

In taikning that all fleschelie paramour,
Quhilk Venus hes in reull and governance,
Is sumtyme sweit, sumtyme bitter and sour,
Richt unstabill and full of variance,
Mingit with cairfull joy and fals plesance,
Now hait, now cauld, now blyith, now full of wo,
Now grene as leif, now widderit and ago.

With buik in hand than come Mercurius,
Richt eloquent and full of rethorie,
With polite termis and delicious,
With pen and ink to report all reddie,
Setting sangis and singand merilie;
His hude was reid, heklit atouir his croun,
Lyke to ane poeit of the auld fassoun.

Boxis he bair with fyne electuairis
And sugerit syropis for digestioun,
Spycis belangand to the pothecairis,
With mony hailsum sweit confectioun;
Doctour in phisick, cled in ane skarlot goun,
And furrit weill, as sic ane aucht to be –
Honest and gude, and not ane word culd lie.

217 sea. **220** foolishly fancy. **222** combed, parted. **224** At times .... **225** dissembling. **226** glances. **229** stinging. **230** take heed. **232** tokening, sexual love. **236** Mingled. **238** withered and gone. **242** make a report. **243** Composing. **244** up over. **245** old fashion **246** syrupy medicines.

Nixt efter him come Lady Cynthia,
The last of all and swiftest in hir spheir;
Of colour blak, buskit with hornis twa,
And in the nicht scho listis best appeir;
Haw as the leid, of colour nathing cleir,
For all hir licht scho borrowis at hir brother
Titan, for of hirself scho hes nane uther.

Hir gyte was gray and full of spottis blake
And on hir breist ane churle paintit full evin
Beirand ane bunche of thornis on his bak,
Quhilk for his thift micht clim na nar the hevin.
Thus quhen thay gadderit war, thir goddes sevin,
Mercurius thay cheisit with ane assent
To be foir-speikar in the parliament.

Quha had bene thair and liken for to heir
His facound toung and termis exquisite
Of rethorick the prettick he micht leir,
In breif sermone ane pregnant sentence wryte.
Befoir Cupide veiling his cap a lyte,
Speiris the caus of that vocatioun,
And he anone schew his intentioun.

'Lo,' quod Cupide, 'quha will blaspheme the name
Of his awin god, outher in word or deid,
To all goddis he dois baith lak and schame
And suld have bitter panis to his meid.
I say this by yone wretchit Cresseid,
The quhilk throw me was sumtyme flour of lufe,
Me and my mother starklie can reprufe,

'Saying of hir greit infelicitie
I was the caus, and my mother Venus
Ane blind goddes hir cald that micht not se,
With sclander and defame injurious.
Thus hir leving unclene and lecherous
Scho wald returne on me and my mother,
To quhome I schew my grace abone all uther.

'And sen ye ar all sevin deificait,
Participant of devyne sapience,
This greit injure done to our hie estait

255 equipped. **257** Bluish-grey. **261** quite plainly. **263** no nearer. **264** these **265** chose. **266** 'speaker' (presiding chairman). **267** (so fortunate as). **268** eloquent **269** practice, learn. **270** In a few words, (how to) write. **271** doffing. **272** He asks, summons. **273** set forward his accusation. **276** insult. **285** living. **286** throw back. **287** granted (i.e. to Cresseid).

Me think with pane we suld mak recompence.
Was never to goddes done sic violence –
As weill for yow as for myself I say –
Thairfoir ga help to revenge, I yow pray!'

Mercurius to Cupide gave answeir
And said, 'Schir King, my counsail is that ye
Refer yow to the hiest planeit heir
And tak to him the lawest of degre
The pane of Cresseid for to modifie:
As god Saturne, with him tak Cynthia.'
'I am content,' quod he, 'to tak thay twa.'

Than thus proceidit Saturne and the Mone
Quhen thay the mater rypelie had degest:
For the dispyte to Cupide scho had done
And to Venus, oppin and manifest,
In all hir lyfe with pane to be opprest
And torment sair with seiknes incurabill,
And to all lovers be abhominabill.

This duleful sentence Saturne tuik on hand
And passit doun quhair cairfull Cresseid lay
And on hir heid he laid ane frostie wand.
Than lawfullie on this wyse can he say:
'Thy greit fairnes and all thy bewtie gay,
Thy wantoun blude, and eik thy goldin hair,
Heir I exclude fra the for evermair.

'I change thy mirth into melancholy,
Quhilk is the mother of all pensivenes;
Thy moisture and thy heit in cald and dry;
Thyne insolence, thy play and wantones
To greit diseis; thy pomp and thy riches
In mortall neid; and greit penuritie
Thow suffer sall and as ane beggar die.'

O cruell Saturne, fraward and angrie,
Hard is thy dome and to malitious!
On fair Cresseid quhy hes thow na mercie,
Quhilk was sa sweit, gentill and amorous?
Withdraw thy sentence and be gracious –
As thow was never: sa schawis throw thy deid,
Ane wraikfull sentence gevin on fair Cresseid.

291 retribution. **293** speak. **296** Sir. **299** decide upon. **303** considered. **309** took charge of. **320** distress. **323** ill-tempered. **324** judgement, too. **328** act. **329** vindictive.

Than Cynthia, quhen Saturne past away,
Out of hir sait discendit doun belyve
And red ane bill on Cresseid quhair scho lay,
Contening this sentence diffinityve:
'Fra heit of bodie I the now depryve
And to thy seiknes sall be na recure
Bot in dolour thy dayis to indure.

'Thy cristall ene mingit with blude I mak,
Thy voice sa cleir unplesand hoir and hace,
Thy lustie lyre ovirspred with spottis blak,
And lumpis haw appeirand in thy face:
Quhair thow cummis, ilk man sall fle the place.
This sall thow go begging fra hous to hous
With cop and clapper lyke ane lazarous.'

This doolie dreame, this ugly visioun
Brocht to an end, Cresseid fra it awoik,
And all that court and convocatioun
Vanischit away. Than rais scho up and tuik
Ane poleist glas and hir schaddow culd luik;
And quhen scho saw hir face sa deformait,
Gif scho in hart was wa aneuch, God wait!

Weiping full sair, 'Lo, quhat it is,' quod sche,
'With fraward langage for to mufe and steir
Our craibit goddis – and sa is sene on me!
My blaspheming now have I bocht full deir;
All eirdlie joy and mirth I set areir.
Allace, this day! allace, this wofull tyde
Quhen I began with my goddis for to chyde!'

Be this was said, ane chyld come fra the hall
To warne Cresseid the supper was reddy;
First knokkit at the dure, and syne culd call:
'Madame, your father biddis yow cum in hy:
He hes mervell sa lang on grouf ye ly,
And sayis your beedes bene to lang sumdeill;
The goddis wait all your intent full weill.'

Quod scho, 'Fair chyld, ga to my father deir
And pray him cum to speik with me anone.'
And sa he did, and said, 'Douchter, quhat cheir?'

332 (formally) read a document. **335** remedy. **337** eyes, mingled. **338** rough and hoarse **339** lovely complexion. **340** greyish. **342** Thus. **343** leper. **347** rose. **348** reflection. **350** woeful, knows. **352** move and provoke. **355** behind me. **358** When. **362** prone on the ground. **363** somewhat.

'Allace!' quod scho, 'Father, my mirth is gone!'
'How sa?' quod he, and scho can all expone,
As I have tauld, the vengeance and the wraik
For hir trespas Cupide on hir culd tak.

He luikit on hir uglye lipper face,
The quhylk befor was quhite as lillie flour;
Wringand his handis, oftymes he said, allace!
That he had levit to se that wofull hour!
For he knew weill that thair was no succour
To hir seiknes, and that dowblit his pane.
Thus was thair cair aneuch betuix thame twane!

Quhen thay togidder murnit had full lang,
Quod Cresseid, 'Father, I wald nat be kend:
Thairfoir in secreit wyse ye let me gang
Unto yone spitall at the tounis end,
And thidder sum meit for cheritie me send
To leif upon, for all mirth in this eird
Is fra me gane – sic is my wikkit weird!'

Than in ane mantill and ane bawer-hat,
With cop and clapper, wonder prively,
He opnit ane secreit yet and out thairat
Convoyit hir, that na man suld espy,
Unto ane village half ane myle thairby,
Delyverit hir in at the spittaill-hous
And daylie sent hir part of his almous.

Sum knew hir weill and sum had na knawledge
Of hir becaus scho was sa deformait,
With bylis blak ovirsprad in hir visage
And hir fair colour faidit and alterait.
Yit thay presumit, for hir hie regrait
And still murning, scho was of nobill kin;
With better will thairfor they tuik her in.

The day passit and Phebus went to rest,
The cloudis blak ovirquhelmit all the sky.
God wait gif Cresseid was ane sorrowfull gest,
Seing that uncouth fair and harbery!
But meit or drink scho dressit hir to ly
In ane dark corner of the hous allone,
And on this wyse weiping scho maid hir mone:

375 lived. **380** known. **381** go. **384** live, earth. **385** cruel fate. **386** beaver-hat (worn by Calchas). **388** gate. **392** alms. **395** boils. **397** lamentation. **398** quiet. **403** fare and lodging. **404** prepared.

The Complaint of Cresseid

'O sop of sorrow, sonkin into cair!
O cative Creisseid! For now and ever mair
Gane is thy joy and al thy mirth in eird;
Of all blyithnes now art thou blaiknit bair;
Thair is na salve may saif the of thy sair!
Fell is thy fortoun, wickit is thy weird,
Thy blys is baneist and thy baill on breird!
Under the eirth God gif I gravin wer,
Quhair nane of Grece nor yit of Troy micht heir'd!

'Quhair is thy chalmer wantounlie besene,
With burely bed and bankouris browderit bene?
Spycis and wyne to thy collatioun,
The cowpis all of gold and silver schene,
The sweit-meits servit in plaittis clene
With saipheron sals of ane gude sessoun?
Thy gay garmentis with mony gudely goun,
Thy plesand lawn pinnit with goldin prene?
All is areir thy greit royall renoun!

'Quhair is thy garding with thir greissis gay
And fresche flowris quhilk the quene Floray
Had paintit plesandly in everie pane,
Quhair thou was wont full merilye in May
To walk and tak the dew be it was day,
And heir the merle and mawis mony ane,
With ladyis fair in carrolling to gane
And se the royall rinkis in thair array,
In garmentis gay garnischit on everie grane?

'Thy greit triumphand fame and hie honour,
Quhair thou was callit of eirdlye wichtis flour,
All is decayit, thy weird is welterit so:
Thy hie estait is turnit in darknes dour.
This lipper ludge tak for thy burelie bour,
And for thy bed tak now ane bunche of stro,
For waillit wyne and meitis thou had tho

407 (thing soaked in). **408** wretched. **410** made pale and bare. **411** heal **412** Cruel. **413** bliss, banished, distress beginning to increase. **414** grant, buried. **415** bear it. **416** luxuriously furnished. **417** With sumptuous bed and finely embroidered seat-covers. **418** evening refreshment. **419** goblets. **421** saffron sauce, flavour. **423** fine linen, brooch. **425** these plants. **427** part. **429** gather, as soon as. **430** blackbird and song-thrush. **431** go. **433** smallest part. **435** creatures. **436** overturned. **438** dwelling. **439** straw. **440** choice.

Tak mowlit brid, peirrie and ceder sour;
Bot cop and clapper now is all ago.

'My cleir voice and courtlie carrolling,
Quhair I was wont with ladyis for to sing,
Is rawk as ruik full hiddeous, hoir and hace;
My plesand port, all utheris precelling,
Of lustines I was hald maist conding –
Now is deformit the figour of my face:
To luik on it na leid now lyking hes.
Sowpit in syte, I say with sair siching,
Ludgeit amang the lipper leid, "Allace!"

'O ladyis fair of Troy and Grece, attend
My miserie, quhilk nane may comprehend,
My frivoll fortoun, my infelicitie,
My greit mischeif, quhilk na man can amend.
Be war in tyme, approchis neir the end,
And in your mynd ane mirrour mak of me:
As I am now, peradventure that ye
For all your micht may cum to that same end,
Or ellis war, gif ony war may be.

'Nocht is your fairnes bot ane faiding flour,
Nocht is your famous laud and hie honour
Bot wind inflat in uther mennis eiris;
Your roising reid to rotting sall retour.
Exempill mak of me in your memour
Quhilk of sic thingis wofull witnes beiris:
All welth in eird away as wind it weiris.
Be war thairfoir, approchis neir the hour:
Fortoun is fikkill quhen scho beginnis and steiris.'

Thus chydand with hir drerie destenye,
Weiping scho woik the nicht fra end to end;
Bot all in vane – hir dule, hir cairfull cry,
Micht not remeid nor yit hir murning mend.
Ane lipper lady rais and till hir wend
And said, 'Quhy spurnis thow aganis the wall
To sla thyself and mend nathing at all?

'Sen thy weiping dowbillis bot thy wo,
I counsall the mak vertew of ane neid:

441 mouldy, perry (pear-cider). **442** Except for. **445** raucous, rook. **446** excelling. **447** worthy. **449** person. **450** Immersed in sorrow, sighing. **451** Lodged, folk. **454** fickle. **460** worse. **463** puffed. **464** rosy. **465** memory. **467** passes away. **469** gets moving. **474** rose, went to her. **476** destroy. **477** Since.

Go leir to clap thy clapper to and fro
And leif efter the law of lipper leid.'
Thair was na buit, bot furth with thame scho yeid
Fra place to place, quhill cauld and houngersair
Compellit hir to be ane rank beggair.

That samin tyme, of Troy the garnisoun,
Quhilk had to chiftane worthie Troylus,
Throw jeopardie of weir had strikken doun
Knichtis of Grece in number mervellous;
With greit tryumphe and laude victorious
Agane to Troy richt royallie thay raid
The way quhair Cresseid with the lipper baid.

Seing that companie come, all with ane stevin
Thay gaif ane cry and schuik coppis gude speid,
Said, 'Worthie lordis, for Goddis lufe of hevin,
To us lipper part of your almous-deid!'
Than to thair cry nobill Troylus tuik heid,
Having pietie, neir by the place can pas
Quhair Cresseid sat, not witting quhat scho was.

Than upon him scho kest up baith hir ene –
And with ane blenk it come into his thocht
That he sumtime hir face befoir had sene;
Bot scho was in sic plye he knew hir nocht –
Yit than hir luik into his mynd it brocht
The sweit visage and amorous blenking
Of fair Cresseid, sumtyme his awin darling.

Na wonder was, suppois in mynd that he
Tuik hir figure sa sone – and lo, now quhy:
The idole of ane thing in cace may be
Sa deip imprentit in the fantasy
That it deludis the wittis outwardly,
And sa appeiris in forme and lyke estait
Within the mynd as it was figurait.

Ane spark of lufe than till his hart culd spring
And kendlit all his bodie in ane fyre;
With hait fewir ane sweit and trimbling
Him tuik, quhill he was reddie to expyre –
To beir his scheild his breist began to tyre.

479 learn. **480** live. **481** remedy, went. **482** until. **484** garrison. **486** fortune of war. **489** rode. **490** waited. **491** voice. **492** with vigour. **494** give a share. **496** pity. **499** glance. **501** state. **505** supposing if. **506** Interpreted her appearance. **507** image, perchance. **510** condition. **514** hot fever, a fit of sweating. **515** until.

Within ane quhyle he changit mony hew,
And nevertheles not ane ane uther knew.

For knichtlie pietie and memoriall
Of fair Cresseid ane gyrdill gan he tak,
Ane purs of gold and mony gay jowall,
And in the skirt of Cresseid doun can swak,
Than raid away and not ane word he spak,
Pensive in hart, quhill he come to the toun,
And for greit cair oft-syis almaist fell doun.

The lipper folk to Cresseid than can draw
To se the equall distributioun
Of the almous, bot quhen the gold thay saw
Ilk ane to uther prevelie can roun,
And said, 'Yone lord hes mair affectioun,
However it be, unto yone lazarous
Than to us all – we knaw be his almous.'

'Quhat lord is yone,' quod scho, 'have ye na feill,
Hes done to us so greit humanitie?'
'Yes,' quod a lipper man, 'I knaw him weill:
Schir Troylus it is, gentill and fre.'
Quhen Cresseid understude that it was he,
Stiffer than steill thair stert ane bitter stound
Throwout hir hart, and fell doun to the ground.

Quhen scho ovircome, with siching sair and sad,
With mony cairfull cry and cald ochane:
'Now is my breist with stormie stoundis stad,
Wrappit in wo, ane wretch full will of wane!'
Than swounit scho oft or ever scho culd refrane,
And ever in hir swouning cryit scho thus:
'O fals Cresseid and trew knicht Troylus!

'Thy lufe, thy lawtie and thy gentilnes
I countit small in my prosperitie,
So elevait I was in wantones
And clam upon the fickill quheill sa hie.
All faith and lufe I promissit to the
Was in the self fickill and frivolous:
O fals Cresseid and trew knicht Troylus!

'For lufe of me thow keipt gude continence,
Honest and chaist in conversatioun.

522 throw. **525** oft-times. **529** whisper. **533** idea. **538** pang. **540** revived. **541** and bitter cries of 'alas!'. **542** beset. **543** bewildered. **547** loyalty. **552** in itself. **555** dealings with others.

Of all wemen protectour and defence
Thou was, and helpit thair opinioun –
My mynd in fleschelie foull affectioun
Was inclynit to lustis lecherous:
Fy, fals Cresseid! O trew knicht Troylus!

'Lovers be war and tak gude heid about
Quhome that ye lufe, for quhome ye suffer paine:
I lat yow wit thair is richt few thairout
Quhome ye may traist to have trew lufe agane –
Preif quhen ye will, your labour is in vaine.
Thairfoir I reid ye tak thame as ye find,
For thay ar sad as widdercok in wind.

'Becaus I knaw the greit unstabilnes,
Brukkill as glas, into myself, I say –
Traisting in uther als greit unfaithfulnes,
Als unconstant and als untrew of fay –
Thocht sum be trew, I wait richt few ar thay:
Quha findis treuth lat him his lady ruse!
Nane but myself as now I will accuse.'

Quhen this was said, with paper scho sat doun,
And on this maneir maid hir testament:
'Heir I beteiche my corps and carioun
With wormis and with taidis to be rent;
My cop and clapper and myne ornament
And all my gold the lipper folk sall have
Quhen I am deid, to burie me in grave.

'This royall ring set with this rubie reid
Quhilk Troylus in drowrie to me send
To him agane I leif it quhen I am deid
To mak my cairfull deid unto him kend.
Thus I conclude schortlie and mak ane end:
My spreit I leif to Diane quhair scho dwellis,
To walk with hir in waist woddis and wellis.

'O Diomeid, thou hes baith broche and belt
Quhilk Troylus gave me in takning
Of his trew lufe!' And with that word scho swelt.
And sone ane lipper man tuik of the ring,
Syne buryit hir withouttin tarying.

557 reputation. **564** in return. **565** Test it out. **567** steadfast, weathercock. **569** Brittle, within. **570** Anticipating. **571** faith. **572** Though, know. **573** praise. **577** commit. **578** toads. **583** as a love-token. **584** leave. **585** death, known. **588** uninhabited woods with pools. **591** swooned to death. **592** took off. **593** Then.

To Troylus furthwith the ring he bair
And of Cresseid the deith he can declair.

Quhen he had hard hir greit infirmitie,
Hir legacie and lamentatioun,
And how scho endit in sic povertie,
He swelt for wo and fell doun in ane swoun;
For greit sorrow his hart to brist was boun,
Siching full sadlie, said, 'I can no moir:
Scho was untrew and wo is me thairfoir.'

Sum said he maid ane tomb of merbell gray
And wrait hir name and superscriptioun
And laid it on hir grave quhair that scho lay,
In golden letteris, conteining this ressoun:
'Lo, fair ladyis, Cresseid of Troyis toun,
Sumtyme countit the flour of womanheid,
Under this stane, lait lipper, lyis deid.'

Now, worthie wemen, in this ballet schort,
Maid for your worschip and instructioun,
Of cheritie I monische and exhort,
Ming not your lufe with fals deceptioun.
Beir in your mynd this schort conclusioun
Of fair Cresseid, as I have said befoir;
Sen scho is deid, I speik of hir no moir.

The Fables

The Fox and the Wolf

The practice of confession was central to the experience of the medieval Christian and a key element in the church's exercise of control over the minds of the faithful. Abuse of the practice was a serious matter, but was widespread, and the high comedy of this fable is an index to some of the forms it took: confession undertaken out of fear rather than penitence, with no intention of breaking the habit of sin, nor of performing penance; and absolution administered with indulgence, especially by friars who were susceptible to flattery or bribes and had no continuing pastoral responsibility. Somehow, amidst all the animal energies and high spirits, it is not easy to remember how serious it all was, though Henryson reminds us, in the three heavy stanzas of the *Moralitas.*

Leif we this wedow glaid, I yow assure,
Of Chantecleir, mair blyith than I can tell,

599 swooned. **600** ready. **603** tombstone. **606** statement. **610** little poem. **612** admonish. **615** here-before. **614** Leave.

And speik we of the fatal aventure
And destenie that to this foxe befell,
Quhilk durst na mair with miching intermell
Als lang as leme or licht wes of the day,
Bot bydand nicht full styll lurkand he lay,

Quhill that Thetes, the goddes of the flude,
Phebus had callit to the harbery,
And Hesperous put up his cluddie hude,
Schawand his lustie visage in the sky.
Than Lourence luikit up, quhair he couth ly,
And kest his hand upon his ee on hicht,
Merie and glade that cummit wes the nicht.

Out of the wod unto ane hill he went
Quhair he micht se the tuinkling sternis cleir
And all the planetis of the firmament,
Thair cours and eik thair moving in thair spheir,
Sum retrograde and sum stationeir,
And of the zodiak in quhat degre
Thay wer ilk ane. As Lowrence leirnit me,

Than Saturne auld wes enterit in Capricorne,
And Juppiter movit in Sagittarie,
And Mars up in the Rammis heid wes borne,
And Phebus in the Lyoun furth can carie;
Venus the Crab, the Mone wes in Aquarie,
Mercurius, the god of eloquence,
Into the Virgyn maid his residence.

But astrolab, quadrant or almanak,
Teichit of nature be instructioun,
The moving of the hevin this tod can tak,
Quhat influence and constellatioun
Wes lyke to fall upon the eirth adoun,
And to himself he said, withoutin mair,
'Weill worth the, father, that send me to the lair.

'My destenie and eik my weird I wait,
My aventure is cleirlie to me kend;
With mischeif myngit is my mortall fait
My misleving the soner bot gif I mend;

618 pilfering, engage in. **620** awaiting. **621** sea. **622** night's lodging-place. **623** (the evening star). **625** from where he lay. **626** (shaded his eyes). **634** each one, taught. **641** Virgo. **642** Without. **644** fox, ascertain. **645** stellar influence. **648** Good befall you, to learning. **649** fate, know. **650** fortune. **652** unless.

It is reward of sin, ane schamefull end.
Thairfoir I will ga seik sum confessour
And schryiff me clene of my sinnis to this hour.

'Allace,' quod he, 'richt waryit ar we thevis:
Our lyif is set ilk nicht in aventure,
Our cursit craft full mony man mischevis,
For ever we steill and ever ar lyke pure;
In dreid and schame our dayis we indure,
Syne "Widdinek" and "Crakraip" callit als,
And till our hyre hangit up be the hals.'

Accusand thus his cankerit conscience,
Into ane craig he kest about his ee,
So saw he cummand, ane lyttill than frome thence,
Ane worthie doctour in divinitie,
Freir Wolff Waitskaith, in science wonder sle,
To preiche and pray was new cummit fra the closter,
With beidis in hand, sayand his Pater Noster.

Seand this wolff, this wylie tratour tod
On kneis fell, with hude into his nek:
'Welcome, my gostlie father under God',
Quod he, with mony binge and mony bek.
'Ha,' quod the wolff, 'schir Tod, for quhat effek
Mak ye sic feir? Ryse up, put on your hude!'
'Father,' quod he, 'I haif grit cause to du'de:

'Ye are mirrour, lanterne and sicker way
Suld gyde sic sempill folk as me to grace;
Your bair feit and your russet coull of gray,
Your lene cheik, your paill and pietious face,
Schawis to me your perfite halines;
For weill wer him that anis in his lyve
Had hap to yow his sinnis for to schryve.'

'Na, selie Lowrence,' quod the wolf, and leuch,
'It plesis me that ye ar penitent.'
'Of reif and stouth, schir, I can tell aneuch,
That causis me full sair for to repent.
Bot father, byde still heir upon the bent,

656 cursed. **657** in jeopardy. **658** injures. **659** alike poor. **661** Then also called "Gallows-neck" and "Crack-rope". **662** for our reward. **667** 'Do-harm', knowledge, clever. **669** prayer-beads. **670** Seeing. **671** around his neck. **673** bow, inclination of the head. **675** behaviour. **676** do it. **677** sure. **679** coarse cloth cowl. **682** once. **683** good fortune. **684** poor simple, smiled. **686** robbery and theft.

I yow beseik, and heir me to declair
My conscience, that prikkis me sa sair.'

'Weill,' quod the wolff, 'sit doun upon thy kne.'
And he doun bair-heid sat full humilly
And syne began with 'Benedicitie'.
(Quhen I this saw, I drew ane lytill by,
For it effeiris nouther to heir nor spy
Nor to reveill thing said under that seill.)
Unto the tod this-gait the wolf couth mele:

'Art thow contrite and sorie in thy spreit
For thy trespas?' 'Na, schir, I can not du'id.
Me think that hennis ar sa honie sweit
And lambes flesche that new ar lettin bluid,
For to repent my mynd can not concluid,
Bot of this thing, that I haif slane sa few.'
'Weill,' quod the wolf, 'in faith thow art ane schrew.

'Sen thow can not forthink thy wickitnes,
Will thow forbeir in tyme to cum, and mend?'
'And I forbeir, how sall I leif, allace,
Haifand nane uther craft me to defend?
Neid causis me to steill quhair-ever I wend:
I eschame to thig, I can not wirk, ye wait,
Yit wald I fane pretend to gentill stait.'

'Weill,' quod the wolf, 'thow wantis pointis twa
Belangand to perfyte confessioun;
To the thrid part of penitence let us ga:
Will thow tak pane for thy transgressioun?'
'Na, schir, considder my complexioun,
Seikly and waik, and off my nature tender;
Lo, will ye se, I am baith lene and sklender.

'Yit nevertheles I wald, swa it wer licht,
Schort, and not grevand to my tendernes,
Tak part of pane, fulfill it gif I micht,
To set my selie saull in way of grace.'
'Thow sall,' quod he, 'forbeir flesch untill Pasche
To tame this corps, that cursit carioun,
And heir I reik the full remissioun.'

691 set. **692** knelt. **694** aside. **695** is fitting. **696** seal (promise of confidentiality). **697** in this way, spoke. **699** do it. **702** make a decision. **705** Since, repent. **707** If, live. **710** am ashamed, dig. **715** accept penitential discipline. **721** a little bit. **725** grant.

'I grant thairto, swa ye will giff me leif
To eit puddingis, or laip ane lyttill blude,
Or heid, or feit, or paynchis let me preif,
In cace I falt of flesch into my fude.'
'For grit mister I gif the leif to du'de
Twyse in the oulk, for neid may haif na law.'
'God yeild yow, schir, for that text weill I knaw.'

Quhen this wes said, the wolf his wayis went;
The foxe on fute he fure unto the flude;
To fang him fisch haillelie wes his intent.
Bot quhen he saw the walterand wallis woude,
All stonist still into ane stair he stude,
And said, 'Better that I had biddin at hame
Nor bene ane fischar, in the Devillis name!

'Now man I scraip my meit out of the sand,
For I haif nouther boittis, net nor bait.'
As he wes thus for falt of meit murnand,
Lukand about, his leving for to lait,
Under ane tre he saw ane trip of gait.
Than wes he blyith, and in ane hewch him hid,
And fra the gait he stall ane lytill kid.

Syne over the heuch unto the see he hyis
And tuke the kid be the hornis twane
And in the watter outher twyis or thryis
He dowkit him, and till him can he sayne,
'Ga doun, schir Kid, cum up, schir Salmond, agane,'
Quhill he wes deid, syne to the land him drewch
And of that new-maid salmond eit anewch.

Thus fynelie fillit with young tender meit,
Unto ane derne for dreid he him addrest,
Under ane busk, quhair that the sone can beit,
To beik his breist and bellie he thocht best;
And rekleslie he said, quhair he did rest,
Straikand his wame aganis the sonis heit,
'Upon this wame set wer ane bolt full meit.'

Quhen this wes said, the keipar of the gait,
Cairfull in hart his kid wes stollen away,

728 paunch-meats (tripe, etc.), taste. **729** lack. **730** In case of great need. **731** week. **732** reward. **734** went, sea. **736** surging angry waves. **737** astonished, a horrified stare. **738** stayed. **739** Than. **740** must. **743** sustenance, seek. **744** troop of goats. **745** little hollow. **755** hiding-place. **757** warm. **759** belly. **760** It would be perfect justice if an arrow went straight through my stomach.

On everilk syde full warlie couth he wait,
Quhill at the last he saw quhair Lowrence lay.
Ane bow he bent, ane flane with fedderis gray
He haillit to the heid and, or he steird,
The foxe he prikkit fast unto the eird.

'Now,' quod the foxe, 'allace and wellaway!
Gorrit I am, and may na forther gane;
Me think na man may speik ane word in play
Bot now-on-dayis in ernist it is tane.'
The hird him hynt and out he drew his flane
And for his kid and uther violence
He tuke his skyn and maid ane recompence.

Moralitas

This suddand deith and unprovysit end
Of this fals tod, without contritioun,
Exempill is exhortand folk to amend,
For dreid of sic ane lyk conclusioun;
For mony gois now to confessioun
Can not repent nor for thair sinnis greit
Because thay think thair lustie lyfe sa sweit.

Sum bene also throw consuetude and ryte
Vincust with carnall sensualitie:
Suppose thay be as for the tyme contryte,
Can not forbeir nor fra thair sinnis fle.
Use drawis nature swa in propertie
Of beist and man that neidlingis thay man do
As thay of lang tyme hes bene hantit to.

Be war, gude folke, and feir this suddane schoit,
Quhilk smytis sair withoutin resistence.
Attend wyislie and in your hartis noit,
Aganis deith may na man mak defence.
Ceis of your sin, remord your conscience,
Do wilfull pennance here, and ye shall wend,
Efter your deith, to blis withouttin end.

The Wolf and the Wether

Qwhylum thair wes, as Esope can report,
Ane scheipheird duelland be ane forrest neir,

763 look. **765** arrow. **766** drew. **767** pinned. **769** Spiked. **772** herdsman, seized. **774** got some of his own back. **775** unforeseen. **780** weep. **782** custom and habit. **783** Vanquished. **786** in the character. **787** of necessity, must. **788** accustomed. **791** take note. **793** examine remorsefully. **794** voluntary. **2455** Once upon a time.

Quhilk had ane hound that did him grit comfort:
Full war he wes to walk his fauld, but weir,
That nouther wolf nor wildcat durst appeir,
Nor foxe on feild nor yit no uther beist,
Bot he thame slew or chaissit at the leist.

Sa happinnit it – as everilk beist man de –
This hound of suddand seiknes to be deid;
Bot than, God wait, the keipar of the fe
For verray wo woxe wanner nor the weid:
'Allace!' quod he, 'now se I na remeid
To saif the selie beistis that I keip,
For with the wolf weryit beis all my scheip!'

It wald have maid ane mannis hart sair to se
The selie scheipirdis lamentatioun:
'Now is my darling deid, allace!' quod he;
'For now to beg my breid I may be boun,
With pyikstaff and with scrip to fair of toun;
For all the beistis befoir that bandonit bene
Will schute upon my beistis with ire and tene!'

With that ane wedder wichtlie wan on fute:
'Maister,' quod he, 'mak merie and be blyith;
To brek your hart for baill it is na bute.
For ane deid dogge ye na cair on yow kyith:
Ga fetche him hither and fla his skyn off swyth,
Syne sew it on me – and luke that it be meit,
Baith heid and crag, bodie, taill and feit.

'Than will the wolf trow that I am he,
For I shall follow him fast quharever he fair.
All haill the cure I tak it upon me
Your scheip to keip at midday, lait and air:
And he persew, be God I sall not spair
To follow him as fast as did your doig,
Swa that I warrand ye sall not want ane hoig.'

Than said the scheipheird: 'This come of ane gude wit;
Thy counsall is baith sicker, leill and trew;
Quha sayis ane scheip is daft, that lieit of it.'
With that in hy the doggis skyn off he flew

2458 sheep-fold, without doubt. **2462** must die. **2464** livestock. **2465** paler than a weed. **2468** worried, will be. **2472** ready. **2473** bag, go out of. **2474** have been cowed. **2475** rush, anger **2476** quickly got up. **2478** sorrow, remedy. **2479** don't show yourself sorrowful. **2480** flay. **2481** well-fitting. **2482** neck. **2484** goes. **2485** Entirely, charge. **2486** early. **2487** If. **2489** be missing one young sheep. **2491** reliable, faithful. **2493** flayed.

And on the scheip rycht softlie couth it sew.
Than worth the wedder wantoun of his weid:
'Now of the wolf,' quod he, 'I have na dreid.'

In all thingis he counterfait the dog,
For all the nycht he stude and tuke na sleip
Swa that weill lang thair wantit not ane hog.
Swa war he wes and walkryfe thame to keip
That Lowrence durst not luke upon ane scheip,
For, and he did, he followit him sa fast
That of his lyfe he maid him all agast.

Was nowther wolf, wildcat nor yit tod
Durst cum within thay boundis all about
Bot he wald chase tham baith throw rouch and snod.
Thay bailfull beistis had of their lyvis sic dout,
For he wes mekill and semit to be stout,
That everilk beist thay dreid him as the deid,
Within that woid that nane durst hald thair heid.

Yit happinnit thair ane hungrie wolf to slyde
Out-throw his scheip quhair that lay on ane le:
'I sall have ane,' quod he, 'quhatever betyde,
Thocht I be werryit, for hunger or I de!'
With that ane lamb intill his cluke hint he.
The laif start up, for thay wer all agast –
But God wait gif the wedder followit fast!

Went never hound mair haistelie fra the hand
Quhen he wes rynnand maist raklie at the ra
Nor went this wedder baith over mois and strand,
And stoppit nouther at bank, busk nor bra,
Bot followit ay sa ferslie on his fa,
With sic ane drift, quhill dust and dirt overdraif him,
And maid ane vow to God that he suld have him.

With that the wolf let out his taill on lenth,
For he wes hungrie and it drew neir the ene,
And schupe him for to ryn with all his strenth,
Fra he the wedder sa neir cummand had sene.
He dred his lyfe and he overtane had bene:

2495 foolishly proud. **2500** watchful. **2505** those. **2506** rough ground and smooth. **2507** Those harmful, such fear. **2509** death. **2510** wood. **2512** open field. **2514** before I die. **2515** clutch, seized **2516** rest. **2518** (when released). **2519** quickly, roe-deer. **2520** Than, moorland and stream. **2521** bush nor hillside. **2523** impetus, covered. **2526** evening. **2527** endeavoured. **2528** From the time that. **2529** feared for, if.

Thairfoir he spairit nowther busk nor boig,
For weill he kennit the kenenes of the doig.

To mak him lycht he kest the lamb him fra,
Syne lap over leis and draif throw dub and myre.
'Na,' quod the wedder. 'in faith we part not swa:
It is not the lamb, bot the, that I desyre!
I sall cum neir, for now I se the tyre.'
The wolf ran till ane rekill stude behind him –
Bot ay the neirar the wedder he couth bind him.

Sone efter that he followit him sa neir
Quhill that the wolf for fleidnes fylit the feild,
Syne left the gait and ran throw busk and breir
And schupe him fra the schawis for to scheild.
He ran restles, for he wist of na beild;
The wedder followit him baith out and in,
Quhill that ane breir-busk raif rudelie off the skyn.

The wolf wes wer and blenkit him behind
And saw the wedder come thrawand throw the breir,
Syne saw the doggis skyn hingand on his lind:
'Na,' quod he, 'is this ye, that is sa neir?
Richt now ane hound and now quhyte as ane freir!
I fled over-fer and I had kennit the cais:
To God I vow that ye sall rew this rais!

'Quhat wes the cause ye gaif me sic ane katche?'
With that in hy he hint him be the horne:
'For all your mowis ye met anis with your matche,
Suppois ye leuch me all this yeir to scorne.
For quhat enchessoun this doggis skyn have ye borne?'
'Maister,' quod he, 'bot to have playit with yow:
I yow requyre that ye nane uther trow.'

'Is this your bourding in ernist than?' quod he;
'For I am verray effeirit and on flocht;
Cum bak agane and I sall let yow se.'
Than quhar the gait wes grimmit he him brocht:
'Quhether call ye this fair play or nocht,

2533 leapt, drove, pool. **2537** broken-down stone wall (?). **2538** dogged his steps. **2540** fright, fouled. **2541** Then, track. **2542** woodland-thickets. **2543** without cease, refuge. **2545** tore. **2546** aware, glanced. **2547** thrusting. **2548** around his loins. **2550** (a Carmelite friar). **2551** if, known the situation. **2552** race/course of action. **2553** chase. **2555** tricks, for once. **2556** Even if, get me laughed at. **2557** reason. **2560** jesting. **2561** afraid, in a flutter. **2563** befouled.

To set your maister in sa fell effray
Quhill he for feiritnes hes fylit up the way!

'Thryis, be my saull, ye gart me schute behind –
Upon my hoichis the senyeis may be sene:
For feiritnes full oft I fylit the wind.
Now is this ye? Na, bot ane hound I wene!
Me think your teith over-schort to be sa kene.
Blissit be the busk that reft yow your array,
Ellis, fleand, bursin had I bene this day!'

'Schir,' quod the wedder, 'suppois I ran in hy,
My mynd wes never to do your persoun ill:
Ane flear gettis ane follower commounly,
In play or ernist – preif quha-sa-ever will;
Sen I bot playit, be gracious me till
And I sall gar my freindis blis your banis;
Ane full gude servand will crab his maister anis.'

'I have bene oftymis set in grit effray,
Bot, be the rude, sa rad yit wes I never
As thow hes maid me with thy prettie play.
I schot behind quhen thow overtuke me ever –
Bot sikkerlie now sall we not dissever!'
Than be the crag-bane smertlie he him tuke,
Or ever he ceissit, and it in schunder schuke.

Moralitas

Esope that poete, first father of this fabill,
Wrait this parabole, quhilk is convenient
Because the sentence wes fructuous and agreabill,
In moralitie exemplative prudent;
Quhais problemes bene verray excellent,
Throw similitude of figuris, to this day,
Gevis doctrine to the redaris of it ay.

Heir may thow se that riches of array
Will cause pure men presumpteous for to be:
Thay think thay hald of nane, be thay als gay,
Bot counterfute ane lord in all degre.

2565 terrible fright. **2566** Until, fear. **2567** made me shoot out. **2568** hocks, signs. **2573** bursted (by his bowels). **2575** intention. **2576** One in flight. **2579** cause. **2580** (is allowed to) annoy. **2582** cross, terrified. **2584** kept catching up with me. **2585** part **2587** asunder. **2589** fitting. **2590** suitable. **2591** furnishing an example. **2592** riddles of interpretation. **2593** Through aptness of figurative application. **2596** poor. **2597** have no feudal obligation.

Out of their cais in pryde thay clym sa hie
That thay forbeir thair better in na steid,
Quhill sum man tit thair heillis over thair heid.

Richt swa in service uther sum exceidis,
And thay haif withgang, welth and cherising,
That thay will lychtlie lordis in thair deidis,
And lukis not to thair blude nor thair ofspring.
Bot yit nane wait how lang that reull will ring;
Bot he wes wyse that bad his sone considder:
'Bewar in welth, for hall-benkis ar rycht slidder!'

Thairfoir I counsell men of everilk stait
To knaw thameself and quhome thay suld forbeir
And fall not with thair better in debait,
Suppois thay be als galland in thair geir:
It settis na servand for to uphald weir,
Nor clym sa hie quhill he fall of the ledder:
Bot think upon the wolf and on the wedder!

2599 situation in life. **2600** no place. **2601** pulls. **2602** some others go too far. **2603** If, success. **2604** disparage. **2606** knows, state of affairs, prevail. **2608** benches, slippery. **2609** estate. **2612** Even if. **2613** is proper, strife. **2615** Only.

William Dunbar (c.1456–c.1515)

Meditation in Winter

Into thir dirk and drublie dayis
Quhone sabill all the hevin arrayis
With mystie vapouris, cluddis and skyis,
Nature all curage me denyis
Of sangis, ballattis and of playis.

Quhone that the nycht dois lenth in houris
With wind, with haill and havy schouris,
My dulie spreit dois lurk for schoir;
My hairt for languor dois forloir
For laik of Symmer with his flouris.

I waik, I turne, sleip may I nocht;
I vexit am with havie thocht.
This warld all ovir I cast about
And ay the mair I am in dout
The mair that I remeid have socht.

I am assayit on everie syde:
Dispair sayis ay, 'In tyme provyde
And get sum thing quhairon to leif,
Or with grit trouble and mischeif
Thow sall into this court abyd.'

Than Patience sayis, 'Be not agast:
Hald hoip and treuthe within the fast
And lat Fortoun wirk furthe hir rage,
Quhome that no rasoun may assuage
Quhill that hir glas be run and past.'

And Prudence in my eir sayis ay,
'Quhy wald thow hald that will away?

1 In these, overcast. **4** heart (for). **5** poems. **8** doleful, cowers under the threat. **9** becomes forlorn. **13** consider. **14** anxiety. **15** remedy. **16** assailed. **18** live. **20** (i.e. James's court). **23** work off. **25** hour-glass. **27** hold on to what.

Or craif that thow may have no space,
Thow tending to ane uther place,
A journay going everie day?'

And than sayis Age, 'My friend, cum neir,
And be not strange, I the requeir:
Cum, brodir, by the hand me tak;
Remember thow hes compt to mak
Of all thi tyme thow spendit heir.'

Syne Deid castis upe his yettis wyd,
Saying, 'Thir oppin sall the abyd;
Albeid that thow wer never sa stout,
Undir this lyntall sall thow lowt:
Thair is nane uther way besyde.'

For feir of this all day I drowp:
No gold in kist, nor wyne in cowp,
No ladeis bewtie nor luiffis blys,
May lat me to remember this,
How glaid that ever I dyne or sowp.

Yit, quhone the nycht begyynis to schort,
It dois my spreit sum pairt confort
Of thocht oppressit with the schowris.
Cum, lustie Symmer, with thi flowris,
That I may leif in sum disport!

Christ in Triumph

Done is a batell on the dragon blak;
Our campioun Chryst confoundit hes his force.
The yettis of hell ar brokin with a crak;
The signe triumphall rasit is of the croce.
The divillis trymmillis with hiddous voce;
The saulis ar borrowit and to the blis can go.
Chryst with his blud our ransonis dois indoce:
Surrexit Dominus de sepulchro.

Dungin is the deidly dragon Lucifer,
The crewall serpent with the mortall stang,
The auld kene tegir with his teith on char,
Quhilk in a wait hes lyne for us so lang,

28 crave what, no length of time. **30** day's journey. **32** distant with me, request. **34** reckoning. **36** gates. **37** These open. **38** Although. **39** stoop. **42** chest. **44** prevent. **50** live. **3** gates. **5** tremble. **6** ransomed. **9** Beaten down. **11** bared ('ajar'). **12** ambush, lain.

Thinking to grip us in his clowis strang;
The merciful Lord wald nocht that it wer so,
He maid him for to felye of that fang:
Surrexit Dominus de sepulchro.

He for our saik that sufferit to be slane
And lyk a lamb in sacrifice wes dicht
Is lyk a lyone rissin up agane,
And as gyane raxit him on hicht.
Sprungin is Aurora radius and bricht,
On loft is gone the glorius Appollo,
The blisful day depairtit fro the nycht:
Surrexit Dominus de sepulchro.

The grit victour agane is rissin on hicht
That for our querrell to the deth wes woundit;
The sone that wox all paill now schynis bricht
And dirknes clerit, our fayth is now refoundit;
The knell of mercy fra the hevin is soundit,
The Cristin ar deliverit of thair wo,
The Jowis and thair errour ar confoundit:
Surrexit Dominus de sepulchro.

The fo is chasit, the battell is done ceis,
The presone brokin, the jevellouris fleit and flemit;
The weir is gon, confermit is the peis,
The fetteris lowsit and the dungeoun temit,
The ransoun maid, the presoneris redemit;
The feild is win, ourcumin is the fo,
Dispulit of the tresur that he yemit:
Surrexit Dominus de sepulchro.

From The Golden Targe

Ryght as the stern of day begouth to schyne,
Quhen gone to bed war Vesper and Lucyne,
I raise, and by a rosere did me rest.
Up sprang the goldyn candill matutyne,
With clere depurit bemes cristallyne,
Glading the mery foulis in thair nest;
Or Phebus was in purpur cape revest

13 claws. **15** fail, attempt to seize his prey. **18** offered. **20** reared. **21** (the dawn), radiant. **22** Aloft, (the sun). **28** having cleared away. **29** bell-ringing. **33** brought to an end. **34** jailers fled and put to flight. **35** war. **36** emptied. **38** won. **39** guarded. **1** day-star, began. **2** were the evening-star and moon. **3** rose, rose-bush. **4** of the morning. **7** Before, cap, clad.

Up raise the lark, the hevyns menstrale fyne,
In May, intill a morow myrthfullest.

Full angellike thir birdis sang thair houris
Within thair courtyns grene, into thair bouris
Apparalit quhite and rede wyth blomes suete.
Anamalit was the felde wyth all colouris;
The perly droppis schake in silvir schouris
Quhill all in balme did branch and levis flete.
To part fra Phebus did Aurora grete:
Hir cristall teris I saw hyng on the flouris,
Quhilk he for lufe all drank up wyth his hete.

For mirth of May, wyth skippis and wyth hoppis,
The birdis sang upon the tender croppis
With curiouse note, as Venus chapell clerkis.
The rosis yong, new spreding of thair knopis,
War powdrit brycht with hevinly beriall droppis
Throu bemes rede birnyng as ruby sperkis.
The skyes rang for schoutyng of the larkis;
The purpur hevyn, ourscailit in silvir sloppis,
Ourgilt the treis, branchis, lef and barkis.

Doun throu the ryce a ryvir ran wyth stremys,
So lustily agayn thai lykand lemys
That all the lake as lamp did leme of licht,
Quhilk schadowit all about wyth twynkling glemis
That bewis bathit war in secund bemys
Throu the reflex of Phebus visage brycht.
On every syde the hegies raise on hicht;
The bank was grene, the bruke was full of bremys,
The stanneris clere as stern in frosty nycht.

The cristall air, the sapher firmament,
The ruby skyes of the orient
Kest beriall bemes on emerant bewis grene.
The rosy garth depaynt and redolent
With purpur, azure, gold and goulis gent
Arayed was by dame Flora the quene
So nobily that joy was for to sene.
The roch agayn the rivir resplendent
As low enlumynit all the leves schene.

9 in a morning. **11** within. **13** Enamelled. **14** shook. **15** Until, dewy fragrance, flow. **16** weep. **20** uppermost shoots. **21** intricate. **22** buds. **23** beryl (crystal-clear). **26** The purple (i.e. scarlet) sky, sprinkled over with little trailing clouds. **27** Gilded over. **28** rushes. **29** So cheerfully reflecting back those pleasant gleams. **30** water-surface. **31** was reflected. **32** boughs. **35** bream. **36** gravel (on the river-bed), stars. **40** garden. **41** noble red. **45** flame.

Quhat throu the mery foulys armony
And throu the ryveris soun rycht ran me by
On Florais mantill I slepit as I lay,
Quhare sone into my dremes fantasy
I saw approch, agayn the orient sky,
A saill als quhite as blossum upon spray,
Wyth merse of gold brycht as the stern of day,
Quhilk tendit to the land full lustily
As falcoun swift desyrouse of hir pray.

And hard on burd unto the blomyt medis
Amang the grene rispis and the redis
Arrivit sche, quharfro anon thare landis
Ane hundreth ladyes, lusty into wedis,
Als fresch as flouris that in May upspredis,
In kirtillis grene, withoutyn kell or bandis;
Thair brycht hairis hang gleting on the strandis
In tressis clere, wyppit wyth goldyn thredis;
With pappis quhite and mydlis small as wandis.

Discrive I wald, bot quho coud wele endyte
How all the feldis wyth thai lilies quhite
Depaynt war brycht, quhilk to the hevyn did glete?
Noucht thou, Omer, als fair as thou coud wryte,
For all thine ornate stilis so perfyte;
Nor yit thou, Tullius, quhois lippis suete
Of rethorike did into termes flete.
Your aureate tongis both bene all to lyte
For to compile that paradise complete.

{The ship disembarks its crew of gods and goddesses, who sing, dance and soon discover the dreamer hiding. He is subjected to a full-scale allegorical siege, in which the Golden Targe (shield) of Reason at first protects him from the assaults of Beauty and Venus. Eventually overcome by 'Perilous Presence', he is made happy, then miserable, then woken up by the noise of the departing ship's gunfire salute (a remarkably modern touch).}

O reverend Chaucere, rose of rethoris all,
As in oure tong ane flour imperiall
That raise in Britane, evir (quho redis rycht)
Thou beris of makaris the tryumph riall:
Thy fresch anamalit termes celicall
This mater coud illumynit have full brycht.
Was thou noucht of oure Inglisch all the lycht

52 ship's topcastle. **53** approached. **55** hard at hand, blooming. **56** sedge. **57** (the vessel). **58** beautifully dressed. **60** caul (hair-net). **61** glittering. **62** bound round. **63** slender. **65** (the ladies). **66** glitter. **70** flowed with terms of rhetoric. **71** inadequate. **72** give an account of. **253** rhetoricians. **255** rose. **257** enamelled, heavenly.

Surmounting eviry tong terrestriall
Als fer as Mayes morow dois mydnycht?

O morall Gower and Ludgate laureate,
Your sugurit lippis and tongis aureate
Bene to oure eris cause of grete delyte;
Your angel mouthis most mellifluate
Oure rude langage has clere illumynate
And fair ourgilt oure spech, that imperfyte
Stude, or your goldyn pennis schupe to write.
This ile before was bare and desolate
Of rethorike or lusty fresch endyte.

Thou lytill quair, be evir obedient,
Humble, subject and symple of entent,
Before the face of eviry connyng wicht.
I knaw quhat thou of rethorike hes spent:
Of all hir lusty rosis redolent
Is non into thy gerland sett on hicht;
Eschame tharof, and draw the out of sicht.
Rude is thy wede, disteynit, bare and rent –
Wele aucht thou be aferit of the licht!

From The Treatise of the Two Married Women and the Widow

Apon the Midsummer evin, mirriest of nichtis,
I muvit furth till ane meid, as midnicht wes past,
Besyd ane gudlie grein garth, full of gay flouris,
Hegeit of ane huge hicht with hawthorne treis,
Quhairon ane bird on ane bransche so birst out hir notis
That never ane blythfullar bird was on the beuche hard.
Quhat throw the sugarat sound of hir sang glaid
And throw the savour sanative of the sueit flouris,
I drew in derne to the dyk to dirkin efter mirthis;
The dew donkit the daill, and dynnit the feulis.
I hard, under ane holyn hevinlie grein hewit,
Ane hie speiche at my hand with hautand wourdis:
With that in haist to the hege so hard I inthrang
That I was heildit with hawthorne and with heynd leveis.
Throw pykis of the plet thorne I presandlie luikit
Gif ony persoun wald approche within that plesand garding.

268 set out. **270** writing. **271** book. **273** knowledgeable. **274** wasted. **277** Be ashamed. **3** garden. **6** bough heard. **7** What with. **8** health-giving. **9** I approached in secret to the fence, to lie hidden on the look-out for amusement. **10** made damp, made a din. **11** holly-tree. **12** loud. **14** hidden, pleasant. **15** prickles, intertwined.

I saw thre gay ladeis sit in ane grein arbeir,
All grathit into garlandis of fresche gudlie flouris:
So glitterit as the gold wer thair glorius gilt tressis,
Quhill all the gressis did gleme of the glaid hewis.
Kemmit was thair cleir hair, and curiouslie sched,
Attour thair schulderis doun schyre schyning full bricht,
With curches cassin thair-abone of kirsp cleir and thin.
Thair mantillis grein war as the gress that grew in May sessoun,
Fetrit with thair quhyt fingaris about thair fair sydis.
Of ferliful fyne favour war thair faceis meik,
All full of flurist fairheid as flouris in June,
Quhyt, seimlie and soft as the sweit lillies,
Now upspred upon spray as new spynist rose,
Arrayit ryallie about with mony riche vardour,
That nature full nobillie annamalit with flouris
Of alkin hewis under hevin that ony heynd knew,
Fragrant, all full of fresche odour fynest of smell.
Ane cumlie tabil coverit wes befoir tha cleir ladeis,
With ryalle cowpis apon rawis, full of ryche wynis.
And of thir fair wlonkes whit, tua weddit war with lordis,
Ane wes ane wedow, iwiss, wantoun of laitis.
And as thai talk at the tabill of mony taill sindry
They wauchtit at the wicht wyne and waris out wourdis,
And syn thai spak more spedelie and sparit no matiris.
'Bewrie,' said the wedo, 'ye woddit wemen ying,
Quhat mirth ye fand in maryage, sen ye war menis wyffis;
Reveill gif ye rewit that rakles conditioun,
Or gif that ever ye luffit leyd upon lyf mair
Nor thame that ye your fayth hes festinit for ever,
Or gif ye think, had ye chois, that ye wald cheis better.
Think ye it nocht ane blist band that bindis so fast
That none undo it a deill may, bot the deith ane?'
Than spak ane lusty belyf with lustie effeiris:
'It that ye call the blist band that bindis so fast
Is bair of blis and bailfull and greit barrat wirkis.
Ye speir, had I fre chois, gif I wald cheis bettir?
Chenyeis ay ar to eschew, and changeis ar sueit;
Sic cursit chance till eschew, had I my chois anis,
Out of the chenyeis of ane churle I chaip suld for evir.
God gif matrimony wer made to mell for ane yeir!

18 arrayed in. **19** wire. **21** Combed, elegantly parted. **22** Over, bright. **23** With kerchiefs of fine and delicate fabric thrown over (their hair). **25** Fastened. **26** wonderful. **29** opened-out. **30** verdure. **31** enamelled. **32** all kinds of, courteous person. **36** these noble creatures. **37** behaviour. **39** quaffed, strong, pour. **40** coherently. **41** Reveal, wedded. **43** carelessly entered-upon. **44** man alive. **45** Than. **48** one bit, alone. **49** a fine woman, at once, manner. **51** misery. **52** ask. **53** Chains. **54** for once. **55** escape. **56** God grant that marriage were made for the purpose of having sex for a year!.

It war bot merrens to be mair, bot gif our myndis pleisit.
It is agane the law of luf, of kynd and of nature,
Togidder hartis to strene that stryveis with uther.
Birdis hes ane better law na bernis, be meikill,
That ilk yeir with new joy joyis ane maik
And fangis thame ane fresche feyr, unfulyeit and constant,
And lattis thair fulyeit feiris flie quhair thai pleis.
Cryst gif sic ane consuetude war in this kith haldin!
Than weill war us wemen that evir we war born:
We suld have feiris as fresche to fang quhen us likit,
And gif all larbaris thair leveis quhen thai lak curage.
'Myself suld be full semlie in silkis arrayit,
Gymp, jolie and gent, richt joyus and gentryce.
I suld at fairis be found, new faceis to se,
At playis and at preichingis and pilgrimages greit,
To schaw my renone royaly quhair preis was of folk,
To manifest my makdome to multitude of pepill
And blaw my bewtie on breid quhair bernis war mony,
That I micht cheis and be chosin and change quhen me lykit.
Than suld I waill ane full weill our all the wyd realme
That suld my womanheid weild the lang winter nicht;
And quhen I gottin had ane grome ganest of uther,
Yaip and ying in the yok ane yeir for to draw,
Fra I had preveit his pith the first plesand moneth,
Than suld I cast me to keik in kirk and in markat
And all the cuntre about, kyngis court and uther,
Quhair I ane galland micht get aganis the nixt yeir,
For to perfurneis furth the werk quhen failyeit the tother –
A forky fure ay furthwart and forsy in draucht,
Nother febill nor fant nor fulyeit in labour,
But als fresche of his forme as flouris in May –
For all the fruit suld I fang, thocht he the flour burgeoun.
'I have ane wallidrag, ane worme, ane auld wobat carle,
A waistit wolroun, na worth bot wourdis to clatter;
Ane bumbart, ane dron-bee, ane bag full of flewme,
Ane skabbit skarth, ane scorpioun, ane scutarde behind;
To se him scart his awin skyn grit scunner I think.
Quhen kissis me that carybald, than kyndillis all my sorrow:
As birss of ane brym bair his berd is als stif,
Bot soft and soupill as the silk is his sary lume –

57 nuisance. **60** than men, by far. **61** enjoys, mate. **62** takes, mate, unspoiled. **63** worn-out. **64** custom, land. **67** impotent, tickets-of-leave. **69** Dainty, ladylike. **72** crowd **73** beauty. **74** abroad. **76** choose, out of all. **78** fitter than any other. **79** Fresh. **80** once, tested. **81** look around. **85** lively fellow, at the ready. **86** worn out. **88** take, cause to bud. **89** weakling, hairy caterpillar churl. **90** worn-out boar. **91** A 'bum', phlegm. **92** monster, shit-shooter. **93** scratch, cause of disgust. **94** ogre (?). **95** bristles, fierce boar. **96** sorry tool.

He may weill to the syn assent, but sakles is his deidis!
With gore his tua grym ene ar gladdereit all about,
And gorgeit lyk tua gutaris that war with glar stoppit.
Bot quhen that glowrand gaist grippis me about
Than think I hiddowus Mahowne hes me in armes:
Thair ma na sanyng me save fra that auld Sathane,
For thocht I croce me all cleine, fra the croun doun,
He wil my corse all beclip and clap to his breist.
Quhen schaiffyn is that ald schaik with a scharp rasour,
He schovis on me his schevill mouth and schendis my lippis,
And with his hard hurcheone skyn sa heklis he my chekis
That as a glemand gleyd glowis my chaftis:
I schrenk for the scharp stound, bot schout dar I nought
For schore of that auld schrew – schame him betide!
The luf-blenkis of that bogill, fra his blerde ene,
As Belzebub had on me blent abasit my spreit,
And quhen the smy on me smyrkis with his smakes molet,
He fepillis like a farcy aver that flyrit one a gillot.
'Quhen that the sound of his saw sinkis in my eris,
Than ay renewis my noy or he be neir cumand;
Quhen I heir nemmyt his name, than mak I nyne crocis
To keip me fra the cummerans of that carll mangit,
That full of eldnyng is and anger and all evill thewis.
I dar nought luke to my luf for that lene gib,
He is sa full of jelusy and engyne fals,
Ever ymagynyng in mynd materis of evill,
Compasand and castand casis a thousand
How he sall tak me with a trawe at trist of ane othir.
I dar nought keik to the knaip that the cop fillis
For eldnyng of that ald schrew that ever on evill thynkis;
For he is waistit and worne fra Venus werkis
And may nought beit worth a bene in bed of my mystirs,
He trowis that young folk I yerne, yeild for he gane is,
Bot I may yuke all this yer or his yerd help.
'Ay quhen that caribald carll wald clym one my wambe,
Than am I dangerus and daine and dour of my will:
Yit leit I never that larbar my leggis ga betueene
To fyle my flesche na fumyll me without a fee gret.

97 blameless. **98** slime, eyes, besmeared. **99** clogged up, mud. **100** ghoul. **102** making of the sign of the cross. **103** though, completely. **104** embrace. **105** 'shack-rag'. **106** twisted, bruises. **107** hedgehog, scratches **108** live coal, jaws. **109** pain. **110** fear. **111** love-glances, bogey. **112** smirked, cast down my spirits. **113** wretch, villainous nether lip. **114** He sticks out his lower lip like a diseased old cart-horse leering at a mare. **115** voice. **116** annoyance. **118** encumbrance, moronic churl. **119** jealousy, qualities. **120** mangy tom-cat. **121** contrivances **123** Devising and planning ways. **124** trick, at tryst with. **125** peep at, lad. **126** jealousy. **128** satisfy, needs. **129** because he has become impotent. **130** have the itch, prick. **132** standoffish and disdainful and wilfully stubborn. **134** defile, grope.

And thoght his pen purly me payis in bed,
His purse pays richely in recompense efter!
For or he clym on my corse, that carybald forlane,
I have conditioun of a curche of kersp alther-fynest,
A goun of engranyt claith, right gaily furrit,
A ring with a ryall stane, or other riche jowell –
Or rest of his rousty raid, thoght he wer rede wod.
For all the buddis of Johne Blunt, quhen he abone clymis,
Me think the baid deir aboucht, sa bawch ar his werkis.
And thus I sell him solace, thoght I it sour think:
Fra sic a syre God yow saif, my sueit sisteris deir!'
   Quhen that the semely had said her sentence to end,
Than all thai leuch apon loft with latis full mery
And raucht the cop round about full of riche wynis
And ralyeit lang, or thai wald rest, with ryatus speche.
   The wedo to the tothir wlonk warpit ther wordis:
'Now, fair sister, fallis yow but fenying to tell,
Sen man ferst with matrimony yow menskit in kirk
How haif ye farne, be your faith? Confese us the treuth:
That band to blise or to ban, quhilk yow best thinkis?
Or how ye like lif to leid into lell spousage?
And syne myself ye exem on the samyn wise
And I sall say furth the soth, dissymyland no word.'
   The pleasand said, 'I protest, the treuth gif I schaw,
That of your toungis ye be traist.' The tothir twa grantit:
With that sprang up hir spreit be a span hechar.
'To speik,' quoth scho, 'I sall nought spar – ther is no spy neir:
I sall a ragment reveil fra rute of my hert,
A roust that is sa rankild quhill risis my stomok.
Now sall the byle all out brist that beild has so lang,
For it to beir one my breist wes berdin our-hevy.
I sall the venome devoid with a vent large
And me assuage of the swalme that suellit wes gret.
   'My husband wes a hur-maister, the hugeast in erd,
Tharfoir I hait him with my hert, sa help me our Lord!
He is a young man ryght yaip, bot nought in youth flouris,
For he is fadit full far and feblit of strenth.
He wes as flurising fresche within this few yeris,
Bot he is falyeid full far and fulyeid in labour.
He has bene lychour so lang quhill lost is his natur.

135 penis, poorly. **137** worthless. **138** I make it a condition that I receive a kerchief of the finest fabric of all. **139** dyed-in-grain scarlet. **141** antique fumbling, stark mad. **142** bribes. **143** long wait, feeble. **146** opinion. **147** laughed aloud, jests. **148** passed. **149** joked. **150** noble lady, uttered. **151** it falls to you, without feigning. **152** honoured. **153** fared. **154** bless or curse **155** faithful. **156** then, examine. **159** trustworthy. **160** higher. **162** long catalogue (of woes). **163** sore, festered. **164** filled with pus. **165** breast, burden. **166** outburst **167** swelling. **168** whore-master. **170** fresh. **173** fallen away, exhausted.

His lume is waxit larbar and lyis into swoune:
Wes never sugeorne wer set na on that snaill tyrit,
For efter sevyn oulkis rest it will nought rap anys.
He has bene waistit apone wemen or he me wif chesit
And in adultre, in my tyme, I haif him tane oft.
And yit he is als brankand with bonet one syde
And blenkand to the brichtest that in the burgh duellis,
Alse curtly of his clething and kemmyng of his hair
As he that is mare valyeand in Venus chalmer.
He semys to be sumthing worth, that syphyr in bour;
He lukis as he wald luffit be, thoght he be litill of valour.
He dois as dotit dog that dankys on all bussis
And liftis his leg apon loft, thoght he nought list pische.
He has a luke without lust and lif without curage;
He has a forme without force, and fessoun but vertu,
And fair wordis but effect, all fruster of dedis.
He is for ladyis in luf a right lusty schadow,
Bot into derne, at the deid, he sal be drup fundin.
He ralis and makis repet with ryatus wordis,
Ay rusing him of his radis and rageing in chalmer,
Bot God wait quhat I think quhen he so thra spekis
And how it settis him so syde to sege of sic materis,
Bot gif himself, of sum evin, myght ane say amang thaim –
Bot he nought ane is, bot nane, of naturis possessoris.
'Scho that has ane auld man nought all is begylit:
He is at Venus werkis na war na he semys.
I wend I josit a gem, and I haif geit gottin;
He had the glemyng of gold and wes bot glase fundin.
Thought men be ferse, wele I fynde, fra falye ther curage,
Thar is bot eldnyng or anger ther hertis within.
Ye speik of berdis on bewch: of blise may thai sing
That on Sanct Valentynis day ar vacandis ilk yer:
Hed I that plesand prevelege to part quhen me likit,
To change and ay to cheise agane, than chastite, adew!
Than suld I haif a fresch feir to fang in myn armys:
To hald a freke quhill he faynt may foly be calit.
'Apone sic materis I mus at mydnyght full oft
And murnys so in my mynd I murdris myselfin;
Than ly I waikand for wa and walteris about,
Wariand oft my wekit kyn that me away cast

175 tool, feeble. **176** rest (from sex), worse waste of time. **177** weeks, 'knock', once. **178** for wife. **180** cocky. **181** winking at. **186** foolish, urinates. **189** the manner without the power. **190** useless. **191** illusory appearance. **192** in the dark, in the act, droopy **193** jests, uproarious noise. **194** boasting of his sexual successes. **195** boldly. **196** suits, extravagantly, speak. **197** Unless, some evening, assay. **200** no worse than. **201** thought, chose, jet. **202** found (to be). **203** as soon as. **204** jealousy. **206** free to take a mate. **207** depart. **209** companion. **210** until he becomes impotent. **213** toss. **214** Cursing, wicked.

To sic a craudoune but curage that knyt my cler bewte
And ther so mony kene knyghtis this kenrik within.
Than think I on a semelyar, the suth for to tell,
Na is our syre be sic sevin – with that I sych oft.
Than he ful tenderly dois turne to me his tume person
And with a yoldin yerd dois yoik me in armys,
And sais, "My soverane sueit thing, quhy sleip ye no betir?
Me think ther haldis yow a hete, as ye sumharme alyt."
Quoth I, "My hony, hald abak, and handill me nought sair;
A hache is happinit hastely at my hert-rut."
With that I seme for to swoune, though I na swerf tak,
And thus beswik I that swane with my sueit wordis.
I cast on him a crabit ee quhen cleir day is cummyn
And lettis it is a luf-blenk quhen he about glemys:
I turne it in a tender luke that I in tene warit
And him behaldis hamely with hertly smyling.
'I wald a tender peronall that myght na put thole,
That hatit men with hard geir for hurting of flesch,
Had my gud man to hir gest, for I dar God aver
Scho suld not stert for his straik a stray breid of erd!
And syne I wald that ilk band that ye so blist call
Had bund him so to that bryght quhill his bak werkit,
And I wer in a beid broght with berne that me likit –
I trow that bird of my blis suld a bourd want!'

[*The widow says she will tell how experience has taught her to manage successfully the business of being a wife, chiefly by bullying, flattering and deceiving her husbands (she has had two) into submission, meanwhile taking young lovers. Widowhood has brought her nothing but happiness and chances to carry on more openly, in what we might call her* salon.]

'Bot yit me think the best bourd, quhen baronis and knyhtis
And othir bachilleris blith blumyng in youth
And all my luffaris lele my lugeng persewis
And fyllis me wyne wantonly with weilfair and joy.
Sum rownis and sum ralyeis and sum redis ballatis,
Sum raiffis furth rudly with riatus speche,
Sum plenis and sum prayis, sum prasis mi bewte,
Sum kissis me, sum clappis me, sum kyndnes me proferis,

215 Sexless coward, hid away. **216** When there are, kingdom. **218** Than, by seven times, sigh. **219** empty. **220** floppy penis. **222** fever, ails. **224** ache. **225** don't actually faint. **226** deceive, fellow. **227** jaundiced eye. **228** pretend, glares round. **229** really meant in anger. **230** kindly. **231** young girl, endure any poking. **232** erect penises. **234** She would not start a straw's breadth of ground for any thrust of his. **236** until his back finally gave out. **238** I believe that woman would be lacking anything to jest about concerning my happiness. **476** sport. **478** resort to my house. **480** One whispers, one cracks jokes. **481** talks wildly. **482** complains (of love). **483** pats.

Sum kerffis to me curtasli, sum me the cop giffis,
Sum stalwardly steppis ben with a stout curage
And a stif standand thing staiffis in mi neiff.
And mony blenkis ben our, that but full fer sittis,
That mai for the thik thrang nought thrif as thai wald;
Bot with my fair calling I comfort thaim all,
For he that sittis me nixt, I nip on his finger;
I serf him on the tothir syde on the samin fasson,
And he that behind me sittis, I hard on him lene,
And him befor, with my fut fast on his I stramp,
And to the bernis far but sueit blenkis I cast.
To every man in speciall speke I sum wordis
So wisly and so womanly quhill warmys ther hertis.
  'Thar is no liffand leid so law of degre
That sall me luf unluffit, I am so loik-hertit,
And gif his lust so be lent into my lyre quhit
That he be lost or with me lig, his lif sall not danger.
I am so mercifull in mynd and menys all wichtis,
My sely saull sal be saif, quhen Sabot all jugis.
Ladyis, leir thir lessonis and be no lassis fundin:
This is the legeand of my lif, thought Latyne it be nane!'
  Quhen endit had hir ornat speche, this eloquent wedow,
Lowd thai lewch all the laif and loffit hir mekle,
And said thai suld exampill take of her soverane teching
And wirk eftir hir wordis, that woman wes so prudent.
Than culit thai ther mouthis with confortable drinkis
And carpit full cummerlik with cop going round.
  Thus draif thai out that deir nyght with danceis full noble
Quhill that the day did up daw and dew donkit flouris.
The morow myld wes and meik, the mavis did sing,
And all remuffit the myst and the meid smellit.
Silver schouris doune schuke as the schene cristall
And berdis shoutit in schaw with ther schill notis:
The goldin glitterand gleme so gladit ther hertis,
Thai maid a glorius gle amang the grene bewis.
The soft sowch of the swyr and soune of the stremys,
The sueit savour of the sward, singing of foulis
Myght confort ony creatur of the kyn of Adam
And kindill agane his curage, thoght it wer cald sloknyt.
  Than rais ther ryall rosis in ther riche wedis
And rakit hame to rest throu the rise blumys,

484 bows. **485** within (into an inner room). **486** thrust, fist. **487** And one who sits full far outside may look within from a distance. **488** thrive. **489** welcome. **494** far without. **497** living man, low. **498** warm-hearted. **499** inclined, skin. **500** lie, be in danger. **501** take pity on. **502** God (the Lord Sabaoth). **503** learn, innocent little girls. **506** laughed, rest, praised. **509** cooled. **510** chatted, intimately. **511** passed. **512** dawn. **516** wood. **518** music, boughs. **519** sough, valley. **522** gone completely cold. **523** rose. **524** went, shrub-blossoms.

And I all prevely past to a plesand arber
And with my pen did report ther pastance most mery.
Ye auditoris most honorable, that eris has gevin
Onto this uncouth aventur, quhilk airly me happinnit:
Of ther thre wantoun wiffis that I haif writtin heir,
Quhilk wald ye waill to your wif, gif ye suld wed one?

'Timor Mortis Conturbat Me'

I that in heill wes and gladnes
Am trublit now with gret seiknes
And feblit with infermite:
Timor mortis conturbat me.

Our plesance heir is all vane-glory,
This fals warld is bot transitory,
The flesch is brukle, the fend is sle:
Timor mortis conturbat me.

The stait of man dois change and vary,
Now sound, now seik, now blith, now sary,
Now dansand mery, now like to dee:
Timor mortis conturbat me.

No stait in erd heir standis sickir;
As with the wynd wavis the wickir,
Wavis this warldis vanite:
Timor mortis conturbat me.

Onto the ded gois all estatis,
Princis, prelotis and potestatis,
Baith riche and pur of al degre:
Timor mortis conturbat me.

He takis the knyhtis into feild
Anarmyt undir helme and scheild –
Victour he is at all melle:
Timor mortis conturbat me.

That strang unmercifull tyrand
Takis on the moderis breist sowkand
The bab full of benignite:
Timor mortis conturbat me.

526 pastime. **528** unusual. **530** choose. **1** health. **4** The fear of death troubles me. **7** frail, sly. **13** sure. **14** willow-branch. **17** death. **18** powerful lords. **21** on the battlefield. **23** every battle. **25** (i.e. Death).

He takis the campion in the stour,
The capitane closit in the tour,
The lady in bour full of bewte:
Timor mortis conturbat me.

He sparis no lord for his piscence,
Na clerk for his intelligence;
His awfull strak may no man fle:
Timor mortis conturbat me.

Art-magicianis and astrologgis,
Rethoris, logicianis and theologgis –
Thame helpis no conclusionis sle:
Timor mortis conturbat me.

In medicyne the most practicianis,
Lechis, surrigianis and phisicianis,
Thameself fra ded may not supple:
Timor mortis conturbat me.

I se that makaris amang the laif
Playis heir ther pageant, syne gois to graif:
Sparit is nocht ther faculte:
Timor mortis conturbat me.

He has done petuously devour
The noble Chaucer, of makaris flour,
The Monk of Bery, and Gower, all thre:
Timor mortis conturbat me.

The gud Syr Hew of Eglintoun,
And eik Heryot, and Wyntoun,
He has tane out of this cuntre:
Timor mortis conturbat me.

That scorpion fell has done infek
Maister Johne Clerk and James Afflek,
Fra balat making and tragidie:
Timor mortis conturbat me.

Holland and Barbour he has berevit;
Allace! that he nocht with us levit
Schir Mungo Lokert of the Le:
Timor mortis conturbat me.

29 battle. **33** puissance. **35** stroke. **39** clever arguments. **41** greatest. **43** deliver. **45** poets, rest. **46** grave. **47** profession. **55** (i.e. Scotland). **57** poisoned. **61** seized.

Clerk of Tranent eik he has tane,
That maid the 'Anteris of Gawane';
Schir Gilbert Hay endit has he:
Timor mortis conturbat me.

He has Blind Hary and Sandy Traill
Slaine with his schour of mortall haill,
Quhilk Patrik Johnestoun myght nought fle:
Timor mortis conturbat me.

He has reft Merseir his endite,
That did in luf so lifly write,
So schort, so quyk, of sentence hie:
Timor mortis conturbat me.

He has tane Roull of Aberdene,
And gentill Roull of Corstorphin –
Two bettir fallowis did no man se:
Timor mortis conturbat me.

In Dunfermelyne he has done roune
With Maister Robert Henrisoun;
Schir Johne the Ros enbrast has he:
Timor mortis conturbat me.

And he has now tane, last of aw,
Gud gentill Stobo and Quintyne Schaw,
Of quham all wichtis has pete:
Timor mortis conturbat me.

Gud Maister Walter Kennedy
In poynt of dede lyis veraly –
Gret reuth it wer that so suld be!
Timor mortis conturbat me.

Sen he has all my brether tane,
He will naught lat me lif alane:
On forse I man his nyxt pray be:
Timor mortis conturbat me.

Sen for the ded remeid is none,
Best is that we for dede dispone,
Eftir our deid that lif may we:
Timor mortis conturbat me.

Quoth Dunbar quhen he wes sek.

66 Adventures. **73** (power of) writing. **74** about love. **81** whispered. **85** all. **87** pity. **93** brothers. **94** let me alone live. **95** Perforce, must. **97** death. **98** make ready. **99** live.

Sir Thomas Wyatt (1503–1542)

'The longe love, that in my thought doeth harbar'

The longe love, that in my thought doeth harbar
 And in myn hert doeth kepe his residence,
 Into my face preseth with bolde pretence
And therin campeth, spreding his baner.
She that me lerneth to love and suffre,
 And willes that my trust and lustes negligence
 Be rayned by reason, shame and reverence,
With his hardines taketh displeasur;
Wherewithall unto the hertes forrest he fleith,
 Leving his entreprise with payn and cry,
And ther him hideth and not appereth.
What may I do when my maister fereth
But in the feld with him to lyve and dye?
For goode is the lif, ending faithfully.

'Who-so list to hunt, I knowe where is an hynde'

Who-so list to hunt, I knowe where is an hynde,
 But as for me, helas, I may no more –
 The vayne travaill hath weried me so sore;
I ame of theim that farthest commeth behinde.
Yet may I by no meanes my weried mynde
 Drawe from the diere, but as she fleeth afore
 Fayntyng I folowe. I leve of therefore,
Sins in a nett I seke to hold the wynde.
Who list her hunt, I put him owte of dowbte,
 As well as I may spend his tyme in vain:
 And graven with diamonds in letters plain
There is written her fair neck rounde abowte,
 '*Noli me tangere*, for Cesars I ame,
 And wylde for to hold, though I seme tame.'

5 teaches. **7** modesty. **1** wishes. **7** leave off.

'Farewell, Love, and all thy lawes for ever'

Farewell, Love, and all thy lawes for ever:
   Thy bayted hookes shall tangill me no more.
   Senec and Plato call me from thy lore
To perfaict welth my wit for to endever.
In blynde error when I did persever,
   Thy sherpe repulse that pricketh ay so sore
   Hath taught me to sett in tryfels no store
And scape forth, syns libertie is lever.
Therefore farewell: goo trouble yonger hertes
   And in me clayme no more authorite;
   With idill youth goo use thy propertie
And theron spend thy many brittil dertes;
   For hetherto though I have lost all my tyme,
   Me lusteth no lenger rotten boughes to clymbe.

'My galy charged with forgetfulnes'

My galy charged with forgetfulnes
   Thorough sharpe sees in wynter nyghtes doeth pas
   Twene rock and rock, and eke myn enemy, alas,
That is my lorde, sterith with cruelnes,
And every owre a thought in redines,
   As tho that deth were light in suche a case;
   An endles wynd doeth tere the sayll apase
Of forced sighes and trusty ferefulnes.
A rayn of teris, a clowde of derk disdain,
   Hath done the weried cordes great hinderaunce,
   Wrethed with errour and eke with ignoraunce.
The starres be hid that led me to this pain;
   Drowned is reason that should me confort,
   And I remain dispering of the port.

'Madame, withouten many wordes'

Madame, withouten many wordes
   Ons, I am sure, ye will or no;
And if ye will, then leve your bordes
   And use your wit and shew it so,

4 well-being. **8** dearer. **11** special power. **12** fragile. **14** I wish. **1** full laden. **5** And every (stroke of the) oar. **6** an unimportant matter. **8** fear to trust. **11** Entangled. **2** One day, (say yes). **3** jests.

And with a beck ye shall me call;
  And if of oon that burneth alwaye
Ye have any pitie at all,
  Aunswer him faire with yea or nay.

Yf it be yea, I shal be fayne;
  If it be nay, frendes as before;
Ye shall anothre man obtain
  And I myn owne and yours no more.

'They fle from me that sometyme did me seke'

They fle from me that sometyme did me seke
  With naked fote stalking in my chambre.
I have sene theim gentill, tame and meke
  That nowe are wyld and do not remembre
  That sometyme they put theimself in daunger
To take bred at my hand; and nowe they raunge
Besely seking with a continuell chaunge.

Thancked be fortune, it hath ben othrewise
  Twenty tymes better – but ons in speciall,
In thyn arraye after a pleasaunt gyse,
  When her lose gowne from her shoulders did fall
  And she me caught in her armes long and small,
Therewithall swetely did me kysse,
And softely saide, 'Dere hert, howe like you this?'

It was no dreme: I lay brode waking.
  But all is torned thorough my gentilnes
Into a straunge fasshion of forsaking,
  And I have leve to goo of her goodenes,
  And she also to use new-fangilnes.
But syns that I so kyndely am served,
I would fain knowe what she hath deserved.

'What no, perdy, ye may be sure!'

What no, perdy, ye may be sure!
Thinck not to make me to your lure
  With wordes and chere so contrarieng,
  Swete and sowre contrewaing;
To much it were still to endure.

5 nod. **5** in my power. **10** thin, in a pleasing way. **12** slender. **1** indeed (par dieu). **2** (bait for a trained hawk). **4** weighing against each other.

Trouth is trayed where craft is in ure;
But though ye have had my hertes cure,
  Trow ye I dote withoute ending?
  What no, perdy!

Though that with pain I do procure
For to forgett that ons was pure,
  Within my hert shall still that thing,
  Unstable, unsure, and wavering,
Be in my mynde withoute recure?
  What no, perdy!

'Marvaill no more all-tho'

Marvaill no more all-tho
  The songes I syng do mone,
For othre lif then wo
  I never proved none.
And in my hert also
  Is graven with lettres diepe
A thousand sighes and mo,
  A flod of teres to wepe.

How may a man in smart
  Fynde mater to rejoyse?
How may a mornyng hert
  Set forth a pleasaunt voise?
Play who that can that part:
  Nedes must in me appere
How fortune overthwart
  Doeth cause my mornyng chere.

Perdy, there is no man
  If he never sawe sight
That perfaictly tell can
  The nature of the light.
Alas, how should I then,
  That never tasted but sowre,
But do as I began,
  Continuelly to lowre?

But yet perchaunce som chaunce
  May chaunce to chaunge my tune;
And when suche chaunce doeth chaunce
  Then shall I thanck fortune;

6 betrayed, use. **7** care. **10** try. **11** what. **14** remedy. **4** experienced. **9** sharp pain. **15** opposed.

And if I have suche chaunce,
  Perchaunce ere it be long
For suche a pleasaunt chaunce
  To syng som plaisaunt song.

'Tho I cannot your crueltie constrain'

Tho I cannot your crueltie constrain
For my good will to favor me again,
  Tho my true and faithfull love
  Have no power your hert to move,
Yet rew upon my pain.

Tho I your thrall must evermore remain
And for your sake my libertie restrain,
  The greatest grace that I do crave
  Is that ye would vouchesave
To rew upon my pain.

Tho I have not deserved to obtain
So high reward but thus to serve in vain,
  Tho I shall have no redresse,
  Yet of right ye can no lesse
But rew upon my pain.

But I se well that your high disdain
Wull no wise graunt that I shall more attain;
  Yet ye must graunt at the last
  This my powre and small request:
Rejoyse not at my pain.

'To wisshe and want and not obtain'

To wisshe and want and not obtain,
To seke and sew ese of my pain,
Syns all that ever I do is vain,
  What may it availl me?

All-tho I stryve both dey and howre
Against the streme with all my powre,
If fortune list yet for to lowre,
  What may it availl me?

If willingly I suffre woo,

2 sue for relief.

If from the fyre me list not goo,
If then I burne, to plaine me so
  What may it availl me?

And if the harme that I suffre
Be runne to farr owte of mesur,
To seke for helpe any further
  What may it availl me?

What tho eche hert that hereth me plain
Pitieth and plaineth for my payn?
If I no les in greif remain,
  What may it availl me?

Ye, tho the want of my relief
Displease the causer of my greife,
Syns I remain still in myschiefe,
  What may it availl me?

Suche cruell chaunce doeth so me threte
Continuelly inward to fret,
Then of relese for to trete
  What may it availl me?

Fortune is deif unto my call,
My torment moveth her not at all,
And though she torne as doeth a ball,
  What may it availl me?

For in despere there is no rede;
To want of ere, speche is no spede;
To linger still alyve as dede
  What may it availl me?

'Some-tyme I fled the fyre that me brent'

Some-tyme I fled the fyre that me brent,
  By see, by land, by water and by wynd,
And now I folow the coles that be quent
  From Dovor to Calais against my mynde.
Lo how desire is both sprong and spent!
  And he may se that whilom was so blynde,
And all his labor now he laugh to scorne,
Mashed in the breers that erst was all to-torne.

11 complain. **14** too far. **23** distress. **33** wise advice (to be found). **34** Where there is no ear, benefit. **3** quenched. **6** once. **7** may laugh. **8** Enmeshed, torn to pieces.

'The furyous gone in his rajing yre'

The furyous gonne in his rajing yre,
When that the bowle is rammed in to sore
And that the flame cannot part from the fire,
Cracketh in sonder and in the ayer doeth rore
The shevered peces. Right so doeth my desire,
Whose flame encreseth from more to more,
Whych to lett owt I dare not loke nor speke:
So now hard force my hert doeth all to-breke.

'My lute, awake! perfourme the last'

My lute, awake! perfourme the last
Labor that thou and I shall wast,
And end that I have now begon;
For when this song is sung and past,
My lute, be still, for I have done.

As to be herd where ere is none,
As lede to grave in marbill stone,
My song may perse her hert as sone;
Should we then sigh, or sing, or mone?
No, no, my lute, for I have done.

The rokkes do not so cruelly
Repulse the waves continuelly
As she my suyte and affection,
So that I am past remedy:
Whereby my lute and I have done.

Prowd of the spoyll that thou hast got
Of simple hertes thorough loves shot,
By whom, unkynd, thou hast theim wone,
Thinck not he hath his bow forgot,
All-tho my lute and I have done.

Vengeaunce shall fall on thy disdain,
That makest but game on ernest pain;
Thinck not alone under the sonne
Unquyt to cause thy lovers plain,
All-tho my lute and I have done.

2 cannon-ball. **3** firing (of the ball). **6** As (easily). **7** lead (metal) to engrave. **13** suit (petition). **17** (Cupid's arrow). **24** To cause thy lovers to complain without being paid back.

Perchaunce the lye wethered and old,
The wynter nyghtes that are so cold,
  Playnyng in vain unto the mone:
Thy wisshes then dare not be told!
  Care then who lyst, for I have done.

And then may chaunce the to repent
The tyme that thou hast lost and spent
  To cause thy lovers sigh and swoune;
Then shalt thou knowe beaultie but lent,
  And wisshe and wante as I have done.

Now cesse, my lute, this is the last
Labour that thou and I shall wast,
  And ended is that we begon;
Now is this song both sung and past;
  My lute be still, for I have done.

'*In eternum* I was ons determed'

In eternum I was ons determed
For to have lovid and my minde affermed
That with my herte it shuld be confermed
  In eternum.

Forthwith I founde the thing that I myght like
And sought with love to warme her hert alike,
For, as me thought, I shulde not se the like
  In eternum.

To trase this daunse I put myself in prese;
Vayne hope ded lede and bad I should not cese
To serve, to suffer and still to hold my pease
  In eternum.

With this furst rule I fordred me apase,
That, as me thought, my trowthe had taken place
With full assurans to stond in her grace
  In eternum.

It was not long or I by proofe had found
That feble bilding is on feble grounde,
For in her herte this worde ded never sounde:
  In eternum.

26 you may lie. **30** pleases. **1** determined. **9** To follow the steps of this dance I went out among the throng. **13** progressed rapidly. **17** before.

In eternum then from my herte I kest
That I had furst determined for the best;
Now in the place another thought doeth rest,
   In eternum.

'Hevyn and erth and all that here me plain'

Hevyn and erth and all that here me plain
   Do well perceve what care doeth cause me cry,
Save you alone to whom I cry in vain:
   'Mercy, madame, alas, I dy, I dy!'

Yf that you slepe, I humbly you require
   Forbere a while and let your rigour slake,
Syns that by you I burne thus in this fire:
   To here my plaint, dere hert, awake, awake!

Syns that so oft ye have made me to wake
   In plaint and teres and in right pitious case,
Displease you not if force do now me make
   To breke your slepe, crieng 'Alas, alas!'

It is the last trouble that ye shall have
   Of me, madame, to here my last complaint.
Pitie at lest your poure unhappy slave,
   For in dispere, alas, I faint, I faint!

It is not now, but long and long ago
   I have you served as to my powre and myght
As faithfully as any man myght do,
   Clayming of you nothing of right, of right,

Save of your grace only to stay my lif,
   That fleith as fast as clowd afore the wynde;
For syns that first I entred in this stryf
   An inward deth hath fret my mynde, my mynd.

Yf I had suffered this to you unware,
   Myn were the fawte and you nothing to blame,
But syns you know my woo and all my care
   Why do I dy? Alas, for shame, for shame!

I know right well my face, my lowke, my teeres,
   Myn iyes, my wordes and eke my driery chiere
Have cryd my deth full oft unto your eres –
   Herd of belefe it doeth appere, appere!

21 cast. **1** complain. **6** slacken. **18** to (the best of). **21** preserve. **32** Hard.

A better prouff I se that ye would have
  How I am dede; therefore when ye here tell
Beleve it not, all-tho ye se my grave.
  Cruell, unkynd! I say farewell, farewell!

'To cause accord or to agre'

To cause accord or to agre
Two contraries in oon degre
And in oon poynct, as semeth me,
To all mans wit it cannot be:
  It is impossible.

Of hete and cold when I complain
And say that hete doeth cause my pain,
When cold doeth shake me every vain
And both at ons, I say again
  It is impossible.

That man that hath his hert away,
If lyf lyveth there, as men do say,
That he hert-les should last on day
Alyve and not to torne to clay,
  It is impossible.

Twixt lyf and deth, say what who sayth,
There lyveth no lyf that draweth breth;
They joyne so nere and eke, i'feith,
To seke for lif by wissh of deth
  It is impossible.

Yet love that all thing doeth subdue,
Whose power ther may no lif eschew,
Hath wrought in me that I may rew
These miracles to be so true,
  That are impossible.

'You that in love finde lucke and habundaunce'

You that in love finde lucke and habundaunce
  And live in lust and joyful jolitie,
  Arise, for shame! Do away your sluggardie!
Arise, I say, do May some observaunce!
Let me in bed lye dreming in mischaunce

12 (i.e. in his heart). **13** one. **16** whatever anyone says. **18** closely.

Let me remembre the haps most unhappy
That me betide in May most comonly,
As oon whom love list litil to avaunce.
Sephame saide true that my nativitie
Mischaunced was with the ruler of the May:
He gest, I prove, of that the veritie!
In May my welth and eke my lif, I say,
Have stonde so oft in suche perplexitie:
Rejoyse! Let me dreme of your felicitie.

'What rage is this? what furour of what kynd?'

What rage is this? what furour of what kynd?
What powre, what plage, doth wery thus my mynd?
Within my bons to rancle is assind
What poyson, plesant swete?

Lo, se myn iyes swell with contynuall terys;
The body still away sleples it weris;
My fode nothing my faintyng strenght reperis,
Nor doth my lyms sustayne.

In diepe wid wound the dedly strok doth torne
To curid skarre that never shall retorne.
Go to, tryumphe, reioyse thy goodly torne!
Thi frend thow dost opresse.

Opresse thou dost, and hast off hym no cure,
Nor yett my plaint no pitie can procure.
Fiers tygre fell, hard rok withowt recure,
Cruell rebell to love!

Ons may thou love, neuer belovffd agayne:
So love thou still and not thy love obttayne;
So wrathfull love with spites of just disdayne
May thret thy cruell hert.

'Is it possible'

Is it possible
That so hye debate,
So sharpe, so sore, and of suche rate,
Shuld end so sone and was begone so late?
Is it possible?

11 I find to be true. **12** well-being. **10** healed. **15** remedy. **17** One day. **2** so great a quarrel. **3** intensity.

Is it possible –
So cruell intent,
So hasty hete and so sone spent,
From love to hate, and thence for to relent?
Is it possible?

Is it possible
That eny may fynde
Within oon hert so dyverse mynd,
To change or torne as wether and wynd?
Is it possible?

Is it possible
To spye it in an iye
That tornys as oft as chance on dy?
The trothe whereof can eny try?
Is it possible?

It is possible
For to torne so oft,
To bryng that lowyst that was most aloft,
And to fall hyest yet to lyght soft:
It is possible!

All is possible,
Who-so lyst beleve;
Trust therfore fyrst, and after preve,
As men wedd ladyes by lycence and leve:
All is possible.

'Forget not yet the tryde entent'

Forget not yet the tryde entent
Of suche a truthe as I have ment,
My gret travayle so gladly spent
Forget not yet.

Forget not yet when fyrst began
The wery lyfe ye know syns whan,
The sute, the servys none tell can,
Forget not yet.

Forget not yet the gret assays,
The cruell wrong, the skornfull ways,
The paynfull pacyence in denays,
Forget not yet.

18 What, at dice. **3** labour. **7** love-suit, reckon up. **9** trials. **11** refusals.

Forget not yet, forget not thys,
How long ago hath ben and is
The mynd that never ment amys,
Forget not yet.

Forget not then thyn owne aprovyd,
The whyche so long hath the so lovyd,
Whose stedfast faythe yet never movyd,
Forget not thys.

'Blame not my lute for he must sownde'

Blame not my lute for he must sownde
Of this or that as liketh me;
For lak of wytt the lute is bownde
To gyve suche tunes as plesith me.
Tho my songes be sumewhat strange
And spekes suche wordes as toche thy change,
Blame not my lute.

My lute, alas, doth not ofende
Tho that perfors he must agre
To sownde such tunes as I entende
To sing to them that hereth me;
Then tho my songes be somewhat plain
And tocheth some that use to fayn,
Blame not my lute.

My lute and strynges may not deny,
But as I strike they must obay;
Brake not them than so wrongfully
But wreke thyself some wyser way;
And tho the songes whiche I endight
Do qwytt thy change with rightfull spight,
Blame not my lute.

Spyght askyth spight and changing change
And falsyd faith must nedes be known;
The faute so gret, the case so strange,
Of right it must abrode be blown.
Then since that by thyn own desart
My songes do tell how trew thou art,
Blame not my lute.

17 acknowledged (lover). **6** touch upon. **12** direct in meaning. **13** are accustomed to. **18** avenge. **20** requite your unfaithfulness.

Blame but theself that hast mysdon
And well desarvid to have blame;
Change thou thy way, so evyl bygon,
And then my lute shall sownde that same.
But if tyll then my fyngeres play
By thy desart their wontyd way,
Blame not my lute.

Farwell, unknown, for tho thow brake
My strynges in spight with gret desdayn,
Yet have I fownde owt for thy sake
Stringes for to strynge my lute agayne;
And if perchance this folysh ryme
Do make the blushe at any tyme,
Blame not my lute.

'What shulde I saye'

What shulde I saye
Sins faithe is dede
And truthe awaye
From you is fled?
Shulde I be led
With doblenesse?
Naye, naye, mistresse!

I promiside you,
And you promiside me
To be as true
As I wolde be;
But sins I se
Your doble herte,
Farewell, my perte!

Though for to take
It is not my minde
But to forsake
One so unkind,
And as I finde
So will I truste –
Farewell, unjuste!

Can ye saye naye
But you saide
That I allwaye
Shulde be obeide?

34 According to your deserving. **22** deny (that).

And thus betraide
Or that I wiste –
Farewell, unkiste!

'Spight hath no powre to make me sadde'

Spight hath no powre to make me sadde
Nor scornefulnesse to make me playne;
It doth suffise that ons I had,
And so to leve it is no payne.
Let theim frowne on that leste doth gaine,
Who ded rejoise must nedes be glad;
And tho with wordis thou wenist to rayne,
It doth suffise that ons I had.

Sins that in chekes thus overthwart
And coyly lookis thou dost delight,
It doth suffise that myne thou wart,
Tho change hath put thy faithe to flight.
Alas, it is a pevishe spight
To yelde thiself and then to part.
But since thou setst thi faithe so light,
It doth suffise that myne thou wart.

And since thy love doth thus declyne
And in thy herte suche hate doth grow,
It doth suffise that thou wart myne,
And with good will I quite it soo.
Some-tyme my frende, farewell my foo:
Since thou change, I am not thyne.
But for relef of all my woo
It doth suffise that thou wart myne.

Prayeng you all that heris this song
To judge no wight, nor none to blame;
It doth suffise she doth me wrong
And that herself doth kno the same.
And tho she change, it is no shame:
Their kinde it is and hath bene long.
Yet I proteste she hath no name:
It doth suffise she doth me wrong.

27 Before I knew. **2** complain. **5** obtain least. **7** think to have power. **9** rebuffs, perverse. **20** repay. **31** reputation for ill-doing.

'I abide and abide and better abide'

I abide and abide and better abide –
  And after the olde proverbe – the happie daye;
  And ever my ladye to me doth saye,
'Let me alone and I will provyde.'
I abide and abide and tarrye the tyde,
  And with abiding spede well ye maye:
  Thus do I abide, I wott, allwaye,
Nother obtayning nor yet denied.
Aye me! this long abidyng
  Semith to me as who sayeth
  A prolonging of a dieng dethe
Or a refusing of a desyred thing.
  Moche ware it bettre for to be playne
  Then to saye 'abide' and yet shall not obtayne.

'Stond who-so list upon the slipper toppe'

Stond who-so list upon the slipper toppe
Of courtes estate, and lett me here rejoyce,
And use me quyet without lett or stoppe,
Unknowen in courte, that hath suche brackishe joyes.
In hidden place so lett my dayes forth passe
That when my yeares be done, withouten noyse
I may dye aged after the common trace.
For hym death greep'th right hard by the croppe
That is moche knowen of other, and of himself, alas,
Doth dye unknowen, dazed, with dreadfull face.

'Throughout the world, if it wer sought'

Throughout the world, if it wer sought,
Faire wordes ynough a man shall finde:
They be good chepe, they cost right nought,
Their substance is but onely winde.
But well to say and so to mene,
That swete acord is seldom sene.

5 prolong the time. **6** you may (but not me). **8** Neither. **1** wishes, slippery. **3** live my life, hindrance. **4** unappetising. **7** course of life. **8** head. **10** bewildered, fearful. **3** a good bargain. **2** tasting. **3** banquets. **6** hold to.

'In court to serve decked with freshe aray'

In court to serve decked with freshe aray,
Of sugred meates felyng the swete repast,
The life in bankets and sundry kindes of play
Amid the presse of lordly lokes to waste
Hath with it joynde oft-times such bitter taste
That who-so joyes such kinde of life to holde
In prison joyes, fettred with cheines of gold.

Henry Howard, Earl of Surrey (1517–1547)

'When ragyng love with extreme payne'

When ragyng love with extreme payne
  Most cruelly distrains my hart;
When that my teares, as floudes of rayne,
  Beare witnes of my wofull smart;
When sighes have wasted so my breath
That I lye at the poynte of death,

I call to minde the navye greate
  That the Grekes brought to Troye towne,
And how the boysteous windes did beate
  Their shyps and rente their sayles adowne,
Till Agamemnons daughters bloode
Appeasde the goddes that them withstode;

And how that in those ten yeres warre
  Full manye a bloudye dede was done,
And manye a lord that came full farre
  There caught his bane, alas, to sone,
And many a good knight overronne,
Before the Grekes had Helene wonne.

Then thinke I thus: sithe suche repayre,
  So longe time warre of valiant men,
Was all to winne a ladye fayre,
  Shall I not learne to suffer then,
And thinke my life well spent to be
Servyng a worthier wight than she?

Therfore I never will repent,
  But paynes contented stil endure,
For like as when, rough winter spent,
  The pleasant spring straight draweth in ure,

16 destruction. **28** comes into being.

So after ragyng stormes of care
Joyful at length may be my fare.

'The soote season, that bud and blome furth bringes'

The soote season, that bud and blome furth bringes,
With grene hath clad the hill and eke the vale;
The nightingale with fethers new she singes;
The turtle to her make hath tolde her tale.
Somer is come, for every spray now springes;
The hart hath hong his olde hed on the pale;
The buck in brake his winter cote he flinges;
The fishes flote with newe repaired scale.
The adder all her sloughe awaye she slinges;
The swift swalow pursueth the flyes smale;
The busy bee her honye now she minges;
Winter is worne that was the flowers bale.
And thus I see among these pleasant thinges
Eche care decayes, and yet my sorow springes.

'Set me wheras the sonne doth perche the grene'

Set me wheras the sonne doth perche the grene,
Or wher his beames may not dissolve the ise;
In temprat heat where he is felt and sene;
With prowde people, in presence sad and wyse;
Set me in base or yet in highe degree,
In the long night or in the shortyst day,
In clere weather or wher mysts thikest be,
In loste yowthe or when my haires be grey;
Set me in earthe, in heaven, or yet in hell,
In hill, in dale, or in the fowming floode,
Thrawle or at large, alive whersoo I dwell,
Sike or in healthe, in yll fame or in good:
Yours will I be, and with that onely thought
Comfort myself when that my hap is nowght.

'Love, that doth raine and live within my thought'

Love, that doth raine and live within my thought
And buylt his seat within my captyve brest,
Clad in the armes wherin with me he fowght

1 sweet. **4** turtledove, mate. **6** antlers, fence. **7** thickets. **11** has mind of. **12** harm **1** pierce. **11** at liberty. **14** fortune. **1** reign.

Oft in my face he doth his banner rest.
But she that tawght me love and suffre paine,
My doubtfull hope and eke my hote desire
With shamfast looke to shadoo and refrayne,
Her smyling grace convertyth streight to yre.
And cowarde love than to the hert apace
Taketh his flight where he doth lorke and playne
His purpose lost, and dare not show his face.
For my lordes gylt thus fawtless byde I payne,
Yet from my lorde shall not my foote remove:
Sweet is the death that taketh end by love.

'Alas, so all thinges nowe do holde their peace'

Alas, so all thinges nowe do holde their peace,
Heaven and earth disturbed in nothing;
The beastes, the ayer, the birdes their song do cease,
The nightes chare the starres aboute doth bring.
Calme is the sea, the waves worke lesse and lesse:
So am not I, whom love, alas, doth wring,
Bringing before my face the great encrease
Of my desires, whereat I wepe and syng
In joye and wo as in a doutfull ease;
For my swete thoughtes sometyme do pleasure bring,
But by and by the cause of my disease
Geves me a pang that inwardly doth sting,
When that I thinke what griefe it is againe
To live and lacke the thing should ridde my paine.

'Geve place, ye lovers, here before'

Geve place, ye lovers, here before
That spent your bostes and bragges in vain:
My ladies beawtie passeth more
The best of yours, I dare well sayn,
Than doth the sonne the candle-light
Or brightest day the darkest night;

And thereto hath a trothe as just
As had Penelope the fayre,
For what she saith, ye may it trust
As it by writing sealed were.

7 (taught me) to. **3** wind. **4** chariot.

And vertues hath she many moe
Than I with pen have skill to showe.

I coulde rehearse, if that I wolde,
The whole effect of Natures plaint
When she had lost the perfit mold,
The like to whom she could not paint:
With wringing handes howe she dyd cry,
And what she said – I know it, I.

I knowe she swore with ragyng mind,
Her kingdom onely set apart,
There was no losse, by lawe of kind,
That could have gone so nere her hart.
And this was chiefly all her payne:
She coulde not make the lyke agayne.

Sith Nature thus gave her the prayse
To be the chiefest worke she wrought,
In faith, me thinke some better waies
On your behalfe might well be sought
Then to compare, as ye have done,
To matche the candle with the sonne.

Epitaph for Wyatt

W. resteth here, that quick could never rest,
Whose heavenly giftes encreased by disdayn
And vertue sank the deper in his brest –
Such profit he by envy could obtain:

A hed, where wisdom misteries did frame,
Whose hammers bet styll in that lively brayn
As on a stithe where that some work of fame
Was dayly wrought to turne to Britaines gayn;

A visage stern and myld, where bothe did grow
Vice to contemne, in vertue to rejoyce,
Amid great stormes whom grace assured so
To lyve upright and smile at Fortunes choyce;

A hand that taught what might be sayd in ryme,
That reft Chaucer the glory of his wit –

20 alone excepted. **1** alive. **2** because of the disdain (of others). **4** from envious malice. **7** anvil. **9** both (qualities). **14** robbed.

A mark the which, unparfited for time,
  Some may approche but never none shall hit;

A toung that served in forein realmes his king,
  Whose courteous talke to vertue did enflame
Eche noble hart – a worthy guide to bring
  Our English youth by travail unto fame;

An eye whose judgement none affect could blinde,
  Frendes to allure and foes to reconcile,
Whose persing loke did represent a mynde
  With vertue fraught, reposed, voyd of gyle;

A hart where drede was never so imprest
  To hyde the thought that might the trouth avance,
In neyther fortune loft nor yet represt –
  To swell in wealth or yeld unto mischance;

A valiant corps, where force and beawty met –
  Happy, alas to happy, but for foes! –
Lived and ran the race that Nature set,
  Of manhodes shape where she the molde did lose.

But to the heavens that simple soule is fled,
  Which left with such as covet Christ to know
Witnesse of faith that never shall be ded,
  Sent for our helth, but not received so.

15 unfinished for want of time. **21** passion. **27** lofty. **33** innocent.

Edmund Spenser (1552–1599)

From *The Shepherd's Calendar*

January

'In this fyrst Aeglogue Colin Cloute, a shepheardes boy complaineth him of his unfortunate love, being but newly (as semeth) enamoured of a countrie lasse called Rosalinde; with which strong affection being very sore traveled, he compareth his carefull case to the sadde season of the yeare, to the frostie ground, to the frozen trees, and to his owne winterbeaten flocke. And lastlye, fynding himselfe robbed of all former pleasaunce and delights, hee breaketh his pipe in peeces and casteth himselfe to the ground.'

A shepeheards boye (no better doe him call),
When winters wastful spight was almost spent,
All in a sunneshine day, as did befall,
Led forth his flock, that had bene long ypent.
So faynt they woxe and feeble in the folde
That now unnethes their feete could them uphold.

All as the sheepe, such was the shepeheards looke,
For pale and wanne he was, alas the while!
May seeme he lovd, or els some care he tooke:
Well couth he tune his pipe and frame his stile.
Tho to a hill his faynting flocke he ledde
And thus him playnde, the while his shepe there fedde.

'Ye gods of love, that pitie lovers payne
(If any gods the paine of lovers pitie),
Looke from above, where you in joyes remaine,
And bowe your eares unto my doleful dittie.
And Pan, thou shepheards god, that once didst love,
Pitie the paines that thou thyselfe didst prove.

Thou barrein ground, whome winters wrath hath wasted,
Art made a myrrhour to behold my plight:

9 Perhaps. **10** he knew how to. **11** Then.

Whilome thy fresh spring flowrd and after hasted
Thy sommer prowde with daffadillies dight,
And now is come thy wynters stormy state,
Thy mantle mard wherein thou maskedst late.

Such rage as winters reigneth in my heart,
My life-bloud friesing with unkindly cold;
Such stormy stoures do breede my balefull smart
As if my yeare were wast and woxen old.
And yet, alas, but now my spring begonne,
And yet, alas, yt is already donne.

You naked trees, whose shady leaves are lost,
Wherein the byrds were wont to build their bowre,
And now are clothd with mosse and hoary frost
Instede of bloosmes wherwith your buds did flowre,
I see your teares that from your boughes doe raine,
Whose drops in drery ysicles remaine.

All so my lustfull leafe is drye and sere,
My timely buds with wayling all are wasted;
The blossome which my braunch of youth did beare
With breathed sighes is blowne away and blasted,
And from mine eyes the drizling teares descend,
As on your boughes the ysicles depend.

Thou feeble flocke, whose fleece is rough and rent,
Whose knees are weake through fast and evill fare,
Mayst witnesse well by thy ill governement
Thy maysters mind is overcome with care.
Thou weake, I wanne; thou leane, I quite forlorne;
With mournyng pyne I, you with pyning mourne.

A thousand sithes I curse that carefull hower
Wherein I longd the neighbour towne to see,
And eke tenne thousand sithes I blesse the stoure
Wherein I sawe so fayre a sight as shee.
Yet all for naught: such sight hath bred my bane.
Ah, God, that love should breede both joy and payne!

It is not Hobbinol wherefore I plaine,
Albee my love he seeke with dayly suit.
His clownish gifts and curtsies I disdaine,
His kiddes, his cracknelles and his early fruit.

27 fits of anguish. **49** times. **51** moment of pain. **58** home-made cakes.

Ah, foolish Hobbinol, thy gifts bene vayne:
Colin them gives to Rosalind againe.

I love thilke lasse (alas, why doe I love?)
And am forlorne (alas, why am I lorne?)
Shee deignes not my good will, but doth reprove,
And of my rurall musick holdeth scorne.
Shepheards devise she hateth as the snake,
And laughes the songes that Colin Clout doth make.

Wherefore my pype, albee rude Pan thou please,
Yet for thou pleasest not where most I would,
And thou unlucky Muse, that wontst to ease
My musyng mynd, yet canst not when thou should,
Both pype and Muse shall sore the whyle abye!'
So broke his oaten pype, and downe dyd lye.

By that the welked Phoebus gan availe
His weary waine, and nowe the frosty night
Her mantle black through heaven gan overhaile;
Which seene, the pensife boy, halfe in despight,
Arose, and homeward drove his sonned sheepe,
Whose hanged heads did seeme his carefull case to weepe.

71 pay for. **73** faded, bring down. **74** cart. **75** draw over. **77** sun-wearied.

Index of Titles and First Lines

'Alas, so all thinges nowe do holde their peace' 174
'Ane doolie sessoun to ane cairful dyte' 112
'Apon the Midsummer evin, mirriest of nichtis' 144

'Blame not my lute for he must sownde' 167

Canterbury Tales, The 7
Christ in Triumph 140

'Done is a batell on the dragon blak' 140

'Experience, thogh noon auctoritee' 27
Epitaph for Wyatt 175

Fables, The 128
'Farewell, Love, and all thy lawes for ever' 156
'Forget not yet the tryde entent' 166
Fox and the Wolf, The 128
'Ful erly bifore the day the folk up rysen' 88
'furyous gonne in his rajing yre, The' 161

General Prologue, The 7
'Geve place, ye lovers, here before' 174
Golden Targe, The 141

'Hevyn and erth and all that here me plain' 163

'I abide and abide and better abide' 170
'I that in heill wes and gladnes' 152
'In a somur sesoun whan softe was the sonne' 72
'In court to serve decked with freshe aray' 171
'*In eternum* I was ons determed' 162
'In Flandres whilom was a compaignye' 62
'In th' olde dayes of the kyng Arthour' 48
'Into thir dirk and drublie dayis' 139
'Is it possible' 165

January 177

'Leif we this wedow glaid, I yow assure' 128
'longe love, that in my thought doeth harbar, The' 155

'Lordynges,' quod he, 'in chirches whan I preche' 58
'Love, that doth raine and live within my thought' 173

'Madame, withouten many wordes' 156
'Marvaill no more all-tho' 158
Meditation in Winter 139
'My galy charged with forgetfulnes' 156
'My lute, awake! perfourme the last' 161

'Oure Hoost gan to swere as he were wood' 57

Pardoner's Prologue, The 58
Pardoner's Prologue, and Tale, The 57
Pardoner's Tale, The 62

'Qwhylum thair wes, as Esope can report' 133

'Ryght as the stern of day begouth to schyne' 141

'Set me wheras the sonne doth perche the grene' 173
'shepeheards boye (no better doe him call), A' 177
Shepherd's Calendar, The 177
Sir Gawain and the Green Knight 88
'Some-tyme I fled the fyre that me brent' 160
'soote season, that bud and blome furth bringes, The' 173
'Spight hath no powre to make me sadde' 169
'Stond who-so list upon the slipper toppe' 170

Testament of Cresseid, The 112
'They fle from me that sometyme did me seke' 157
'Tho I cannot your crueltie constrain' 159
'Throughout the world, if it wer sought' 170
Timor Mortis Conturbat Me 152
'To cause accord or to agre' 164
'To wisshe and want and not obtain' 159
Treatise of the Two Married Women and the Widow, The 144

Vision of Piers Plowman, The 72

'W. resteth here, that quick could never rest' 175
'Whan that Averill with his shoures soote' 7
'What no, perdy, ye may be sure!' 157
'What rage is this? what furour of what kynd?' 165
'What shulde I saye' 168
'When ragyng love with extreme payne' 172
'Who-so list to hunt, I knowe where is an hynde' 155
Wife of Bath's Prologue, The 27
Wife of Bath's Prologue and Tale, The 27
Wife of Bath's Tale, The 48
Wolf and the Wether, The 133

'You that in love finde lucke and habundaunce' 164